Culture, Biology, and Anthropological Demography

Culture, Biology, and Anthropological Demography attempts a rapprochement of anthropological demography and human evolutionary ecology through recognition of common research topics and the construction of a broad theoretical framework incorporating both cultural and biological motivation. Two distinctive approaches to the study of human demography exist within anthropology today – anthropological demography and human evolutionary ecology. The first stresses the role of culture in determining population parameters, whereas the second posits that demographic rates reflect adaptive behaviors that are the products of natural selection. Both these approaches are utilized to search for demographic strategies in varied cultural and temporal contexts ranging from African pastoralists through North American postindustrial societies. Although both of these approaches have achieved notable successes, each has ignored or actively disparaged the other. In an attempt to initiate a discussion between the two fields, this book develops a framework recognizing cultural and biological demographic strategies.

Eric Abella Roth is Professor of Anthropology in the Department of Anthropology, University of Victoria, and an Affiliate, Center for Studies in Demography and Ecology, University of Washington – Seattle. He has conducted demographic anthropological fieldwork in the Canadian Subarctic, the Sudan, and northern Kenya. He is coeditor of *African Pastoralist Systems: An Integrated Approach* (1994, Lynne Rienner).

New Perspectives on Anthropological and Social Demography

Demography deals with issues of great social importance, and demographic research fuels some of the central current policy debates of our time. Nevertheless, demographic theory has not changed much over the years, and old and sometimes inappropriate models are still being applied to new problems. Increasingly, however, demographers have become aware of the limitations of standard surveys and statistics, and they are moving to incorporate theoretical and methodological approaches from other disciplines, in particular anthropology. For their part, anthropologists have generally failed to take account of the advances in modern demography, but they are now beginning to take part in the central debates on questions of theory and policy in population research. A new wave of interdisciplinary research is emerging, combining the interests and approaches of demographers, anthropologists, and other social scientists. Some of the most interesting products of this new wave will be published in *New Perspectives on Anthropological and Social Demography*.

Books in the series include

1. *Census and Identity*
   The Politcs of Race, Ethnicity, and Language in National Censuses
   edited by David Kertzer and Dominique Arel
   ISBN 0 521 80823 5 HB/0 521 00427 6 PB
2. *Demography in the Age of the Postmodern*
   Nancy E. Riley and James McCarthy
   ISBN 0 521 82626 8 HB/0 521 53364 3 PB
3. *Culture, Biology, and Anthropological Demography*
   Eric Abella Roth
   ISBN 0 521 80905 3 HB/0 521 00541 8 PB

Culture, Biology, and Anthropological Demography

Eric Abella Roth
University of Victoria

CAMBRIDGE
UNIVERSITY PRESS

PUBLISHED BY THE PRESS SYNDICATE OF THE UNIVERSITY OF CAMBRIDGE
The Pitt Building, Trumpington Street, Cambridge, United Kingdom

CAMBRIDGE UNIVERSITY PRESS
The Edinburgh Building, Cambridge CB2 2RU, UK
40 West 20th Street, New York, NY 10011-4211, USA
477 Williamstown Road, Port Melbourne, VIC 3207, Australia
Ruiz de Alarcón 13, 28014 Madrid, Spain
Dock House, The Waterfront, Cape Town 8001, South Africa

http://www.cambridge.org

First published 2004

Printed in the United States of America

Typeface Plantin 10/12 pt. *System* LaTeX 2ε [TB]

A catalog record for this book is available from the British Library.

Library of Congress Cataloging in Publication Data

Roth, Eric Abella.
Culture, biology, and anthropological demography / Eric Abella Roth.
p. cm. – (New perspectives on anthropological and social demography)
Includes bibliographical references and index.
ISBN 0-521-80905-3 – ISBN (invalid) 0-521-00544-8 (pbk.)
1. Demographic anthropology. 2. Human ecology. 3. Human behavior. 4. Mate selection. 5. Social ecology. I. Title. II. Series.
GN33.5.R68 2004
304.6 – dc22 2003068838

ISBN 0 521 80905 3 hardback
ISBN 0 521 00541 8 paperback

Contents

Figures

Tables

Acknowledgments

I am indebted to many people for their help with this book. My gratitude goes to Dr. David Kertzer, Series Editor, for the time and effort he expended in shepherding the project along from original outline to the finished book. I also thank Jessica Kuper and Andrew Beck of Cambridge University Press for their initial guidance and help in keeping the project moving. Thanks as well to two anonymous reviewers who provided both encouragement and very constructive criticism of the original draft. The book would not have been finished without the professional expertise (and kindness) of Kenneth Karpinski, Project Manager, Professional Publishing Group, at TechBooks; and Susan Zinninger, Copyeditor. To all the above, please accept a very sincere thank you for your professional help, academic guidance, and personal courtesy.

My Canadian, American and Kenyan colleagues and friends helped me in a multitude of ways, with data collection and analysis, reading the text, and not least, talking and listening to me talk about this project. Thanks to all these people, particularly Larion Aliaro, Moyra Brackley, Tom Burch, Merwan Engineer, Elliot Fratkin, Masako Fujita, Korea Leala, Margaret Leala, Daniel Lemoille, John McPeak, Judith Mitchell, Martha Nathan, Elizabeth Ngugi, and Kevin Smith. If I've forgotten anyone, please accept my apologies along with my thanks. I conclude this list by acknowledging my biggest academic debt of all, to my mentor and friend, Nancy Howell.

None of the fieldwork on which this book is based would have been possible without the consent and participation of the Rendille, Samburu and Ariaal people of northern Kenya. Thank you to all those folks who welcomed me into their homes, fed me, took care of me when I was sick, entertained me when I was well, and just put up with me for long periods of time.

Finally, since any demographic study starts, and ends, with children, I dedicate this book, with love, to my children, Hollis and Aidan Roth.

1 Anthropological Demography and Human Evolutionary Ecology

Two Solitudes

With the twenty-twenty vision of hindsight, I can easily identify two events that initiated this book. The first was a 1996 American Anthropological Association (AAA) Invited Session titled "Evolutionary Biology and Human Social Behaviour: 20 Years Later." Organized by human behavioral ecologists Lee Cronk and Napoleon Chagnon, this two-part session took its name from the AAA session twenty years earlier that culminated in the edited volume, *Evolutionary Biology and Human Social Behavior: An Anthropological Perspective* (Chagnon and Irons 1979). This work became the flagship for the anthropological application of E. O. Wilson's (1975) thesis of sociobiology. During the 1996 session (now represented in the edited text, *Adaptation and Human Behavior: An Anthropological Perspective*, by Cronk, Chagnon, and Irons 2000), paper presenters spoke passionately of the importance of evolutionary perspectives in understanding and explaining human behavior, including demographic behavior. They also clearly spoke to the converted; not one member of the audience questioned the speakers' basic assumptions of fitness maximization as the underlying motivation for human behavior.

Presenters emphasized biology, at the expense or even exclusion, of culture. In doing so they echoed past evolutionary ecologists' thoughts on the nonimportance of human culture, exemplified by Wilson's (1978:171) famous statement that "genes hold culture on a leash." Although contemporary human evolutionary ecologists, today also called human behavioral ecologists, distance themselves from such blatant statements of genetic determinism, they still have little time for culture. For example, a recent major review of the evolutionary perspective within anthropology appeared in the prestigious *Annual Review of Anthropology* under the title, "Is there a role for culture in human behavioral ecology?" (Cronk 1995). Even more succinctly, the human evolutionary ecologist Laura Betzig (1997a:49), in her introduction to an important collection of evolutionary ecological works titled *Human Nature: A Critical Reader* (Betzig

1997b), issued the terse statement that, in the investigation of human motivation, "I, personally, find 'culture' unnecessary."

The second event leading to the present work was the 1997 volume edited by David Kertzer and Tom Fricke, titled *Anthropological Demography: Toward a New Synthesis*. Rather than proposing a synthesis between cultural and biological demographic perspectives, the authors used the term *anthropological demography* as shorthand for cultural anthropological studies of demography. That the book sought a synthesis between cultural anthropology and demography, rather than a anthropological reconciliation between cultural and biological perspectives, was evident in the text's relegation of the evolutionary approach to an unflattering footnote (Hammel and Friou 1997:193):

> Where evolutionary theory and particularly sociobiology use concepts of selection and adaptation to explain individual behaviour they often seem thoroughly teleological and not mindful of the fundamental contributions of Darwin and Huxley.

Both *Anthropological Demography: Toward a New Synthesis* and *Adaptation and Human Behaviour: An Anthropological Perspective* do an excellent job in presenting their particular analytical framework, one emphasizing culture, the other stressing the evolutionary biology, of human demographic behavior. Both also share an air of apathy and downright disdain toward the other paradigm. The result is to ignore the other perspective, often apparently without even an attempt at understanding the other school's basic concepts and initial assumptions. This situation has not improved. For example, recently the anthropological demographer John Caldwell (1997) called for a uniform theory of fertility to describe historic and modern fertility decline, whereas the human evolutionary ecologist John Bock (2002) urged the formation of an overarching unified field theory of fertility. The former contains no reference to human evolutionary ecology; the latter contains no references to anthropological demography. The result of this continued intentional ignorance is akin to the "Two Solitudes" of Anglophone and Francophone traditions in Canada (MacClellan 1945) or C. P. Snow's (1993) "Two Cultures," denoted by what he termed "literary intellectuals" and natural scientists.

This book attempts to initiate a discussion between the fields of anthropological demography and human evolutionary ecology. One way to do so is to delineate largely unrecognized common ground, both theoretical and methodological, shared by both perspectives. I have no doubts that even this modest goal will not please dogmatists within either

Table 1.1. *Chapter titles from* Adaptation and Human Behavior: An Anthropological Perspective *and* Anthropological Demography: Toward a New Synthesis

Anthropological Demography (Kertzer and Fricke 1997)	*Adaptation* (Cronk, Chagnon, and Irons 2000)
Culture Theory and Demographic Process: Towards a Thicker Demography (Fricke)	Fertility, Offspring Quality, and Wealth in Dotoga Pastoralists: Testing Evolutionary Models of Intersexual Selection (Sellen et al.)
Demography Without Numbers (Scheper-Hughes)	The Evolutionary Economics and Psychology of the Demographic Transition to Low Fertility (Kaplan and Lancaster)
Kinship Systems and Demographic Regimes (Das Gupta)	An Adaptive Model of Human Reproductive Where Wealth is Inherited: Why People Have Small Families (Mace)
Population and Identity (Kreager)	Manipulating Kinship Rules: A Form of Yanomamo Reproductive Competition) (Chagnon)
Family Systems and Demographic Processes (Skinner)	The Grandmother Hypothesis and Human Evolution (Hawkes et al.)

group. This group of dogmatists, sadly both numerically large and powerfully influential, is not my target audience. Rather I hope to address open-minded scholars on both sides of this debate who value, but perhaps are not reconciled to, opposing premises, approaches, interpretations, and conclusions. The book also is addressed to demographers interested in learning about both approaches and who are not burdened by the academic blinkers of the two anthropological schools.

I am not so naive as to think that the goal of interested mutual discussion will be an easy task, because both perspectives have radically different basic concepts and methodological approaches; this results in dramatically different vocabularies. The gulf separating the two approaches is exemplified in Table 1.1, which lists chapter titles from the two aforementioned texts, human evolutionary ecology's *Adaptation and Human Behavior: An Anthropological Perspective* (Cronk, Chagnon, and Irons 2000) and *Anthropological Demography: Toward a New Synthesis* (Kertzer and Fricke 1997). These titles point to the divergent roots and subsequent trajectories of these two demographic approaches. From the most pessimistic view, the resulting chasm is too broad to span and the prevailing dogma within anthropology too strong to permit any type of rapprochement among anthropologists.

However, I have a sense of hope outside anthropology, generated by demography's current interest in culture and evolution. My optimism stems from the recent inclusion of evolutionary approaches to demography in scheduled sessions at the meetings of the Population Association of America (PAA). These sessions now coexist with regularly scheduled sessions on anthropological demography. Unlike the situation at the AAA, I see the same scholars at both PAA presentations. Even more encouraging, these demographers actually seem keen to understand both perspectives.

This openness on the part of demographers is particularly encouraging given the initial skirmishes between demography and human evolutionary ecology, epitomized by the latter's aggressively negative view of Caldwell's Wealth Flow Theory (Turke 1989; Kaplan 1994) appearing in *Population and Development Review*. Today, however, evolutionary perspectives on subjects as diverse as human aging (Kaplan 1997; Carey and Judge 2001; Carey and Tuljapukar 2003), the demographic transition (Foster 2000; Clark and Low 2001; Haaga 2001), the evolutionary importance of meat eating (Smil 2002), and kin selection (Sear et al. 2002) appear in this and other mainstream demographic journals. In the same editions, these journals feature anthropological demographic studies (Watkins 2000; Johnson-Hanks 2002).

In simultaneously considering evolutionary and cultural perspectives, demographers may actually hold more potential for uniting anthropological demography and human evolutionary ecology than do anthropologists. In part, the difficulty of reconciling these two paradigms within anthropology lies in the fact that each side brings a vastly different time depth to their analyses. Anthropological demography, which today borrows heavily from the traditions of political economy (Wolf 1982), dependency theory (Frank 1967), and world systems theory (Wallerstein 1976) in examining local, non-Western cultures in light of larger Western capitalistic expansion, features a time depth measured in decades, or, at the most, centuries. In contrast, human evolutionary ecologists' view behavior as the long-term product of natural selection, leading to a far greater time depth. Or, as stated by a doyenne of evolutionary theory, Sara Blaffer Hrdy (1999:xi), "My depth of field is millions of years longer, and the subjects in my viewfinder have the curious habit of spontaneously taking on the attributes of other species: chimps, platypuses, australopithecines."

Recently, the biological anthropologists Goodman and Leatherman (1998:31–32) urged their colleagues to study biological adaptations within broader historical contexts, focusing on the roots of socioeconomic variation; or, as they put it, to "refocus upstream" rather than on the temporal immediate. However, human evolutionary ecologists could argue that Goodman and Leatherman severely limit themselves by concentrating on the few centuries of Old World–New World contact. To truly go "upstream" requires a time depth measured in millions, not hundreds, of years. Again demography, with its interest in paleodemography, the evolution of human population numbers, and human longevity, seems well positioned to bridge these two temporal scales.

Why is demography, but not anthropology, so open to pursuing these issues? Why does the ensuing gap between anthropological demography and human evolutionary ecology within anthropology continue to widen? Because both subfields are fully capable of developing their own theory and methodology, I suggest the central question for practitioners of each approach is this: Why bother learning anything about the other perspective? The remainder of this book uses detailed case studies to address this question. Let me give a brief overview now. If, following this section, you are not persuaded by my argument, then you will not find the rest of this book worth your time.

Why Bother?

I begin by asking this question: Why should anthropological demographers learn about human evolutionary ecology when their perspective seems, as described by Hammel and Friou (1997:193), "thoroughly teleological"? The converse question is this: Why should human evolutionary ecologists invest their time and effort in learning about anthropological demography, because, in terms of behavioral motivation, culture is, in the words of Betzig (1997a:49), "unnecessary"? I believe the answer to these questions lies in the overturning of historic paradigms and their replacement with contemporary data.

For anthropological demographers, this means rejecting the now-outdated Standard Social Science model that emphasizes nurture, in the form of society and culture, to the total exclusion of biology. Pinker (2002) traces the development of this model from two historic notions, the tabula rasa, or blank slate, and "the ghost in the machine." The first is the idea that we are born without an innate human nature and therefore all human behavior is molded entirely by one's lifetime experiences. The second proposes a strict mind–body dichotomy, with only the latter ruled by mechanical laws. Both concepts are entrenched in anthropology, where culture historically was seen as *superorganic*; that is, it was an entity totally removed from the biological world of heredity. Two historic quotes from the anthropologist Leslie White (1949; quoted in Degler 1991) exemplify this perspective: "the cultural process may be regarded as a thing *sui generis*, culture is explainable in terms of culture" (p. 208) and "much of what is commonly called 'human nature' is merely culture thrown against a screen of nerves, glands, sense organs, muscles, etc." (p. 161).

In direct contrast to this vision, both biologists and social scientists in the latter half of the twentieth century began to consider human social behavior from an evolutionary perspective. Their research, exemplified by Hamilton's (1964) work on kin selection, Trivers' (1974) analysis of reciprocal altruism, Axelrod's (1984) simulation studies on the emergence of cooperation, and Maynard-Smith's (1982) application of game theory to social strategies, demonstrated that aspects of human social interaction such as cooperation, nepotism, and altruism, which Darwin had difficulty explaining in his original model of evolution by means of natural selection, could now be incorporated by means of the new concepts of kin selection and inclusive fitness. The former proposes that altruistic acts between relatives will be favored by selection if the benefit to the recipient exceeds the cost to the donor, devalued by the degree of relatedness between them (Barrett, Dunbar, and Lycett 2002:386). Inclusive fitness expands Darwin's original consideration of the individual as the sole unit of analysis to include behavior conferring reproductive advantages to relatives who share the same genetic material by common descent.

Incorporating these results into new syntheses of biosocial behavior (Wilson 1975; Dawkins 1976, 1979) resulted in the recognition that basic aspects of human behaviour, such as nepotism, cooperation, and altruism, should be considered evolutionary products of natural selection with biological roots (for recent book-length compilations of this scientific revolution in biology and social behavior, see Hamilton 1998, 2002; Trivers 2002). It also suggested that these basic behaviors formed a biological basis for human culture (see Tooby and Cosmides 1989, 1990; Cosmides and Tooby 1992) somewhere in our evolutionary past. If so, then the two previous quotes should be reworked to read, "much of what is commonly called culture is merely human nature," and "the evolutionary process may be regarded as a thing *sui generis*; biology is explainable in terms of biology."

At the same time as these developments, the long-held notion of culture as the sole source of all human variation was dealt a series of devastating blows by publications refuting long-standing anthropological claims. These claims included arguments that life-cycle stages are experienced differently in distinct cultures (Mead 1927) and that the Hopi peoples of the southwestern United States had no linguistic or psychological concept of time (Carroll 1956); they also included "the doctrine of extreme linguistic relativity," exemplified by the arbitrary linguistic description and classification of color by various cultures. (For additional anthropological claims to the primacy of cultural diversity and in-depth discussions of these three examples, see Brown 1991; Durham 1991; and Cronk 1999.) One by one these claims were falsified by careful anthropological fieldwork. Research in Samoa revealed that Mead's utopian view of Samoan adolescent as a time of socially sanctioned sexual freedom arose from her young female informants' playing a practical joke on the overeager young ethnographer (Freeman 1983). In reality, Samoan adolescence is as sexually conflicted and stressful as that experienced by Western cultures. Ekkehart Malotki's book *Hopi Time* (1983) unequivocally demonstrated that Hopi possess elaborate ceremonial and technical concepts of time fully comparable with other cultures. Berlin and Kay's (1969) cross-cultural research on color classification revealed far more uniformity than disparity. For example, their study populations acknowledged from two to eleven basic colors, but they all start with the colors *black* and *white* and then, if they possess more color classifications, invariably add the same colors. Thus a culture with seven basic colors starts with *black* and *white*, and then it always adds *red, blue, yellow, green*, and *brown*.

Ascribing biological roots to primary social behaviors and dispelling long-held anthropological myths concerning the supremacy of cultural diversity had profound ramifications within academia. In psychology, this gave rise to evolutionary psychology (Barrett et al. 2002); in economics, the linkage between rational choice theory and natural selection led to an adoption of evolutionary theory (Lam 2003). Darwinism became a mainstay of philosophical naturalism, with its proponents arguing for the evolution of free will (Dennett 2003) and the adaptive properties of biologically based human emotions (Frank 1988). In biology, E. O. Wilson's (1975) synthesis of Hamilton and Trivers' work formed the backbone of sociobiology. Today, within the biological sciences, this paradigm is so pervasive that the animal behavioralist John Alcock's (2001) book is correctly labeled *The Triumph of Sociobiology*. Darwin's adaptationist perspective also led to the emergent field of evolutionary medicine (Nesse and Williams 1994; Strassmann and Dunbar 1999).

In anthropology, reactions to these developments were mixed. Some practitioners abandoned studies of cultural singularities to concentrate on the search for human universals. This is best represented by Brown's (1991) cross-cultural research that constructed a Universal People, based on a compilation of shared traits ranging from sexual jealousy through notions of time to incest avoidance and the proscription of rape. Others launched concerted attacks on the new adaptationist perspective (see Sahlins 1976). However, the great majority of anthropologists simply ignored the debate about cultural versus biological roots to human behavior. This lack of interest is truly lamentable, for anthropology still has much to offer in the study of human ethology. In response to Betzig's imperial statement that "personally I can do without culture," one of the founders of behavioral ecology, John R. Krebs, stated that he and his colleague Alex Kacelnik, "personally find culture necessary" (Kacelnik and Krebs 1997:27). In defending this statement, they make the following argument (1997:28):

> Cultural evolution has its own dynamics, constrained but not fully determined by human evolutionary adaptations. A satisfactory understanding of human behavior requires examining the articulation of formerly adaptive traits with present cultural circumstances.

A recent example of the necessity of considering culture along with evolutionary biology is provided by the phenomenon of partible paternity in Lowland South America (Beckerman and Valentine 2002a). Throughout this region, many indigenous cultures believe that multiple males are necessary to form a fetus because fetuses are "sculpted" out of successive coitus, and that only after a sufficient amount of semen accretion can a complete child be formed in women's wombs. Beckerman and Valentine (2002b) show that the belief in partible paternity, specifically the cultural recognition and acceptance of multiple biological fathers, is widespread throughout many Lowland South American societies separated by significant linguistic and geographical and with no history of cultural contact.

This indigenous concept of multiple fathers has notable demographic consequences. Consider the case of Ache foragers of northern Paraguay, reported by Hill and Hurtado (1996). Within Ache society, men and women engage in a series of short, sequential marriages, leading to a high degree of paternal uncertainty. As a result, Ache recognize "primary" and "secondary" fathers. The former consist of men who had intercourse with a woman prior to pregnancy, or when "her blood flow ceased to be found" (Hill and Hurtado 1996:249). Secondary fathers are men who had sexual intercourse with woman in the year preceding pregnancy as well as the man married to the woman at childbirth. Children call both groups by the same term for "father," and both groups contribute food and childcare for offspring they "fathered." The prevalence of both types of fathers is evident in Hill and Hurtado's (1996:273) survey of 321 Ache adults between 1980 and 1989, which included 632 reported fathers, for an average of close to two fathers per birth (mean = 1.97, standard error = 0.06, and median = 2; mode = 2 and maximum = 10).

Among the Ache, there is a long history of infanticide. Hill and Hurtado's data showed that, during the period of early contact with Europeans, 14% of all male and 23% of all female children were killed before they reached the age of ten. Logistic regression analysis revealed that children without fathers were 3.9 times as likely to be killed in each year of childhood, relative to children with fathers. Adopting an evolutionary position, the authors considered Hrdy's (1979) suggestion that female nonhuman primates may counteract the threat of infanticide by spreading paternity confidence among several males. To test this among the Ache, Hill and Hurtado (1996:442) hypothesized that a female Ache strategy is to accumulate multiple sexual partners under the belief that males with some probability of paternity would protect or care for the child in question. A logistic regression analysis of yearly mortality rates and number of secondary fathers for the period 1890–1970 showed that the lowest child mortality rate (ages newborn through nine years) was for offspring with one primary and one secondary father, whereas the highest mortality rate was for those with no secondary fathers. Hill and Hurtado's interpretation is that the optimal effective female strategy is to have an intermediate number of fathers, represented here by one primary and one secondary father. Having more than one secondary father led to a sharp rise in offspring mortality, associated with the dissolution of paternal confidence and subsequent loss of male parental investment.

The same type of mortality differentials associated with the presence of multiple fathers is reported by Beckerman et al. (2002) for the Bari of Venezuela. In this society, the presence of secondary fathers resulted in food provisioning for pregnant mothers, rather than extra male investment in food and time for the offspring. As a result, the most important pathway linking the presence of secondary fathers with differential offspring mortality was by means of lower fetal wastage; the odds ratio of being a stillborn was significant both between those offspring who had no and one secondary parent ($p = 0.001$) and those offspring with one and those with more than one ($p = 0.0034$).

Whether achieved by provisioning of mothers or offspring, the presence of multiple parents in the Bari and Ache flies directly in the face of what Beckerman and Valentine (2002b:3) call the "Standard Model of Human Evolution" (Alexander and Noonan 1979; Lovejoy 1981), which heavily stresses paternal certainty as a vital determinant of human social evolution. This posits a strict sexual division of labor in hominid prehistory, so that males forage and provision females and their dependent offspring, who are under the constant supervision of their mothers. In this scenario, paternal investment is directly linked to paternal certainty, heightened by pair-bonding and monogamy. Only high levels of paternal confidence allowed for the heavy paternal investment of time and energy seen in human evolution but rare in nonhuman primates (Kaplan and Lancaster 2003).

Beckerman and Valentine (2002b:3) also note that the social acceptance of multiple fathers also contradicts previous notions of human universals that include sexual jealousy arising from concerns with paternal confidence. In this regard, Pinker (1997:488–490) writes the following:

> in no society do men readily share a wife. A woman having sex with another man is always a threat to the man's genetic interests, because it might fool him into working for a competitor's genes.

Likewise, the founder of sociobiology, E. O. Wilson, writes in his text, *Consilience* (1998:170), that "in courtship men are predicted to stress exclusive sexual access and guarantees of paternity."

Incorporating the Standard Model of Human Evolution, the widespread cultural phenomenon of partible paternity in Lowland South America constitutes a very strong example of the admonition of Kacelnik and Kreb (1997:28) that "a satisfactory understanding of human behavior requires examining the articulation of formerly adaptive traits with present cultural circumstances." Because analyses from both the Bari and Ache indicate improved offspring mortality rates associated with secondary fathers, it is legitimate to see partible paternity as constituting adaptive cultural behavior, whether or not it is consciously recognized by individuals within these societies. In this interpretation, culture is the *ideational model* of parenting that posits multiple sexual acts with different males are necessary to develop a fetus. It is adherence to, and deviation from, this ideational model, represented by children with one or multiple fathers, that constitutes *social behavior* within these societies. Although I return to this point in subsequent sections, it is important to stress here the difference between culture, which consists of socially recognized ideas that act as potential paths of behavior, and subsequent social behavior, in which individuals choose and enact one possible pathway.

Because in this perspective culture offers an array of choices, it follows that these choices can have adaptive, neutral, or even maladaptive consequences for individual fitness levels. Staying with the topic of paternity, Vickers (2002) describes the sexual belief and behavior of two other native groups of Lowland South America, the Siona and Secoya of northeast Ecuador, who do not recognize multiple fathers. Instead, these groups believe men should not engage in "excessive" sexual matters, because of the underlying cultural construct that menstrual blood will contaminate, weaken, and perhaps even kill men. It can also make their wives suffer, affect men's hunting skill and luck, and inhibit their receiving visions when they drink a potion made from the *yahe* vine (*Banisteriopsis caapi*). Given these dire consequences, it is perhaps not surprising that these two groups believe that fetuses are formed from a single genitor, adultery is viewed with "consternation and stigmatization," the vast majority of Siona–Secoya marriages are monogamous, and women and newborns undergo a period of postpartum isolation (Vickers 2002:233–238). In essence, these two groups differ radically from the Bari and Ache, and they conform much more closely to the Standard Model of Human Evolution with respect to paternal certainty.

There are two alternative interpretations of this marked cultural diversity within the same environmental region. Both highlight the importance of ideational models of culture, but they differ in assessing the link between culture and adaptive social behavior. Vicker's interpretation stems from the human evolutionary ecology perspective, and it posits that Siona–Secoya sexual beliefs are adaptive. Following life history theory terminology, he argues that Siona–Secoya are investing in *parenting*, rather than *mating effort* (much more on this dichotomy, which organizes subsequent chapters, later), evidenced by the cultural ideal of a birth spacing interval of four to six years and a relatively small (four to six children) model family size. Postpartum sexual abstinence and social disparagement of mothers who closely space births, for example, "we aren't opossums to live like that!" (Vickers 2002:238), enforce these two related demographic measures. The alternative explanation is that the Siona–Secoya cultural ideational models of sex and procreation are neither adaptive nor maladaptive, but rather not even formed, consciously or unconsciously, to raise fitness levels. In this view, the widespread distribution of cultures recognizing multiple fathers is analogous to random genetic mutations in Kimura's (1979) Neutrality Theory; the great, great majority does not either adversely or beneficially affect fitness levels.

In this example, and in many other case studies presented in following chapters, I leave it to the reader to decide between these alternative views of cultural links to adaptive behavior. However, one thing is clear: cultural anthropologists, human biologists, and demographers should all "find culture necessary" for any explanation of human behavior. Just as the anthropological myths of Hopi time keeping, culturally arbitrary color schemes, and the Standard Social Science Model to which they belonged were nullified, so too do examples such as partible paternity negate serious consideration of a Standard Model of Human Evolution. Quite simply, people do not behave like either model, and neither model is fully capable of explaining human social behavior. Both, however, can contribute to our understanding of human behavior as it pertains to reproduction and mortality. What is needed is some "flow," in the form of discussion between the adherents of each model, particularly anthropological demographers and human evolutionary ecologists. I begin my appeal to initiate a discussion focusing on common ground by offering a necessarily brief overview of both fields. In doing so, I make the assumption that readers are not very familiar with either anthropological demography or human evolutionary ecology. To this end I attempt to lay out basic theoretical premises of each field and then exemplify their application in specific research.

Anthropological Demography: Culture, not Biology

Within cultural anthropology there is a long history of demographic studies, focusing largely on the theme of population regulation in noncontracepting populations; this is a topic that has been explored from the time of Carr-Saunders' (1922) work, *The Population Problem: A Study in Human Evolution*, through Harris and Ross' (1987) text, *Death, Sex and Fertility: Population Regulation in Preindustrial and Developing Societies*. However, until recently, anthropological demographic studies were either ignored or derided by demographers (see Caldwell, Caldwell, and Caldwell 1987).

Demography's current interest in culture and anthropology arises from two separate lines of inquiry. First, there was the failure of Princeton University's European Fertility Project to explain the timing of the European Demographic Transition in purely economic terms. Instead, historic fertility change appeared to be linked to "cultural change," with culture operationally defined as language, geographical region, or religion (Knodel and van de Walle 1979; Coale and Watkins 1986). Suddenly, demographers were forced to consider incorporating culture into models of demographic change.

Second, these unexpected results dovetailed with the work of Australian demographer John Caldwell, who expressed dissatisfaction with the contextual depth represented by survey data, specifically the World Fertility Survey data (Caldwell 1982, 1985). This dissatisfaction led Caldwell to incorporate anthropological field methods in the construction of small-scale demographic studies, a field he called *microdemography* (Caldwell, Hill, and Hull 1988a). This approach represented a radical development for a classically trained demographer, as apparent in the following quote from Caldwell (1982:4):

> Most demographers work on large data sets, often with little contact with the people whom the statistics describe. Fortunately, in early 1962 it became clear that the 1960 Ghana Census was not going to yield material quickly enough to absorb my time. We thereupon used our limited funds for cheap and relatively small scale investigations which meant borrowing methodology from the anthropologists (and reading them) and becoming intimately acquainted with village

and family in turn. For a demographer with traditional training, the experience was illuminating – so illuminating that we have attempted to use similar methods ever since.

These "illuminating experiences" led Caldwell to actively promote culture as a vital factor in demographic theory. The result was his Wealth Flows Theory (Caldwell 1982), which took its name came from its central tenet that, in patrilineal societies characterized by household modes of production and low levels of female autonomy, children represent wealth because of their early and heavy participation in the household labor pool. Offered as an alternative to traditional Demographic Transition Theory, Caldwell's Wealth Flows Theory marked an important watershed in demography by advancing the radical proposition that high fertility in Third World countries was economically rational. It also was revolutionary in considering culture, represented in both political and economic spheres, as a major force in demographic stability and change.

Together these separate research events propelled culture to the forefront in demography's search for explanatory variables. Unfortunately, in doing so, demography's earlier neglect of anthropology led to the adoption of outmoded anthropological concepts, leading Hammel (1990:456) to lament that "the use of culture in demography seems mired in structural-functional concepts that are about 40 years old, hardening rapidly and showing every sign of fossilization." The "fossilization" that Hammel refers to was demography's view of culture as consisting of group-derived social norms. Adherence to these norms was deemed capable of fully explaining individual behavior. It is not surprising that demographers adopted this view, for, as Bledsoe and Hill (1998:268) note, the father of demography, Thomas Malthus, believed firmly in social norms as preventative checks on population growth, exemplified by conjugal norms supporting premarital sexual restraint and the postponement of marriage for economically unprepared couples.

Inherent problems in this view of culture as a set of social norms are exemplified in Lockwood's (1995) critique of the demographic explanation of sub-Saharan African postpartum taboos and long lactation periods. Using aggregate data collected from past ethnographers (Murdock 1967) along with World Fertility Survey data, Lesthaeghe (1980) and Schoenmaeckers et al. (1981) tested Saucier's (1972) gerontocratic model of sub-Saharan reproductive regimes. This model proposes that older men maintain control over the labor of women and younger men through the use of social structures such as polygyny, unilineal descent, and gerontocracy. These factors in turn permit long postpartum abstinence periods for women without sexual deprivation for older, polygynously married men. The overall interpretation was that long postpartum abstinence periods represented underlying social norms reinforcing adaptive social structures (Lesthaeghe 1989).

Lockwood (1995) argues that this structural–functionalist perspective fails to distinguish between collective norms and individual actions. The structural-functionalist assumption that individual behavior is governed by norms driven by social structure necessitates strong links between social structure and norms, and between collective norms and individual actions. However, Lockwood (1995:1) stresses that these links are "theoretically weak and empirically indeterminate" (see Fricke 1997a and Kertzer 1995, 1998 on this point). Lockwood (1995:1) points out that, if these links exist, then it is difficult, if not impossible, to fully study the relationship between the two phenomena. Similarly, Hammel (1990) notes that the assumption of such a seamless relationship between social norms and individual behavior harkens back to the work of Radcliffe-Brown and Durkheim, who saw culture as a "guidance system" for behavior. However, from this starting point, culture by necessity is "silent on the mechanisms for conformity and deviance" (1990:462) to social norms, even though early structural–functional models admitted to individual deviance from social norms. Holy and Stuchlik (1983) stress that at least three types of data are needed to analyze the relationships between group norms and individual action: (1) data consisting of the reporting of social norms, (2) data consisting of reported behavior and, (3) data consisting of observed action.

Recognizing these pitfalls, recent anthropological demography works abandoned the structural–functionalist model in search of richer contextual pictures of culture's role in demography (see Greenhalgh 1995a; Jones et al. 1997; Kertzer and Fricke 1997; Basu and Aaby 1998). Although certainly not monolithic in their focus, methodologies, or research interests (for reviews of the different contemporary aspects of anthropological demography, see Greenhalgh 1995b and Kertzer and Fricke 1997), these works share common elements that serve to define the field of anthropological demography.

The first is the concept of agency. This reflects Hammel's (1990:456) recommendation that anthropology move away from the institutionalized structural–functional approach and "toward the elucidation of local culture-specific rationalities, in the building of which actors are important perceiving, interpreting and constructing agents." Anthropologists term this viewpoint *social constructionism*, which is "the view that social organization is not determined by broad societal norms, but is a human product, actively constructed by human agents" (Greenhalgh 1995b:14). Hammel and Friou (1994:179) express the central position of agency in anthropology, as opposed to sociology or economics, in the following manner:

> The effect of agency to the economist or sociologist is some measurable amount of residual variance in outcome; to the anthropologist it is a beam from the human soul, which will only be extinguished if its source is found.

This perspective raises two immediate potential points of conflict. The first is the perceived dichotomy between human agency and cultural constraints. Carter (1995, 1998) notes that human agency is frequently interpreted as rational decision making, which is itself seen as an universal property of autonomous individuals. In contrast, culture is perceived as a body of rules represented by social institutions and norms lying outside and constraining individual action. Carter (1998:262) collapses this false dichotomy by emphasizing the work of Giddens (1979) and Lave (1988). The former argues that human action is correctly understood as reflexive monitoring and rationalization of a continuous flow of conduct. In a similar vein, Laves (1988:1) uses the concept of "activity in setting," arguing that agency is "socially distributed," that is, "stretched over, not divided among – mind, body, activity and culturally organized settings (which includes other actors)."

The second potential point of conflict is the degree to which agency can be applied to preindustrial populations. This qualm arises from classic Demographic Transition Theory's position that social norms reigned supreme in Pre-Transitional populations; this is exemplified by Leibenstein's (1981:397) view of decision making in these populations as "passive" or bound by cultural convention. To wit:

> Those living in a village in a developing country are likely to exhibit a considerable amount of routine behavior, and hence this would appear to be a desirable context within which to study passive decision-making. In other words, the general hypothesis is that so-called traditional behavior is likely to involve a great many passive decisions.

Anthropological demographic studies conclusively dissuade us from accepting a passive–active decision-making dichotomy between Pre- and Post-Transitional populations by showing that the former feature heirship strategies to ensure intergenerational property transfer (Bledsoe 1990; Roth 1994a), the use of infanticide or "benign neglect" of children to manage family size or gender composition (Scrimshaw 1978, 1983; Scheper-Hughes 1992; Roth 2000), and the regulation of birth spacing by both traditional and modern contraceptive practices (Bledsoe 2002).

A second unifying factor of current anthropological demography is concern with gender. Here again, anthropology is highly critical of demography's historic use of the concept of gender. As reviewed by Riley (1997a) and Greenhalgh (1995b), demography traditionally studied women in terms of "status" (see Mason 1993) or "autonomy" (Jejeebhoy 1995). Such an approach has strong methodological and theoretical appeal; although female status and autonomy are problematic to define accurately, proxy measures can be incorporated into demographic surveys. This situation is evident in the strong, though still incompletely understood, effects that female education has on both fertility and mortality parameters across different societal settings (see reviews in Bledsoe et al. 1999). With education used as a proxy for female status or autonomy, changing gender relationships emerged in the demographic literature as a powerful engine for social and demographic change, as first put forth in Caldwell's Wealth Flows Theory (Caldwell 1982, 1994). This reasoning is later seen in Jejeebhoy's (1995) recognition of five different types of female autonomy capable of initiating fertility change: knowledge, decision making, and physical, emotional, economic and social autonomy. In her model, these forms of autonomy are synonymous with status and are amenable to analysis by use of Bongaarts' (1982) model of proximate fertility variables.

Anthropologists, however, point to potential problems associated with the use of female status or autonomy as a proxy for gender. The most important is that focusing on individual female attributes such as status and autonomy isolates women from any cultural context, as well as from the opposite sex. Consequently, women and men are seen to inhabit separate, sometimes mutually exclusive, spheres, resulting in a noted absence of men's perspectives in demographic studies (Green and Biddlecom 2000).

A second shortcoming of the emphasis use of female status or autonomy is that it represents discrete states, for example, "low" versus "high" status, without yielding information about the processes leading to their attainment. Thus Levine et al. (1991:459) clearly state that there is "scant information" on the precise mechanisms through which "the formal education of women affects their reproductive and health behaviors" (cited in Carter 1998:49). Nevertheless, it is easy, if not particularly illuminating, to comprehend the corresponding transition from low to high status for educated women.

A third and final failing of the use of status or autonomy to describe gender is that it presupposes unilinear change; for example, as women's status increases, fertility and infant mortality fall, while living conditions for women and families improve. Again, when female education is used as a proxy for status or autonomy, there does appear to be a strong "dose and response" relationship between mother's years of education and infant mortality (Cleland and Kaufmann 1998). However, fertility and mother's education relationships are much more varied and remain largely unexplained. For example, for Western Kenya, Bradley (1995) showed that, in poorer areas where women posted recent political, economic, and educational gains, one net result was increased competition for scarce resources with men, resulting in an increase in domestic violence against women. Likewise, educating young women in sub-Saharan Africa may make them more vulnerable prey to sugar daddies, that is, rich older men, who can help pay their school costs. Heise and Elias (1995:939) capture the juxtaposition of increased status and autonomy with increased risk of sexually transmitted disease:

> Subsidizing the uniform and school fees for adolescent girls in Africa might actually do more to reduce HIV transmission – by eliminating the need for Sugar Daddies – than the most sophisticated "peer education" campaigns.

To avoid these pitfalls, anthropologists replace the concept of female status or autonomy with gender. This is a far more inclusive concept, as noted in the demographer Mason's (1997:159) definition of "gender system" as "the entire complex of roles, rights and statuses that surround being male or female in a given society or culture." This definition fits well with the anthropologist Greenhalgh's (1995b:24) observation that gender (1) entails the study of men as well as women, (2) is a cultural construction, rather than a culture-free idea, (3) denotes power differentials and sex-related ideologies as well as material inequalities, and (4) is a structuring principle of social life rather than simply an individual attribute. From this framework, Greenhalgh (1995b:25) argues that "gender connotes agency" and that gender analyses recognize power differentials and material inequalities. This is expressed succinctly by Kertzer (1997:153):

> People do have some autonomy to make choices; they are not simply "cultural dopes." Yet the choices made by some – those in a position of greater power – are more influential than those made by others.

The third prominent thread in contemporary anthropological demography is the use of a political economy perspective (Greenhalgh 1990, 1995b; Kertzer 1997). Akin to McNicoll's (1994) institutional approach in demography, this perspective stresses that individual agency is inevitably embedded in the social, historic, and economic fabric of local community institutions, which themselves are nested within larger national and international structures. These models emphasize that all behavior is constrained within larger contexts, and that these contexts are frequently linked in terms of historic causation. As a result, this perspective attempts to implement a multilevel framework, with an individual's behavior viewed in the context of larger political, social, or economic processes, all of which may possess deep historical roots. Thus, processes as diverse as the past spread of different religions (e.g., Islam throughout Southeast Asia) and contemporary financial restructuring by the World Bank can be viewed as both constraints and opportunities for new demographic behavior.

Anthropological demography's conceptualization of culture featuring the trinity of individual agency, gender, and political economy is illustrated in Bledsoe and Hill's (Bledsoe et al. 1994; Hill 1997; Bledsoe and Hill 1998; Bledsoe 2002) analyses of West African postpartum patterns. Their study site in Gambia was the center of medical intervention programs carried out by the British Medical Research Council, and the demographic profiles of their village populations fit the pattern previously called "natural fertility." That is, they were characterized by high fertility with evenly spaced birth intervals, which lengthened only with age. Birth intervals formed the focus of their study, particularly in relationship to international religious and local social norms.

Cultural norms are represented by the Quronic decree that a husband and wife abstain from sex for a period of *at least* forty days postpartum. Resumption of conjugal sexual relationships (euphemistically referred to in the local communities as "contact") may begin on or after this date, often accompanied by a cleansing ritual. This norm of course has a deep political and historical basis, reflecting the spread of Islam throughout West Africa from its Arabian hearth. It also has the support of many Gambian men, who interpret the norm as a mandate to initiate sexual relationships precisely on the fortieth day. Together these factors exemplify the influence of both political economy and gender on a specific cultural behavior.

However, this particular Islamic religious decree conflicts with equally strong local social perceptions of proper maternal childcare. These stress long interbirth periods, preferably two or two and one-half years in duration, to facilitate the health of both mother and child. In interviews and surveys, both men and women stated that this period is necessary to sustain maternal health and ensure child survival through a long period of breastfeeding without competition for breast milk from newborn siblings.

These two social norms, one promoting long interbirth intervals to ensure child health and the other calling for relatively quick resumption of sexual relations, pose a conflict for mothers. If women observe the forty-day decree, they can be accused of being poor mothers who put their own sexual desires ahead of concern for their offspring. Alternatively, if a woman delays the resumption of postpartum sexual relationships, her behavior can be seen as irreligious and lacking in wifely virtues, with the latter reflecting poorly on both her natal and her husband's family.

Such a situation is not novel. Bledsoe and Hill recall Van Velson's statement (1967:131) that "individuals are often faced by a choice between alternative norms." What Bledsoe and Hill's research clearly shows is that, in this particular situation, both men and women use cultural norms, rules, and the surrounding ambiguities to their own advantage. Interpreting the Islamic edict, men claim it dictates that a woman should initiate a sexual relationship with her husband immediately on the fortieth day postpartum. In contrast, women commonly interpret it as an obligation to make themselves available to their husbands at any time following the forty-day interval.

This male–female dichotomy is too simplistic, for men commonly recruit elderly women, either from their own family or their in-law's, to help persuade their wives that long periods of abstinence are unacceptable. Furthermore, men make subtle distinctions about the resumption of postpartum contact, reflecting the following criteria (Bledsoe and Hill 1998:289):

- whether the wife in question is young or old;
- whether the union has been in existence for a long or a short time;
- where the wife is in her fertility cycle;
- whether a wife has more children of one sex or another; and
- the status of the wife, for example, an "outside" wife versus an "inside" wife, or an educated wife versus a less educated rural wife.

In detailing these variable criteria, Bledsoe and Hill (1998:288) rightfully note that "even in a setting as small as the domestic contexts in which most demographically relevant behaviors occur, a welter of normative ambiguities and conflicts emerge at once."

Bledsoe and Hill detail the myriad ways women attempt to solve these conflicts. Women who do not want to become pregnant find reasons to take trips to their mother's residence, search out young co-wives, or take herbal indigenous medicines. Others adopt the use of Western contraceptives to avoid pregnancy while resuming postpartum sex. The irony of adopting more "liberal" or "modern" fertility control to enforce traditional social mores does not escape the authors' attention.

These diverse strategies result in great variability in the actual resumption of postpartum sexual relationships. Interpreting this variation, Bledsoe and Hill (1998:273) observe that, in this case, cultural rules may be seen "less as rigidly binding prescriptions for conduct than as resources." This view of culture as a framework of opportunities and constraints, dependent on one's place within local social hierarchies, has the dual advantages of avoiding the false "agency versus culture" dichotomy shown by Carter (1998) while simultaneously incorporating Greenhalgh's (1995b) political economy framework, which stresses power and gender differentials over time and across different regional hierarchies. Focusing on individual variation in relation to social norms further avoids the pitfall of normative reductionism (Bledsoe and Hill 1998:273; see also Cronk 1999), in which people are unthinking "cultural dopes," to use Kertzer's (1997:153) tongue-in-cheek description. Instead, as Kertzer (1997:153) notes,

> [T]his perspective also sheds a quite different light on the notion of the individual; from an unthinking follower of rules and believer of established categories to a strategic actor who may attempt to use rules to achieve desired outcomes.

In summary, unlike earlier efforts, today anthropological demographers see the presence and effect of culture while also recognizing individual variation representing individual agency stemming from gender differences or from one's position within a political economy functioning on multiple levels (local, national, and international).

Human Behavioral Ecology: Biology, not Culture

Unfortunately, another unifying theme of anthropological demography is that it totally ignores the substantial body of demographic studies analyzed from the perspective of *human evolutionary ecology* (Chagnon and Irons 1979; Betzig, Borgerhoff Mulder, and Turke 1988; Borgerhoff Mulder 1992; Smith and Winterhalder 1992a; Betzig 1997b; Cronk, Chagnon, and Irons 2000). Also known as *human behavioral ecology*, this field is defined as the application of natural selection theory to the study of adaptation and biological design in an ecological setting (Smith and Winterhalder 1992a:5). Central to this application is the tenet that human behavior functions to enhance human fitness levels. The unit of analysis is the individual, expressed by means of the concept of methodological individualism that holds that the properties of groups are viewed as a result of the actions of its individual members. Combining these methodological and theoretical tenets, Borgerhoff Mulder (1996:205) summarizes human evolutionary ecology as a field in which

> individuals are viewed as facultative opportunists who assess, either consciously or not, on either the behavioural or the evolutionary time scale, a wide array of environmental conditions (both social and ecological) and determine the optimal fitness-maximizing strategy whereby they can out compete conspecifics in terms of the number of genes transmitted to subsequent generations.

The key phrase in this quotation is the "wide array of environmental conditions (both social and ecological)." Incorporating social conditions within the rubric of "environment" and stressing environmental variation across both space and time avoids the trap of genetic determinism associated with human sociobiology. Defined as "the systematic study of the biological basis of all social behaviour" (Wilson 1975:4), sociobiology views all behavioral variations, including human culture, as genetically coded and therefore the direct result of genetic variation. From this totally adaptationist perspective comes the sense that "the genes hold culture on a leash. The leash is very long, but inevitably values will be constrained in accordance with their effects on the human gene pool" (Wilson 1978:167).

Human evolutionary ecologists reject this doctrine of genetically determined human behavior; instead they use the conceptual tool known as "the phenotypic gambit" (Grafen 1984), in which phenotypes are assumed to be the product of natural selection but the exact nature of the genetic control of phenotypic design is ignored. This flexible perspective stresses interaction between behavior and local environments. Thus, human evolutionary ecologists adhere to the view expressed by Cronk (1991b:27):

> [V]ariations in human behavior are seen as expressions of a human genotype that is essentially similar across human populations, but that has endowed our species with psychological predispositions, mental capacities, and physical abilities that have tended to be adaptive in the environments of human evolution.

Freed from the sociobiological need to link behavior directly to genetic variation, human evolutionary ecology nevertheless shares in the application of the concept of natural selection to human behavior to judge its adaptive value or fitness (see Borgerhoff Mulder 1987). The process of natural selection was succinctly defined by Darwin as the preservation of favorable traits and the elimination of those that are injurious. Darwin's genius lay in delineating the mechanisms that drove this force – differential individual fertility and mortality. Today these two forces determine Darwinian fitness, as measured between reference groups and quantified as Lifetime Reproductive Success.

Currently most commonly invoked in terms of purely genetic inheritance, the original concept of natural selection as developed by Darwin is applicable to any phenomena, providing three conditions are met: (1) phenotypic variation (differences between individuals); (2) some of this variation must be heritable, that is, transmitted to offspring; and (3) variants differ in their ability to survive and reproduce, resulting in fitness differences (Smith and Winterhalder 1992b:26). Phenotype refers to characteristics of an organism other than its DNA, and it may include morphology, physiology, or behavior. With the use of these criteria, two modes of phenotypic transmission, genetic and cultural, are recognized (see Boyd and Richerson 1985; Smith and Winterhalder 1992a), even if the resulting heritability is not perfect. Indeed, imperfections in transmitting biological and cultural information give rise to variation. The resulting variation powers evolution, both biological and cultural, as variants will possess unequal Lifetime Reproductive Success in differing environments.

The fitness of an organism or a cultural trait, defined as "its propensity to survive and reproduce in a particularly specified environment and population (Mills and Beatty 1984:42), is therefore the sum of interactions between the organism and its particular environment. Comparing fitness measures derived from calculations of reproductive success leads to the concept of *adaptation*. Differences arise between evolutionary biologists in their interpretation and application of this concept. One school considers traits shown to increase bearers' fitness relative to other individuals adaptations (Williams 1966). Others extend the concept to any traits that are products of natural selection, thus not only conferring reproductive benefits on its contemporary bearers but also being designed to enhance the reproductive benefits of it bearers in the past. As a compromise, Caro and Borgerhoff Mulder (1987:69) restrict the use of adaptation to any reproductive advantage conferred on its bearers in both modern and traditional societies, in the hopes of "freeing researchers from speculation about gene influences, environmental stability and past selection pressures."

This quick summary glosses over many subtleties within the field of human evolutionary ecology or human behavioral ecology. For these subleties to be understood, it is necessary to present the bewildering multitude of names these two fields have had applied to them. Included here are human sociobiology (Draper and Pennington 1991), human reproductive ecology (Borgerhoff Mulder 1992), Darwinian anthropology (Symons 1989), human behavioral ecology (Cronk 1991a), evolutionary psychology (Barkow, Cosmides, and Tooby 1992), and dual inheritance theory (Boyd and Richerson 1985). Blurton-Jones (1990) and Smith (2000) suggest that the final three, human behavioral ecology, evolutionary psychology, and dual inheritance theory, form distinct yet related major approaches to the study of human behavior in an evolutionary context under the inclusive banner of human evolutionary ecology. Following this lead, this text adopts the overall term *human evolutionary ecology* while distinguishing between these three approaches. Recognizing three distinctive subfields means that the following summary of human evolutionary ecology is longer and more detailed than the preceding review of anthropological demography. More extensive reviews of these three fields are found in the recent book-length manuscripts *Sense and Nonsense: Evolutionary Perspectives on Human Behaviour* (Laland and Brown 2002) and *Human Evolutionary Psychology* (Barrett et al. 2002).

Human Behavioral Ecology

The subfield termed *human behavioral ecology* focuses on measures of reproductive success as human adaptation, stressing the adaptiveness of a behavior by measuring the net effect it has on fitness (see reviews by Borgerhoff Mulder 1992; Winterhalder and Smith 2000). Turke and Betzig (1985:79) formally state this emphasis on reproductive differentials as measures of human adaptation: "modern Darwinian theory predicts that human behaviour will be adaptive, that is designed to promote maximum reproductive success (RS) through available descendants and non-descendent relatives."

Recognizing both descendants and nondescendent relatives means that fitness is assessed in two related manners. The more straightforward of these is Darwinian Fitness, calculated as individual Lifetime Reproductive Success (LRS), which is the combined effects of differential fertility and mortality (Betzig et al. 1988). The second is the concept of *inclusive fitness* (Hamilton 1964), which calculates not only LRS for individuals but also for genetically related kin.

Human behavioral ecology acknowledges the importance of culture in maximizing reproductive success. This is a view of culture embraced earlier by demography, with Levine and Scrimshaw (1983:688) arguing that culture "has helped to increase our reproductive success and to compete in a wide variety of environments." From this starting point, human behavioral ecologists make the more specific hypothesis that "success in achieving culturally defined goals would tend to correlate with reproductive success" (Irons 1979:258). Cultural success is thus viewed as a mechanism for maximizing reproductive success. At the heart of this proposition is the view that humans *competitively* use finite resources to maximize their LRS. Therefore, cultural success in acquiring resources should correlate with reproductive success. To date, this hypothesis has been confirmed cross-culturally for groups as diverse as !Kung hunter–gatherers, East African pastoralists, Mormons, and wealthy Americans (Betzig 1997a).

To test this and other hypotheses, human behavioral ecologists increasingly turned to optimality models composed of *currencies, decision rules*, and *constraints* (Borgerhoff Mulder and Sellen 1994:206). In these models, currencies are outcomes acting as proxies for fitness, such as maximization of reproductive success and minimization of variance, that serves as the model's payoff. The *decision rule* is the behavioral trait whose adaptiveness is being tested, and *constraints* represent assumptions linking decision rules to currencies. One of the best known examples of this work remains Blurton-Jones' (1987; Blurton-Jones and Sibley 1978) modeling of !Kung San South African hunter–gatherers' interbirth intervals based on Howell's (1979, 2000) data. These showed, on average, four-year interbirth intervals for postreproductive !Kung women, resulting in total fertility rates of less than five children. Anthropological demographers argued that this low level of fertility represented a long-standing attempt to achieve group–resource equilibrium (Lee 1979). In contrast, Blurton-Jones' models showed that, considering harsh environmental conditions and child mortality associated with shorter interbirth intervals, the forty-eight-month interbirth interval actually maximized reproductive success. More recent optimality models utilize dynamic simulation models to focus on male decision rules concerning the number of children to bear, and the number of wives to marry, in instances where wealth is inherited (Mace 1996a, 1996b; Luttbeg, Borgerhoff Mulder, and Mangel 2000).

A final tenet of human behavioral ecology is that humans respond to novel, or rapidly changing environments in adaptive ways; adaptive is defined here as "likely to be fitness enhancing in the current environment" (Borgerhoff Mulder 1996:205). This means that biology can quickly "track" changing environments, whether social or cultural, making rapid adjustments to reduce misalignments that result in maladaptive, that is, not fitness enhancing, behavior. Therefore, an important corollary is that natural selection has favored human behavioral plasticity, rather than genetically determined, rigidly fixed traits. Hill and Hurtado (1996:14) refer to humans who adapt to environmental change by utilizing a particular set of behaviors from a much larger set of "reaction norms" that are the product of natural selection operating in past diverse environments, whereas Chisholm (1999:82) states that "theory, observation, and formal models alike suggest that selection is likely to favour phenotypic plasticity when environmental conditions are 'predictably unpredictable.'"

Evolutionary Psychology

This last point serves as a good starting point to distinguish human behavioral ecology from evolutionary psychology. Like the former, evolutionary psychology holds that natural selection works to adapt human behavior to particular environments. However, evolutionary psychology differs in three important respects. First, in contrast to the emphasis that human behavioral ecology places on differential reproductive success, evolutionary psychologists stress "evolved psychological tendencies" (Symons 1989:132), represented by hard-wired cognitive mechanisms underlying human behavior. Although agreeing that differential reproductive success is the measure of fitness, evolutionary psychologists hold that this is only the end result of psychologically induced behaviors. Therefore, finding that reproductive success and cultural success are often linked through the cultural practice of polygny is evaluated by one of evolutionary psychology's main proponent, Jerome Barkow (1989:206–207), as inherently uninteresting:

> But in any society in which polygyny is permitted and depends upon the ability to amass bride-wealth, it would be startling if wealth and reproductive success were not correlated. . . . Because in these cases wealth is obviously directly instrumental in enhancing male reproductive success, it is probably the least interesting way of testing the predicted correlation between culturally defined and genetically defined success.

A second major difference is that Darwinian psychology accepts that some human behavior is maladaptive, which is defined as socially transmitted behavior likely to lead to fitness-reducing behavior on the part of individuals accepting it, relative to that resulting from its rejection (Barkow 1989:294). Darwinian psychologists believe that because culture can change so much faster than the forces of natural selection, culture can "stretch" the fit between behavior and fitness, resulting in maladaptation. As an example, Barkow and Burley (1980) cite the case of using effective contraceptives while making love. Their explanation for such a "culture stretch" is that previously the close connection between sex and reproduction ensured that selection favoring the enjoyment of copulation was sufficient to ensure frequent pregnancy. However, as a result of our changing technological environment, this link was broken, and culture was allowed to "stretch" in a fitness-reducing direction.

The aforementioned example directly relates to the third defining characteristic of evolutionary psychology. Invoking the evolution of psychological tendencies by means of natural selection inherently assumes that such tendencies possess a temporal dimension. Evolutionary psychologists therefore posit that our species' psychological patterns evolved during an "environment of evolutionary adaptiveness" commonly considered as our Pleistocene hunter–gatherer past. The ramifications of applying psychological patterns selected from this distant past to today's modern, technologically rich, and fast-changing world are considerable. For example, many of our current environmental excesses in terms of resource overexploitation may be explicable in terms of the misfit between what Low (1996, 2000) calls "old rules and new environments," that is, our long-evolved psychological tendency to gather resources to support our immediate families and the rapid increase in technological efficiency of extractive technology.

An application of evolutionary psychology to demographic concerns is found in Draper's (1989) article, "African Marriage Systems: Perspectives From Evolutionary Ecology." Draper begins by noting that, with the one glaring exception of sub-Saharan Africa, global fertility levels have declined dramatically over the past twenty years. She argues that this exception arises from a historical African psychological perception of abundant resources, maintained by social institutions promoting high fertility while simultaneously lowering parental investment. Included here is the pre-Colonial African land use system, which minimized individual ownership in favor of group membership rights. In this system, land use rights required only demonstration and acceptance of group membership, usually within a corporate descent group (i.e., the lineage). Because the prevailing technology, that is, shifting cultivation without use of animal-powered ploughing (see Goody 1976; Caldwell and Caldwell 1989), was notoriously land hungry, the descent group's holdings were of necessity large. At the same time, only a small portion of these holdings could be under cultivation at any one time, as extensive fallow periods were required to allow previously used soils to recover.

This system of shifting cultivation gave rise to the psychological perception, or what Draper (1989:148) terms psychological "cognitions" (defined as culturally encoded representations about resource availability), that land was always available. When these cognitions were coupled with social institutions including polygyny, female farming, sexual division of social and economic spheres, and child fostering, the end result was to encourage high fertility while depressing parental investment in children. In Draper's model, the historical result of the interaction of these social institutes with psychological cognitions first led to early, universal marriage for women, establishing the potential for high fertility. Then the sexual division of social and economic spheres for women led them to establish and maintain separate residences from their husbands, which further enhanced this potential. In addition, the widespread pattern of female farming characterizing sub-Saharan Africa led to largely self-sufficient wives, at least with respect to household food needs. Finally, child fostering, also known in the literature as the "borrowing" or "lending" of children, meant that offspring would periodically reside at kinship-related households. All these factors lower parental investment, particularly that of the father, whose reproductive effort was not, in Draper's (1989:154) words, "channelled into parenting (meaning direct provisioning of children) but into mating."

These social institutions are recognizable as parts of Caldwell's (1982) Wealth Flows Theory, with wealth flowing from children to parents. In this model, offspring represent valuable commodities, yielding high returns for low parental investment costs. Writing in 1989, Draper noted that continued sub-Saharan high fertility in the face of several decades of falling infant and child mortality suggests that real economic constraints may not yet be felt by many sub-Saharan African societies. However, should the robust, long-standing system she describes not change quickly when such constraints are incurred, the result will be culture stretch, with a previously adaptive cultural system now leading to maladaptive behavior. Since the publication of her model, fertility has fallen within sub-Saharan Africa, a finding that argues for human behavioral ecology's stance that populations adaptively "track" environmental change, thus reestablishing a fit between parameters of environment and population.

Dual Inheritance Theory

The final entry under the banner of human evolutionary ecology is called, Dual Inheritance Theory (see Boyd and Richerson 1985, 1990, 1992; Durham 1991). This school recognizes culture as a system of inheritance in its own right, evolving in parallel with and yet separate from our genetic system of inheritance. Although viewing natural selection as central to both modes of inheritance, Dual Inheritance Theory differs in several key points from both human behavioral ecology and evolutionary psychology. One immediate difference is that, although only parents can transmit genes, individuals occupying a variety of other social roles, such as grandparents, siblings, and teachers, can transmit culture. Furthermore, cultural behavior can be adopted at various points of the life cycle because behavior can be learned during the lifetime of the organism rather than solely genetically programmed at inception. In this way, cultural evolution is Lamarckian, whereas genetics is Mendelian; dual inheritance is both.

In the fullest treatment of Dual Inheritance Theory, Boyd and Richerson (1985) use algebraic models borrowed from population genetics to model gene–culture coevolution. Just as a finite number of microevolutionary processes, that is, mutation, natural selection, random genetic drift, and gene flow, constitute the only means for the transmission of genetic material across generations, Boyd and Richerson believe social learning, or cultural traditions, are transmitted in specific, limited ways. In their theoretical framework, three different forces, that is, guided variation, biased transmission, and natural selection, underlie cultural evolution.

Guided variation pertains to the "cultural transmission of the results of learning" (Boyd and Richerson 1985:174), and it concerns the impact of individual learning on the frequency of cultural variants. It is particularly relevant to "naive individuals," that is, young, incompletely acculturated persons, who are guided in the acquisition of behavioral phenotypes from their "cultural parents," that is, those who are not kin, in the form of teachers or adult role models. Because so-called favored variants are transmitted from one generation to the next by fully acculturated adults, their adoption is "guided" in their subsequent acceptance frequencies.

In contrast, biased transmission entails naive individuals' selecting from a set of culture-specific behavioral alternatives. In this case at least three possible sources of bias exist (Boyd and Richerson 1985:135):

1. *Direct bias* – one cultural variant is simply more attractive than the alternatives, as judged by the naive individuals.
2. *Indirect bias* – defined as imitating the behaviour of a highly successful role model.
3. *Frequency-dependent bias* – selection of a cultural variant based on the most commonly occurring alternative.

From this general framework, two unique features of Boyd and Richerson's Dual Inheritance Theory emerge. First, although cultural behavior and genetic systems coevolve, natural selection pressures for cultural adaptation may lower genetic fitness. As an example, Boyd and Richerson (1985:199–202; Richerson and Boyd 1992:76–77) point to the Demographic Transition. Whereas sociobiology posits that all species, including our own, attempt to maximize their fitness, the historic European Demographic Transition witnessed decreasing reproductive success in the face of vastly increased per capita resources, resulting in an uncoupling of cultural and reproductive success (Vining 1986). Boyd and Richerson (1985:199) hypothesize that the Demographic Transition represented natural selection acting upon cultural variation learned during the lifetime of organisms. In this instance, cultural selection for the status associated with social mobility would result in decreased Darwinian fitness:

> Conflict with ordinary fitness will occur if one's success or that of one's children in professional roles is negatively correlated with family size. This is plausible since individuals with small families will have more time, money and other resources to devote to the attainment of these social roles.

The second major theoretical position unique to Dual Inheritance Theory is that it recognizes cultural group selection arising from frequency-dependent, conformist decision-making forces as an important force in human evolution. In contrast, the other two subfields cite flaws in Wynne-Edwards' (1962) original model of group selection (see Smith and Winterhalder 1992b) as negating the importance of group selection in human evolution (for detailed histories of the rise, fall, and resurgence of group selection models, see Sober and Wilson 1998; Wilson 2002). Proponents of Dual Inheritance Theory note that these flaws pertain to genetic inheritance and are not relevant to cultural inheritance. Instead, they argue that, under specific conditions, group selection that acts on cultural variation favors cooperators, that is, individuals whose behavior reduces their own welfare but increases the probability of group survival. On the basis of this premise, Boyd and Richerson (1985:230) state the following:

> Group selection occurs whenever the fitness of an individual depends on the behaviours of other individuals in a local group.... If the incremental benefit of investing in the public good exceeds its incremental cost... then groups with more than the average number of cooperators have higher average fitness.

One problem with this model of cultural group selection is its lack of empirical examples, or, as Smith (2000:32) notes, "Dual Inheritance Theory is theoretically rich and sophisticated, but empirically impoverished." My work with Rendille pastoralists of northern Kenya yielded one example of cultural group selection in which selection for group cultural behavior lowers individual fitness levels to preserve group survival; the practice of female genital mutilation (FGM) known as infibulation exemplifies the debate over adaptive versus maladaptive cultural selection. As I believe that Dual Inheritance Theory can provide the strongest bridge between anthropological demography and human evolutionary ecology, I find it worth pausing here to consider these two examples.

Today numbering approximately 25,000 people, the Cushitic-speaking Rendille are linguistically, physically, and culturally related to Somali populations, from whom they claim descent. In pre-colonial times, Rendille featured a subsistence base of nomadic mixed-species pastoralism, herding camels, goats, and sheep in the arid lowlands of the Kaisut and Chalbi Desert, in what today is Marsabit District, northern Kenya (see Figure 1.1). Severe droughts from the 1970s to the present resulted in large livestock losses (Roth 1991, 1996) and led to increased sedentarization for the Rendille (Nathan, Fratkin, and Roth 1996; Fratkin, Roth, and Nathan 1999).

The Rendille were first described as a noncontracepting, parity-independent population regulating their fertility by means of cultural practices by Mary Douglas (1966), who listed the Rendille, along with three other cultures, the Pelly Bay Eskimo, Tikopian Islanders, and

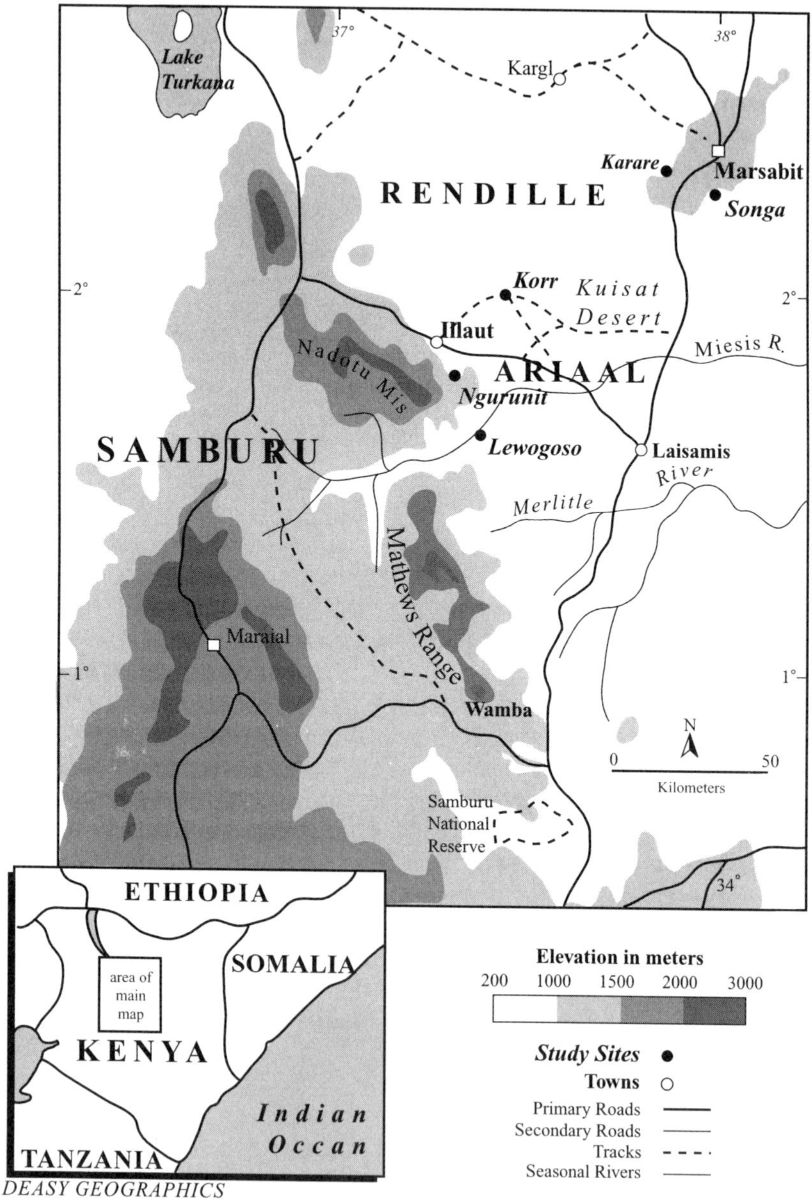

Figure 1.1. Rendille–Ariaal settlements and land, Marsabit District, northern Kenya (after Bates and Fratkin 1998:205).

Nambudiri Brahmins, as exemplifying "population control in primitive groups." Douglas (1966:270–271) ascribed population control to the Rendille's dependence on their slow-growing camel herds:

> Rendille believe their population to be a fixed resource. A static stock population cannot support an increasing human population. . . . Rendille have a problem of over-population in relation to camels.

Douglas (1966:270) cited four specific population-regulating behaviors for the Rendille: (1) infanticide, (2) monogamy, (3) emigration, and (4) late-age marriage. Unlike most other human cultures, Rendille practice infanticide against boys, not girls. Infanticide is practiced only in highly specific circumstances, all related to the society's inheritance pattern of primogeniture, so that only the first-born son inherits his parents' herd (Roth 2000). The second practice, monogamy, reflects the inability to generate multiple bridewealth payments as a result of the lack of "surplus" livestock (i.e., not needed for basic household subsistence requirements), caused by camels' slow reproduction. The third factor, migration, features Rendille emigration to Samburu or Ariaal populations. Latter-born sons, faced with the prospect of little or no livestock inheritance, migrate to these groups, seeking the support of kin and serving as labor in the livestock economy (Spencer 1973:140). For their labor they are given small gifts of livestock, and they begin to build their own herds. Young Rendille women, unable to find a mate in the highly monogamous marital system, or unwilling to wait for age-set marriage dates, also gravitate to Samburu or Ariaal groups that feature higher polygyny rates.

Delay of marriage for both sexes, the fourth and final mechanism, derives directly from the elaborate Rendille age-set system. Age-set formation occurs every fourteen (lunar) years, with the circumcision of eligible young men. These men then serve as warriors (known as *herre*, or bull in Rendille) for the subsequent eleven years until they marry en masse and become elders. A central age-set rule is that a son should marry with the age set three removed from his father's. Thus a first-born son could theoretically be as old as forty-two years (i.e., $3 \times 14 = 42$) before marriage. While leading to late mean age at marriage for males, a far more important demographic characteristic of Rendille age sets is the creation of three "age-set lines," linking every third age set in a father–son pattern. This cyclical aspect of Rendille age sets translates into the creation of three age lines, one of which is termed *teeria*, synonymous with "first born" (see Spencer 1973:3–34; Beaman 1981:398), and which assumes an elevated, high-status position within Rendille society. Daughters of teeria men are designated *sepaade* and are forbidden to marry until all their brothers wed. Thus a first-born sepaade will delay her marriage for

Table 1.2. *Historic dates in Rendille age-set formation*

Rendille age-set name	Samburu equivalent	Circumcision year	Marriage year	First-born child
Libaale	Il-Kiteku	1853	1864[b]	1865–1866[b]
D'bgudo	Il-Tarigirik	1867[b]	1878[b]	1879–1880[b]
Dismaala[a]	Il- Marikon	1881[b]	1892[b]	1893–1894[b]
Irbaangudo	Il-Terito	1895[b]	1908[c]	1909–1910
D'fgudo	Il-Merisho	1909–1910[c]	1920	1921–1922
Irbaalis[a]	Il-Kiliako	1923	1934	1935–1936
Libaale	Il-Mekuri	1937	1948[d]	1949–1950
Irband'if	Il-Kamaniki	1951	1962	1963–1964
D'fgudo[a]	Il-Kachili	1965	1976	1977–1978
Irbaangudo	Il-Kororo	1979	1990	1991–1992

[a]teeria.
[b]Assumed dates, given cyclical regularity.
[c]Irregularities based on Grum (1977:81, cited in Beaman 1981:394).
[d]Irregularities based on Grum (1977:81, cited in Beaman 1981:394).
Source: (Table is after Roth (1993:601)). Also see Spencer 1973:33; Grum 1977:79, 81, 109; Sobania 1980:135; Beaman 1981:394; Schlee 1989:76.

the intervening three age sets until all her brothers marry along with their age mates. Consequently, a first-born sepaade could be above forty years of age when married, representing a tremendous "wastage" of reproductive potential. Table 1.2 presents the Rendille historic age-set calendar, using both Rendille and Samburu age-set names, age-set circumcision and marriage years, the years for first-born children following marriage, and notation of which age-set lines are teeria.

Classic cultural ecology (Moran 1979; Sato 1980) and cultural materialist (Harris and Ross 1987) perspectives on Rendille demography interpret all of the aforementioned behaviors as population-regulating cultural traits arising from the need to achieve and maintain resource–population equilibrium, yet these claims for demographic regulation by cultural means were never supported by demographic data. Indeed, the most complete argument for Rendille fertility and population growth regulation comes from Sato's (1980) painstakingly complete modeling of Rendille camel herds, for which he produces far more complete fertility, mortality, and growth estimates than for Rendille human populations.

Through fieldwork in the 1980s and 1990s, I was able to compile a data set capable of testing the claim that Rendille age-set rules resulted in fertility and population growth regulation. Working in the Rendille community of Korr (see Figure 1.1), I undertook household surveys in 1987, 1990,

Table 1.3. *Women's age at first marriage, arranged by their father's age-set membership, with Rendille–Samburu names*

Father's age set	$\bar{x}$	*SD*	Range	*n*
Dismaala–IL-Marikon (1892)	24.2	6.6	13–38	28
Irbaangudo–Il-Terito (1908)	21.9	5.4	13–33	31
D'fgudo–Il-Merisho (1920)	22.3	3.5	14–28	57
Irbaalis–Il-Kiliako (1934)	29.2	10.2	13–54	110
Libaale–Il-Mekuri (1948)	21.5	4.3	14–34	93
Irbaandif–Il-Kaminiki (1962)	21.3	4.2	12–28	81

Note: Marriage years are given in parentheses.

and 1996. These generated data that enabled me to fit marriages, births, and deaths to a historic event calendar, and the historic Rendille age-set sequence (see Beaman 1981). These data showed that sepaade daughters of teeria age sets do indeed feature statistically significant lower fertility levels and population growth levels, relative to their non-sepaade counterparts (see Roth 1993, 1999). Fertility differentials stem from much later ages at first marriage for sepaade women. In Rendille society, childbirth outside marriage is severely discouraged because of possible inheritance conflicts.

Table 1.3 presents the distribution of first-marriage ages for Rendille women, grouped by their father's age-set membership. For four nonsepaade groups there is remarkable consistency, with average ages ranging only from 21.3 to 22.3 years. For the two sepaade groups, daughters of the *Dismaala* and *Irbaalis* age sets separated by forty-two years (respective marriage years are 1892 and 1934), mean age at marriage is much higher at 24.4 and 29.2 years of age. As a way to model one age-set line, two nonsepaade samples, representing daughters of the *D'fgudo* (marriage year = 1920) and *Libaale* (marriage year = 1934), were combined into one group and compared with the sepaade group formed by the daughters of the Libaale age set shown in Table 1.2 by means of survival analysis. The SAS (2000) LIFETEST procedure yielded a highly a highly significant log-rank statistic (89.0; $p < 0.0001$) for the two distributions of first birth. Figure 1.2 plots the estimated survival values of these two groups, clearly showing the difference between nonsepaade and sepaade age distributions for first marriage.

The demographic result of delaying female marriage for sepaade is shown in Table 1.4. This compares final achieved parity levels for postreproductive Rendille women, divided into sepaade (daughters of the Irbaalis age set; $n = 94$) and nonsepaade (daughters of the Libaale age

Table 1.4. *Demographic characteristics of sepaade and nonsepaade postreproductive women*

Variable	Nonsepaade (Libaale; $n = 75$)	Sepaade (Irbaalis; $n = 94$)
Mean parity	6.1	3.7
Mean generation length	26.8	32.8
Net reproductive rate	1.4	0.8
Growth rate (r)	0.0105	−0.0092

set; $n = 75$). Average parity for the latter is 6.1, whereas their sepaade counterparts only achieve an average of 3.7 births, constituting a decrease of 39%. Table 1.4 also shows the resultant dampening of sepaade fertility, measured by the intrinsic growth rate (r). For this last measure, the non-sepaade sample shows a modest 1% growth rate. In contrast, the sepaade group features negative growth.

Although they delineate delayed age of female marriage as an important Rendille proximate fertility variable, these data do not address the motivation for the origin of the sepaade. I collected oral histories in 1993 and 1996 that linked the origin not to population regulation, as originally

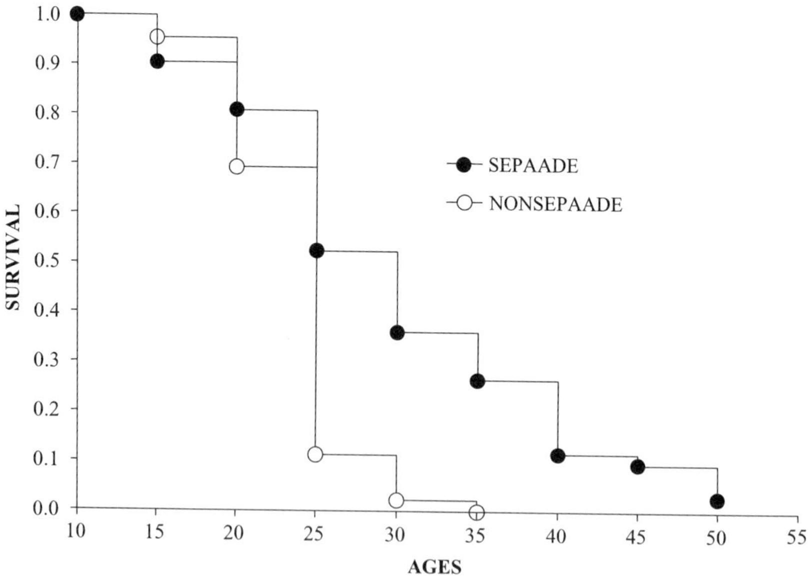

Figure 1.2. Survival curves, sepaade versus nonsepaade first marriages; one age-set line.

espoused by cultural ecologists and materialists, but rather to a specific historic period of intertribal warfare. Rendille stated that sepaade arose in the mid-nineteenth century, during a period of intensive, large-scale warfare between Rendille and Borana, a neighboring pastoral group. At this time, Borana rode horses to raid large Rendille settlements. Rendille camels, left untended by warriors during battles, ran away from the Borana horses. To protect their resources, Rendille appointed the daughters of one age set to look after the camels during battles. These women became the first sepaade. During interviews conducted in 1990, a sepaade woman told me the following:

> The sepaade began when the warriors were going for wars. The warriors needed to go in large numbers. The elders decided to send the elder girls to help water and herd the livestock while the warriors [were] going in the fighting.

Today the linkage of sepaade women with unmarried men, or warriors, continues in both symbolic and real forms. Sepaade women are circumcised one year after their brothers' circumcision, maintaining the linkage between sepaade and warriors (nonsepaade women are circumcised at the time of their marriage). In a 1993 interview with a Rendille elder, Falkenstein (1995:9) independently reported this emic interpretation of the origins of the sepaade:

> In the case of an attack on a Rendille camel camp by Boran cavalry Rendille girls had to prevent a stampede of the camel herd, since the camels would have instinctively followed the horses of the raiders.

Although certainly far different from earlier interpretations linking sepaade with population–resource equilibrium, this newer perspective does not negate claims for sepaade arising from cultural group selection. Indeed, this case provides a strong example of guided group selection arising from emergency situations, as proposed by Boehm (1996). In this model, during times of collective group stress and pressure arising from either ecological disasters or social conditions, exemplified here by warfare, the group is the unit of analysis, and it is the group that provides conscious, deliberate solutions to specific problems. Boehm's (1996) model differs from the earlier models of "naive" group selection invoking neofunctional mechanisms in which actors produce a positive feedback loop through some unintended, and perhaps unrecognized, behavior (see Smith and Winterhalder 1992:42). In contrast to these earlier models, the origin of the sepaade tradition appears to be a conscious group decision aimed at a specific problem, that is, intertribal warfare. In this way, the sepaade tradition constitutes an empirical example of cultural group selection stressed by Boyd and Richerson (1985, 1992) in formulating the Dual

Inheritance Theory, featuring the reduction of fitness for one specific subpopulation, daughters of teeria men, for the survival of the cultural group.

A second example of dual inheritance invoking the concept of adaptive and maladaptive group selection involves the form of female circumcision called infibulation or "pharaonic circumcision" as practiced in northern Sudan. The term *infibulation* evidently stems from the Latin term *fibula*, or clasp, in this case a clasp fastened through the labia majora in an attempt to prevent women from having extramarital sex. Pharaonic refers to the practice's possible origin in Egypt (Shell-Duncan and Hernlund 2000a), and today it refers to the practice of completely removing the labia minora and clitoris, as well as most, or all, of the labia majora. The resulting edges are then stitched together, covering the urethra and the vagina, excluding only a small opening for the passage of urine and menstrual blood. The actual operation is performed within a wide range of ages. Balk (2000:56) reports that, in Sudan, initial circumcision takes place between the ages of four and eleven. Two recent Sudanese surveys reported a mean age of 6.5 years. Women who are infibulated need to be "deinfibulated" for sexual intercourse and childbirth.

In the excellent text, *Female "Circumcision" in Africa: Culture, Controversy and Change* (Shell-Duncan and Hernlund 2000b), Gruenbaum (2000) and Balk (2000) question the adaptiveness, or maladaptiveness, of this practice. Both authors begin by noting the symbolic aspects of infibulation in Sudanese culture, where the practice is a critical part of gender identification, serving as an "assertive, highly meaningful act that emphasizes female fertility by de-emphasizing female sexuality" (Boddy 1982:682; also see Boddy 1989). In particular, because a husband must open the sutures before initiating sexual relations, infibulation acts as a signal that his wife is a virgin while simultaneously identifying his control over his wife's reproduction (Balk 2000:69).

Balk and Gruenbaum emphasize that infibulation also signals a woman's eligibility for marriage. Because fertility outside marriage is heavily discouraged in Islamic northern Sudan, it also serves to act as a signal for the initiation of reproduction. Furthermore, Demographic Health Survey data show that the odds of infibulation rise with increasing education and social status (Balk 2000:59), a finding interpreted by Gruenbaum (2000:50) that infibulation

> reinforces social class and ethnic group superiority by functioning as a ideological marker of superior morality and propriety for the dominant ethnic groups of specific areas, and by serving as justification for the socioeconomic subordination of West African and southern Sudanese groups that do not practice pharaonic "circumcision."

Because infibulation symbolizes so many aspects of northern Sudanese Islamic culture, such as family honor, patriarchy, ethnic identity, and moral superiority, some of the most vocal resistance to discontinuing the practice comes from Sudanese mothers, who fear that not circumcising their daughters would render them ineligible for marriage and leave them childless.

The biological sequelae of infibulation are overwhelmingly negative. Balk's (2000:57–59) review of the medical literature notes an increased risk of urinary tract infections, pelvic inflammatory disease, and reproductive tract infections for infibulated women; all of these factors are linked to female sterility and hence lowered fertility. Furthermore, Balk cites evidence linking infibulation to increased stillbirths and neonatal severe asphyxia, which in turn leads to brain damage or infant death. Biologically, the practice clearly appears maladaptive.

Nevertheless, Gruenbaum (2000:44) strongly disagrees with McElroy and Townsend's (1989:102–104) description of female circumcision as an example of a "maladaptive cultural pattern." The rationale for this seeming paradox is that, without infibulation, Sudanese women may be considered ineligible for marriage, reducing a noninfibulated woman's fitness level, as measured by lifetime reproductive success (LRS), to effectively zero.

Balk reaches the same conclusion, despite her analysis of Sudanese Demographic Health Survey data showing that infibulation, marriage dissolution, and low fertility were all strongly related. Infibulated women were twice as likely (odds ratio = 2.034) to have low fertility, defined as two or fewer children ever born, than noninfibulated women. In addition, infibulated women were 2.3 times more likely to be divorced. The two results are linked, as low fertility is a cause for divorce in Sudan. Indeed, throughout northeast Africa, El Din (1977) reports that low fertility is a major cause of divorce, resulting in the recompense of bridewealth paid by the groom's family.

Using multinomial logistic regression analysis, Balk estimated the joint probabilities of being divorced and having low fertility for the Demographic Health Survey data set. Her results indicated that infibulation raises the likelihood of divorce regardless of a woman's fertility. For example, an infibulated woman with more than two children has 6.6 times the likelihood of divorce than an noninfibulated wife, whereas having fewer than two children raises the likelihood of divorce 7.5 times. In a separate analysis composed only of women in intact marital unions and that controlled for marriage type (monogamous vs. polygynous), she further found infibulated women 1.79 times more likely to have low fertility ($p = 0.054$).

Despite the strong evidence linking infibulation with low fertility or increased risk of divorce, Balk also echoes Gruenbaum's reluctance to classify the practice as maladaptive. In doing so, Balk (2000:71) poses this question: "Are the risks posed by the consequences – marital disruption and childlessness – less than those posed by not adhering to the practice – that is rendering one's daughters 'unmarriagable'"?

These interpretations support Boy and Richerson's notion that cultural selection can override biological natural selection, even though the practice in question leads to lowered fertility and raised offspring mortality. Analogous to their argument for the adoption of small family size during the Demographic Transition, northern Sudanese parents may adopt infibulation because it is associated with high status. In Boyd and Richerson's (1985) Dual Inheritance Theory framework, this is known as indirect bias – imitating the behavior of a highly successful role model. Following adoption of the cultural variant by increasing numbers of families, infibulation could then be supported and spread throughout the rest of the population by means of frequency-dependent bias – or the selection of a cultural variant based on the most commonly occurring alternative. Finally, Balk (2000:71) points out that infibulation may be maintained in the Sudanese culture because those women who have suffered the heaviest costs, that is, low fertility or divorce, will have the lowest LRS. In this regard, Balk (2000:71) cites Mackie's (1996:1,009) observation that, "once in place conventions regulating access to reproduction are deeply entrenched, in part because dissenters fail to have children." In all these scenarios, selection works against the biological or demographic consequences of infibulation while simultaneously favoring the cultural phenotype of infibulation.

Discussion: Cultural and Biological Reductionism

Following the overview of anthropological demography and human evolutionary ecology, I should pause to consider relevant criticisms of each approach. Indeed, it is the weaknesses inherent in each perspective that makes the search for common ground potentially rewarding. Of particular importance is the disparate role allotted culture in the separate fields. Adopting Bongaarts' (1982) terminology and framework for the analysis of intermediate fertility variables, as shown in Table 1.5, we see that each field interprets the role of culture in human demography quite differently. Within anthropological demography culture is often viewed as a *distal variable*, representing a source of motivation for demographic behaviour. Biology, represented by variables such as age at first birth, breastfeeding duration and subsequent interbirth intervals, takes on the role of *proximate, or intermediate variables*, denoting the finite pathways

Table 1.5. *Differing perspectives on the causal ordering of variables among Bongaarts' intermediate or proximal variables framework, anthropological demography, and human evolutionary ecology*

Variable level	Distal	Proximate	Final
Bongaarts' demographic model	Culture Environment Economy Physiology Genetics	Proportions marrying Abortion + Contraception Duration of lactation	TFR NRR IBI
Anthropological demography	Culture	Biology	TFR NRR IBI
Human evolutionary ecology	Biology (Natural selection)	Culture	TFR NRR IBI

determining *final or realized variables*, exemplified by standard demographic measures such as Total Fertility Rates (TFR), Net Reproductive Rate (NRR) and/or interbirth intervals (IBIs). In contrast, human evolutionary ecologists view culture as a proximate variable, merely doing the bidding of biological distal variables, sometimes termed *ultimate* variables by ethologists (see Tindenbergen 1963). From this perspective, also shown in Table 1.5, with the notable exception of Dual Inheritance Theory, culture is merely the handmaiden of biology, at best a necessary tool to achieve fitness maximization.

This perspective is exemplified by human evolutionary ecology's consideration of the cultural feature of polygyny. Within their field this can be viewed as purely a means of maximizing male Lifetime Reproductive Success. In Pre-Transitional populations wealthy men can afford multiple bridewealth payments, reinforcing the linkage between reproductive success and cultural success. In contrast, anthropological demographers accord culture the status of a distal variable determining the pattern and level of the final variables. An example of this would be changes in culturally constructed gender relationships, which in Caldwell's Wealth Flows Theory may lead to increased levels of female education and culminate in lowered fertility and infant/child mortality. In this model biology is only present as a final variable, measurable in standard demographic variables, e.g. child mortality rate, total fertility rate.

Given these two very different starting points, it is little wonder that each paradigm has been heavily criticized by the other. Cultural anthropologists (see Sahlins 1976; Vayda 1995a, 1995b; Rose and Rose 2000) and biologists (Gould and Lewontin 1979; Lewontin, Rose, and

Kamin 1984) have decried human evolutionary ecology's ahistorical approach to explaining human behavior by means of biological reductionism. These criticisms focus on two perceived shortcomings of evolutionary biology, understandably emanating from the critics' particular discipline. In the first, biologists bemoan evolutionary ecologists' reliance on natural selection leading to adaptation in all matters as teleological. In their now-classic spoof of the adaptationist perspective, Gould and Lewontin (1979:) evoke the spirit of Voltaire's Dr. Pagloss from *Candide*, giving the following Pollyanna view of life:

> Things cannot be other than they are. . . . Everything is made for the best purpose. Our noses were made to carry spectacles, so we have spectacles. Legs were clearly intended for breeches, and we wear them.

Although agreeing that natural selection is the most powerful of the Neo-Darwinian forces of evolution, Gould and Lewontin argued that adaptationist emphasis on natural selection to the exclusion of all possible alternatives ironically lessens the explanatory power of natural selection, for it can never be disproved. As Flannery and Reynolds (1989:29) note, this leads to increasingly complicated "Rube Goldberg" explanations when original theoretical predictions are not met. Gould (1982:258) argues that the final result is sociobiological "story telling on the level of Kipling's 'just-so' stories."

More recent criticisms of evolutionary ecology and sociobiology echo past complaints about recognizing only adaptation arising from natural selection, at the expense of random patterns generated by stochastic events such as random genetic drift. In this regard, Hrdy (1990:35) criticizes her own field of sociobiology for its "general lack of respect for irrational processes and accidental phenomena." This blind spot to the importance of random effects or historical accidents is seen in even the very best of human evolutionary ecology. For example, one, if not the, best application of human evolutionary ecology to date is the text *Ache Life History: The Ecology and Demography of a Foraging People*, by Kim Hill and A. Magdalena Hurtado (1996). In one logistic regression analysis, they stress the lack of significant relationships between either hunting skill or body size and age-specific male and female mortality (Hill and Hurtado 1996:304–305). Yet this is hardly surprising, because, as the authors previously stated, the leading cause of adult mortality is accidental death.

In contrast to biologists' complaints, cultural anthropology's major criticism of human evolutionary ecology is that it views culture as merely a minor, sometimes annoyingly ineffective, means of achieving biological ends. This view is perfectly exemplified in the section titled "The Problem of Culture" in evolutionary biologist Richard Alexander's (1987) seminal text, *The Biology of Moral Systems*. Certainly anthropological demographers do not view culture as a "problem." Instead their view is that human culture is highly flexible and adaptive, addressing if not solving a myriad of human problems from basic subsistence to philosophical and religious issues. Anthropological demographers reject the "fossilized" idea of culture equated with invariantly accepted social norms, yet many hold that culture provides behavioral motivation for group members, because culture generates, in Geertz' (1973) words, "models of reality." and "models for reality." Processing and internalizing these models on differing individual levels and degrees is seen as providing the impetus for human behavior, as well as offering an explanation for the variance in adhering to and deviating from social norms (see D'Andrade and Strauss 1997; Strauss 1992).

Not all anthropological demographers or cultural anthropologists hold this position. One of the true deans of anthropological demography, Eugene Hammel, recently stated (Hammel and Friou 1997:180) that "the use of culture as a causal force in explanations that depend on motivation can have, operationally, only a heuristic value" while at the same time informing anthropological demographers that "we can continue to accept the motivational principles of these (motivational) models as analytically useful, but we had better not believe them in any actual sense." Likewise, the cognitive anthropologist Roy D'Andrade (1992:23) observes the following:

> Of course we can say, "people do what they do because their culture makes them do it." The problem with this formulation is that it does not explain anything. Do people always do what their culture tells them to do? If they do, why do they? If they don't, why don't they? And how does culture make them do it? Unless there is some specification of how culture "makes" people do what they do, no explanation has been given.

Human evolutionary ecologist Lee Cronk (1999) also criticizes anthropological demographers for the view that "culture made me do it," by rightfully pointing out that commonly held views of culture as all inclusive negate its explanatory power, just as complete faith in natural selection weakens this principle among human evolutionary ecologists. For example, by defining culture as "everything that people have, think and do as members of a society" (Ferraro, Trevanthan, and Levy 1994:18), nothing is really gained, or explained. Quite simply, if culture is "everything," then it runs the risk of being nothing that could be identified, operationalized, or studied as either discrete parts or as, in the words of the famous nineteenth-century anthropologist, Edward Tylor (1871), "that complex whole."

Cronk (1999:4) stresses that such sweeping definitions negate the chance to make what philosophers call "fundamental" explanations, that is, explanations defining phenomena outside themselves. To exemplify this point, Cronk (1999:132–133) constructed a table with twenty similarly inclusive definitions of culture gleaned from introductory anthropology textbooks, each of which conflates *behavior* with *culture*. If all human behavior is culture, or *cultural behavior*, then it is impossible to study the two separately in order to assess their effects on each other. By adopting such a broad definition, which really states that culture is everything we do, as well as the motivation for doing it, cultural anthropologists are starting with the tautological and uninteresting basic premise that "culture is culture." The explanatory power of this premise is akin to the statement that "a dog is a dog."

A second criticism of the cultural approach featured in anthropological demography is that it is merely descriptive, rather than explanatory, a point raised by Pollak and Watkins (1994). Anthropological demography's emphasis on what Geertz termed "thick" ethnographic description is elegant, but it does not generate or test hypotheses. Thick description is still only description, and the anthropological demographers' search for cultural meaning is not necessarily a search for explanation or motive.

Anthropological demography as an outgrowth of cultural anthropology and human behavioral ecology as a branch of evolutionary biology come with these inherent, historical shortcomings. The question is whether they can both escape the perils of *normative* and *biological reductionism* (Bledsoe and Hill 1998:270). If they can, there is the potential for cross-perspective communication and the creation of new, truly multidisciplinary approaches to human demography. Hrdy (1990:34) offers a glimpse of this potential when she writes the following:

> With the emergence of graduate students literate in both traditions [biological and cultural anthropology], my own hope would be that these separate approaches will increasingly merge, even if it means that the "cannibalization" of other disciplines once prophesized for sociobiology actually ends in the vivisection of sociobiology by traditional disciplines.

This urge for common ground is a strong starting point, and one that I intend to utilize to expand on points of common interest between anthropological demography and human behavioral ecology in the following chapter.

2 Reconciling Anthropological Demography and Human Evolutionary Ecology

Common Ground

Despite their mutual disdain, anthropological demography and human evolutionary ecology share common, though unrecognized, interests. This chapter's goals are to delineate and exemplify common ground between the two perspectives. In contrast to previous texts that constructed coevolutionary frameworks for culture and biology (see Cavalli-Sforza and Feldman 1981; Durham 1991), this chapter has the far more modest objective of simply initiating a dialogue between anthropological demography and human evolutionary ecology. In doing so, it focuses mainly on my work with Rendille pastoralists of northern Kenya.

What do anthropological demography and human evolutionary ecology have in common? Surprisingly, in light of the differences outlined in the previous chapter, I can begin by noting common ground in the very concept of culture. Here evolutionary behavioral ecologists such as Lee Cronk (1999) and cultural anthropologists such as Clifford Geertz (1973) and Roger M. Keesing (1974) are united in proposing that culture is ideational, not behavioral, in nature. In this regard Geertz (1973:144–145) states the following:

> one of the most useful ways – but far from the only one – of distinguishing between culture and social systems is to see the former as an ordered system of meaning and symbols, in terms of which social interaction takes place; and to see the latter as the pattern of social interaction itself. . . . Culture is the fabric of meaning in terms of which humans express their experience and guide their action; social structure is the form that action takes; the actual existing network of social relationship.

Certainly within demography, despite Hammel's (1990) earlier warning that demography has utilized "fossilized" concepts of culture, there are recent, strong attempts to view culture as ideation. In the 1980s, this was represented by "value of children" studies (Bulatao and Lee 1983) that attempted to measure the demand for children throughout the Third World. These studies made a clear distinction between the ideology of high fertility and consequent fertility behavior, with the former driving the latter. Today the increasing use of diffusion models and network analysis in family planning studies (Rutenberg and Watkins 1997; Reed, Briere, and Casterline 1999) reflects the premise that new ideas about fertility and its control operate as ideological innovations spread by local networks within different cultures. In this same vein, Watkins (2000) successfully applied the concept of historically changing ideational models of fertility to both global and local situations.

Viewing culture as ideational also means that cultural change, and demographic change, is ideational change. Anthropological demographers have utilized this concept, exemplified by Fricke (1997a, 1997b), explaining marriage change among Nepalese agropastoralists as reflecting changes in group morals. As discussed later in Chapter 3, interpreting demographic change as changing group moral ideologies may provide fertile common ground with evolutionary perspectives that ascribe biological origins to human moral systems, a theme running from the work of Huxley (1894) to modern human evolutionary ecologists (Alexander 1987, 1993; Irons 1991, 1996). Kertzer (1995:44) reminds us that moral systems are directly linked to culture by calling attention to Kreager's (1986:136) definition of culture, which stresses "the application of criteria of right and wrong." The interaction among demography, culture, and moral systems is inherent in Kreager's (1986:131) statement that "vital processes are the true playground of moral systems."

In all these cases, analysts inherently, if perhaps implicitly, accept Geertz' (1973:89) viewpoint:

> Culture denotes a historically transmitted pattern of meaning embodied in symbols, a system of inherited conceptions expressed in symbolic forms by means of which men [and women] communicate, perpetuate and develop their knowledge about and attitudes towards life.

From this starting point, recall Geertz' quote from Chapter 1 that cultural patterns function as both models *of* and models *for* reality. The distinction is vitally important, for it separates human behavior from the ideological concept of culture, that is, models of reality, from the realized models for reality, represented by actualized behavior. By defining culture as ideation and separating it from behavior, cultural anthropologists such as Geertz and human behavioral ecologists such as Cronk avoid the inherent pitfalls in Tylor's (1871) "complex whole" definition of culture, in which culture is everything and consequently nothing. As Keesing (1974:13) notes, the movement to "narrow the concept of culture so that it includes less and reveals more" paints culture as a set of symbolic rules, norms, and guides operating as both constraints and opportunities for individual and social behavior. This view is identical to Bledsoe and Hill's (1998:273) statement in the previous chapter that cultural rules may be seen "less as rigidly binding prescriptions for conduct than as resources."

Demographic Strategies

Beginning with this shared view of culture as ideation rather than behavior, the next task is to ascertain possible common approaches to analyzing how humans use "resources" provided by culture. One practicable approach is that provided by anthropological demography's and human evolutionary ecology's shared use of the concept of *strategies*. In anthropology, Viazzo and Lynch (2002) trace the concept of strategies to Frederick Barth's (1959a) classic work *Political Leadership Among the Swat Pathans*, and Barth's (1959b) seminal application of game theory to Pathan social organization. In historical demographic work, it was featured in Goody's (1976) idea of "inheritance strategies" and Bourdieu's (1976) vision of "marriage strategies." Today it remains prominent in anthropological demography, exemplified by Fuchs and Moch's (1995) work, "Invisible Cultures: Poor Women's Networks and Reproductive Strategies in Nineteenth Century Paris."

Strategies are a central tenet in human evolutionary ecology also, as witnessed by a recent review article by Winterhalder and Smith (2000) titled "Analysing Adaptive Strategies: Human Behavioural Ecology at Twenty-Five." This review stresses that human behavioral ecology (what this book is lumping together as human evolutionary ecology) studies adaptation by means of examination of decision rules or conditional strategies. The latter term is glossed as "in context X, do α, in context Y, switch to β" (Winterhalder and Smith 2000:54). Although the term *decision rules* is attributable to classic evolutionary ecological work on optimal foraging (see Krebs 1978), Axelrod (1984) effectively links decision rules and strategies by defining a strategy as a decision rule. This simple working definition of a strategy is used throughout the rest of this book.

Considering strategies as a conceptual and methodological tool raises at least three immediate questions. First, on what level of analysis does the concept effectively work? Second, what motivates particular strategies, that is, what are their goals? Third, how can strategies be identified in demographic data? Low, Clarke, and Lockridge (1992:9) succinctly phrase this first concern as "who benefits?" Within human evolutionary ecology, strategies are viewed from the perspective of methodological individualism. They therefore work on the individual, not group, level. Viazzo and Lynch (2002) note that this was also the level originally envisioned by Barth, who wanted the analysis of individual strategies to replace the structuralist approach focusing on unilineal descent groups with the brand of methodological individualism known as "transactionalism." However, the idea's later incorporation, both within anthropology and historical demography, was with reference to "family strategies," usually associated with the transmission of land-based resources from one generation to the next (see Bourdieu 1976; Goody 1976; Kertzer 1984; Moch 1987).

Anthropology's early rejection of methodological individualism is understandable given the field's concern with cultures rather than individuals. In this context, Hill (1997:239) quotes the social anthropologist I. M. Lewis (1976:16):

> we study *peoples* rather than *people*. Our primary units of reference are "societies," that is distinct and relatively autonomous communities whose member's social relationships are embedded in, and expressed through, the medium of a common culture. Culture is the key term here.

Demography can be a mediating force in this debate. Despite the assertion that "biologists tend to look at individual lifetimes and how they vary, while classical demographers look at groups" (Low, Clark, and Lockridge 1992:11), demography has a long tradition of recognizing the individual. This is expressed in Wrigley's (1978:136) statement:

> While the benefit of a culturally embedded fertility strategy is usually analyzed in terms of the group, it is clear that it must influence individual behavior if it is to operate at all.

Today, a new generation of group selection models within biological and social sciences (Richerson and Boyd 1992; Wilson and Sober 1994, 1996; Sober and Wilson 1998; Wilson 2002) attempts to link individual and group advantage. They have reintroduced the concept of multilevel selection and may provide crucial links between human evolutionary ecology and anthropological demography. The reintroduction of group selection models within the social and biological sciences revived interest in the question of who benefits, which is a question once thought dead with the ascendancy and domination of individual-level selection theory in biology. These models are aligned with Dual Inheritance Theory, whose proponents easily acknowledge that "group level adaptations may be more common in the human species than in any other species" (Richerson and Boyd 1992:83).

Ironically, at the same time that evolutionary biology reopened the question of multilevel selection, anthropological demography began to lean toward methodological individualism. This shift away from *peoples* to *people* is evident in the statement by Bledsoe and Hill (1998:273) that the new perspective focusing on the individual

> sheds quite a different light on the notion of the individual from an unthinking follower of rules and believer of established categories, to a strategic actor who may attempt to use rules to achieve desired outcomes.

Anthropological demography's new emphasis on individuals as actors or agents represents what Hammel (1990:466) calls "culture by the people" rather than the outmoded perspective of "culture for the people." Fricke (1997b:61) exemplifies this view of individual strategies within the context of cultural constraints and opportunities by quoting J. C. Alexander (1988:88): "Culture and society form the two contextual levels within which individuals with their own contingent histories and circumstances pursue goals."

The two aforementioned statements are virtually indistinguishable from human behavioral ecology's position that people frequently manipulate culture to achieve individual goals. In the strongest statement on this point, Cronk (1991a, 1994, 1995) applies communication theory to the concept of culture to argue that culture is most often used to manipulate others for individual goals. Chagnon (1988, 1999) operationalizes this position in his highly detailed analysis of Yanomamo men manipulating kinship terminology to move women from marriage ineligible categories into marriage eligible classes. In Chapter 1, we saw this same interpretation of individual agents using and manipulating cultural rules in Bledsoe's (2002; also see Bledsoe and Hill 1998) analysis of Gambian men's interpretation of Islamic edicts on the resumption of postpartum sexual relations. The two interpretations are so similar that Chagnon's analysis of Yanomamo kinship terminology could be summarized by Bledsoe and Hill's (1998:273) observation that cultural rules may be seen "less as rigidly binding prescriptions for conduct than as resources."

Common interest in individual agency operating within the constraints of a particular cultural context brings into focus the second question arising from the use of strategies within human demography, which is that of underlying goals and motivation. Here human evolutionary ecology fares far better than anthropological demography. The former's emphasis on fitness-maximizing strategies whereby individuals attempt to outcompete conspecifics in leaving more descendents in subsequent generations provides a clear set of goals. In addition, the notion that behavior to achieve this goal may be either consciously or unconsciously motivated suggests an underlying, innate biological drive.

In contrast, anthropological demography seems largely silent in ascribing motivation for demographic behavior. This may reflect anthropology's history of description, rather than explanation, or the position that culture does not provide motivation, as represented by the Hammel and Friou (1997) quote in Chapter 1. Those who do attribute motivation to culture face the serious problem of explaining how culture, represented by symbols, translates into action or behavior (Handwerker 2002). In the past, anthropologists proposed a process of *internalization* (see Spiro 1987) by which cultural meanings and symbols are adopted and transformed into motivation. In this rather vague process, "it follows that we might expect those individuals who engage in practices closely linked to cultural models of the good or moral will be more likely to have internalized cultural motivations than those who do not" (Fricke 1997b:190). However, lacking specific processes or mechanisms through which symbolic culture translates directly into action, internalization alone does not address Cronk's (1991a) criticism that "culture made me do it," and it is an insufficient explanation for human motivation.

Today a small group of anthropologists, drawn from cognitive anthropology, biological anthropology, and demographic anthropology, propose specific mechanisms for motivation, stressing the interaction of biology and culture. From cognitive anthropology comes the idea of cognitive schemas, or conceptual structures identifying objects and events, processed by connectionist or parallel distributed processing (PDP) systems consisting of multilayered constellations of neurons linking individual genotypes, emotions, and temperaments and group-level cultural patterns (see Strauss and Quinn 1997). For the biocultural study of human emotions, Worthman (1999) incorporated Lock's (1995:370–374) concept of "local biologies" to study how physiological processes shape and are shaped by specific cultures. The result was the development of a stochastic, epidemiological model in ontogenetic development and personal interactions with a particular culture resulting in what she terms "variable psychobehavioral outcomes." Similarly, for human morals, Rottschaefer (1998) developed a model of moral agency based on the evidence for the biological and psychological ontogeny of human morality.

All these models are largely untested at present: Their importance lies in their potential to explain motivational variation within and between groups. As D'Andrade (1992:23) stressed, stating that culture makes people behave in certain ways does not explain why all people conform to, or do not conform to, cultural norms. The aforementioned models signal the end to such simplistic explanations as "culture made me do it" and mark the opening of a new era of models with the far more plausible catch phrase of "biology and culture made me do it, or not do it."

Human evolutionary ecology could also benefit from more consideration of biological–cultural interactions. Concluding his review of twenty years of human evolutionary ecology, Gray (2000:490) states that "the most important task in the next twenty years will be to incorporate culture into selectionist models in ways more subtle than has been previously possible." He suggests that one way to do so is to view culture as providing the external cues that enable human demographic systems to adaptively track environmental changes. Attempting to understand peoples' culture as a set of transmitted symbols comprising their "models of reality" is a good starting place for delineating the cue and clues for adhering to old "reaction norms," or abandoning them for new ones.

Methodological advances in quantifying shared cultural factors by means of multivariate statistics now permit an effective search for the linkage between cultural cues and decision rules, or what I am simply calling strategies. Largely developed in accordance with Romney's (Romney, Weller, and Batchelder 1986) "culture as consensus" models, these approaches have been utilized by evolutionary (Jones 2000) and cultural anthropologists (Handwerker 2002), and they have the potential to separate cases in which behavioral differences reflect underlying cultural differences from those operating with cultural homogeneity. If future research finds the former pattern on a regular basis, then human evolutionary ecology will have to accept the premise of the "ethnographic mind" (Shore 1996) as well as that of the "adapted mind" (Barkow, Cosmides, and Tooby 1992).

Recognizing that biocultural interaction, rather than only biological factors, underlies human motivation offers a far more realistic perspective. On the negative side, this acceptance complicates our third question posed, how to recognize strategies, because with the recognition of cultural motivation we have to search for more than fitness-maximizing behavior. One straightforward approach is to adopt and expand Alexander's (1987) concept of human reproductive interests. Alexander limited reproductive interests to human concerns with ensuring the indefinite survival of genes and their copies. This narrow definition of reproductive concepts can be expanded to recognize the incontrovertible fact that humans also have *cultural reproductive interests*. Included here is a myriad of motivations, for example the continuation of family names, the inheritance of resources or titles, and parental use of children as old-age security, to name just a few cultural strategies delineated by historical and anthropological demography (Wachter 1978; Caldwell 1982; Knodel 1988; Roth 2000; Bledsoe 2002).

Broadening Alexander's original concept of reproductive interests to include cultural factors permits construction of an expanded framework for examining what Alexander termed "life effort" and "social interactions." For the latter, Alexander focused on different forms of reciprocity designed by natural selection to enhance Darwinian or inclusive fitness (Trivers 1971; Axelrod 1984). This can be enlarged to include cultural behavior on both an individual and group level, reflective of Geertz' concept of ideational culture providing models *of* culture.

Equally important is Alexander's second concept of life effort. In evolutionary ecology, this concept remains practicable today in life history theory (Stearns 1992; Hill and Hurtado 1996; Kaplan 1997; Hill and Kaplan 1999; Worthman 2003). As we shall see in subsequent chapters, life history theory is commonly compartmentalized into mating and parental effort (Fisher 1958), but all life history theory rests on the *principle of allocation*, which states that energy used for one purpose cannot be used for another. Energy allocations are made within three specific domains: (1) maintenance, (2) growth, and (3) reproduction (Worthman 2003:293). Energy allocation among these three domains is viewed as a series of trade-offs made over an individual's life course; this is exemplified by the trade-off in continuing to allocate energy to growth or switching to reproduction, represented by either puberty (Worthman 1999) or first birth (Hill and Hurtado 1996). In addition, energy allocations must be made within these domains, exemplified by the decision to invest in current or future reproduction; in primates, this may link the unusually long longevity of human postmenopausal women to grandchild provisioning by means of the so-called Grandmother Hypothesis (Hill and Hurtado 1996; Hawkes et al. 1999).

Life history theory undeniably has been successfully applied to animal studies, yet its applicability to the analysis of humans is questionable. One of its leading proponents, the anthropologist Carol Worthman (2003:305), pinpoints the theory's limitations:

> [L]ife history theory recognizes ecological, cognitive, and behavioral dimensions but does not adequately consider sociality. Humans must belong to social groups to survive and develop and even to reproduce. Human reproduction depends on relationships, and on sharing resources with others. . . . Yet life history models include neither social production and consumption nor social costs and benefits.

To correct this deficiency, and in recognition of both cultural and biological aspects of human ideology, motivation, and behavior, I propose a rearrangement of Alexander's original scheme so that the social interactions component represents cultural and social factors whereas the life effort category pertains only to biological, that is, evolutionary, concerns. Adopting this expanded model provides three great advantages for our purpose of multidisciplinary reconciliation. First, it recognizes individual

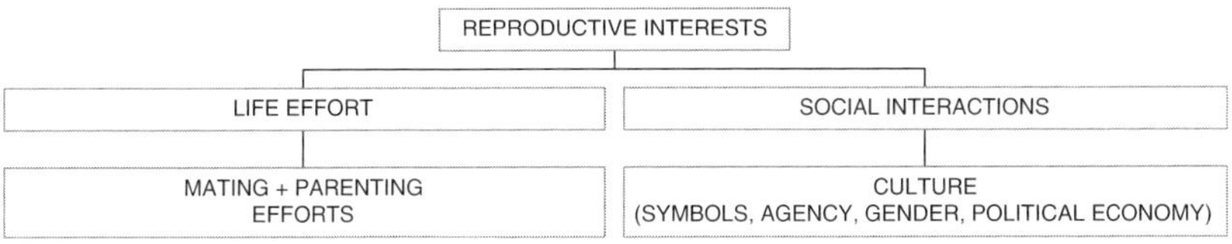

Figure 2.1. Proposed modification of Alexander's model of reproductive interests, incorporating both evolutionary ecology and culture.

human agency, in the form of decision making or strategies, both conscious and unconscious, in either a biological (life effort) or a cultural (social interaction) context. Second, it provides for an evaluative framework of these strategies by means of natural selection's basic mechanisms of fertility and mortality differentials. Third, this expanded framework considers both evolutionary biology and culture as independent variables, capable of interaction between each other and demographic variables, as shown in Figure 2.1.

I can illustrate this framework by focusing on inheritance strategies. Inheritance strategies are a particularly rich potential source for the delineation of strategies, because, in the terminology of evolutionary ecology, they constitute both mating and parenting effort. In addition, anthropologists, demographers, and historians have all investigated both mating and parental-based inheritance strategies among cultures ranging from East African agropastoralists (Borgerhoff Mulder 1988a, 1988b; Mace 1996a, 1996b, 1999) through historic Indian (Dickemann 1979a, 1979b; Schlegel and Elou 1987; Gaulin and Boster 1990), European (Boone 1988; Howell 1976; Goody, Thrisk, and Thompson 1976; Voland 1984, 1989), Japanese (Smith 1977), and North American cultures (Judge and Hrdy 1992).

As with other shared but perhaps not well-recognized concerns of anthropological demography and human evolutionary ecology outlined earlier, inheritance studies sometimes only emphasize the specific concern of one field or approach. Bourdieu's (1976) classic work on French historical marriage strategies focused exclusively on social reproduction. Similarly, Hill and Hurtado (1996:293) tersely outline life history theory's position on the interaction between resources and vital processes: "The only reason living organisms should care about acquiring resources at all is if energy and other limiting components of life can be turned into greater genetic contribution." However, some scholars have constructed models that consider the linkage of biology and culture, either implicitly (Goody 1973) or explicitly (Mace 1996a, 1996b; Hartung 1976, 1981, 1982; Rogers 1995). In this spirit, I now offer a specific example illustrating the potential breadth and flexibility of this approach that considers cultural as well as biological adaptation.

Reproductive Interests: Social Interactions, Life Effort, and Demographic Strategies: A Rendille Example

My example is drawn from my work with Rendille culture and the identification and analysis of indigenous demographic strategies. In particular, it focuses on the Rendille inheritance system of primogeniture, by which the eldest son inherits almost all the family's livestock upon the death of the male household head.

As outlined in Chapter 1, marriage and inheritance are interrelated in Rendille culture. Specifically, they are linked by the culture's dependence on slow-growing camel herds. Fearing environmental disaster in the form of recurrent, severe droughts and livestock epidemics, Rendille view their herds as fixed assets and refuse to divide them among their sons. Instead they keep herds built up over a lifetime intact through impartible inheritance in the form of primogeniture. Marriage, which determines inheritance rights, is likewise perceived as directly linked to the slow growth of camel herds. Low growth rates translate into little surplus animals for bridewealth, reinforcing monogamy as the prevalent marriage form. These patterns appear to be linked to environmental conditions, for among the neighboring Samburu who inhabit adjacent highland areas, a faster reproductive rate of cows in their cattle-based subsistence system features polygny and partible inheritance.

For the Rendille, inheritance is a matter of importance running though the life cycle. Concern with inheritance begins at birth, with Rendille infanticide aimed at males, not females, as overwhelmingly common in the ethnographic record. The rationale for this is found in the categories of males for whom infanticide is prescribed. These are as follows (Kreager 1982:253): (1) first-born twins, which, if sons, could constitute close and confusing competition for inheritance rights; (2) sons born out of wedlock, who therefore lack established paternity; (3) boys born after the circumcision of the household's eldest son, for such children may find themselves in competition for the family herd with the eldest son's own children; and (4) boys born on moonless Wednesday nights, for they are thought to be particularly jealous of their elder brothers and willing to use sorcery against them.

For marriage, the effect of inheritance is less direct but equally important. Without the prospect of inheriting sufficient livestock to start and maintain a viable household herd, latter-born sons leave Rendille society and herd livestock for distant kin in either Samburu or Ariaal economies

(Spencer 1973; Fratkin 1991). As Kreager (1986:256) notes, the basic contradiction in the Rendille social system is that it conserves camels at the expense of young people. Although a large supply of physically fit young men is needed to herd camels, many of these will leave to establish households of their own. As a result, in the 1960s, Spencer (1973) found that at least one-third of Samburu families in his censuses claimed Rendille descent.

Rendille men and women are acutely, perhaps obsessively, aware of these features of their culture, and in particular how they are affected by the sepaade tradition. This was made obvious in male focus groups I conducted in 1990, when men frequently noted that sepaade marriages often result in the taking of additional wives. This emic, or internally derived, view linking sepaade with polygynous marriages stems from the Rendille fear of not having a surviving male heir at the time of the male household head's death. In this case a man is said to be "disinherited," with his livestock holdings passing on to relatives, usually his brothers, or their children. Although the patrilineal nature of Rendille society softens this blow by keeping livestock within the male descent line, Rendille men frequently expressed their fear of this fate befalling them.

Concern with not producing an heir is not limited to the Rendille; it is found in patrilineal cultures ranging from Hindu Indians, where males perform important religious rites at their fathers' funerals (May and Heer 1968), to historic English society, where the extinction of patrilines coincided with the termination of honorary titles (Wachter 1978). This concern and its concomitant behaviors have been examined through the concept of "heirship strategies" (Goody 1973, 1976; Wrigley 1978). According to Wrigley (1978:138), these in large part stem from the recognition that, in Pre-Transitional families,

> a man had to walk a delicate path between the danger, on the one hand, that he might be without a male heir at his death, and, on the other, that he might have difficulty in providing for several sons, each with a claim on his resources.

Such a predicament confronts Rendille male household heads, who seek a balance in which a male heir is secured but not too many "surplus" sons are produced to support through childhood and who may latter cause friction in matters of inheritance. Therefore Rendille men may strive, in Goody's (1976:90–93) terms, to both "add" and "subtract" children. Goody recognized that the former may be achieved directly, through adopting or fostering children, or indirectly, by adding wives by means of polygyny, serial monogamy, or plural marriage with concubines. Because Rendille are also highly concerned with "balancing people against property" to ensure the "viability of the estate" (Goody

Table 2.1. *Distribution of living male heirs by the end of the first wife's reproductive period*

First wife	No heir	Heir(s)	Total
Nonsepaade	9	85	94
Sepaade	24	34	58
TOTAL	33	119	152

Note: Log-likelihood ratio $\chi^2 = 21.05$; $p < 0.001$. First wives are given for 152 men.
Source: Table is after Roth (1993:606).

1976:94), they must frequently subtract children. Social practices related to this concept include contraceptive techniques, infanticide and abortion, celibacy, emigration, and service for part of the developmental cycle as means of reducing the number of heirs (Goody 1976:94).

Although subtraction of male heirs is undeniably important for Rendille males, a concern repeatedly raised in private and group interviews with Rendille men in 1990 was the addition of sons to ensure a male heir at the time of the male household head's death. This was particularly true if men had taken a sepaade first wife, because men recognized that these women have lowered fertility levels. As one Rendille men said to me in a focus group in 1990, "It is a miracle if they even have four children."

Faced with the cultural problem of disinheritance, Rendille men may develop parenting and mating strategies in an effort to balance the number of heirs. As a first step in delineating possible strategies, Table 2.1 presents data for 152 marriages in which the first wife had completed her reproductive period. These data are divided into sepaade and nonsepaade first wives and distinguish between success and failure in producing a surviving male heir at the end of the woman's reproductive career. As expected, sepaade women's overall lower fertility levels translate into a significantly higher number of households without surviving male heirs (without surviving male heir in nonsepaade first marriages = 9/94 or 9.6%; without surviving male heirs in sepaade first marriages = 24/58 or 41.4%). Furthermore, consideration of heirship distributions to these same males, only now including all wives, as shown in Table 2.2, reveals that although the significantly different distribution holds, a further reduction in households without heirs for both nonsepaade (2/94 or 2.1%) and sepaade (15/58 or 25.9%) is also evident. Considering the results of these tables together suggests that (1) heirship concern is evident throughout the sample and (2) such concern is heightened in marriages to sepaade first wives who frequently fail to produce a surviving male

Table 2.2. *Distribution of living male heirs by the end of wives' reproductive period*

All wives	No heir	Heir(s)	Total
Nonsepaade	2	92	94
Sepaade	15	43	58
TOTAL	17	135	152

Note: Log-likelihood $\chi^2 = 20.842$; $p < 0.001$. All wives are listed for 152 men.

heir. These results indicate that the sepaade tradition, acting through its negative influence on heirship patterns, could be a primary determinant of Rendille polygyny, as originally suggested by Rendille informants.

For the importance of heirship concerns as a determinant of Rendille polygyny to be assessed, a multivariate model incorporating measures of both livestock wealth and completed family composition from a first wife was constructed and tested. Based on the same 152 marriages in which the first wife had completed her reproductive career, this model has marital status of the husband, Monogamous versus Polygynous, as the dependent variable. Independent variables reflect specific characteristics of Rendille culture associated with polygyny. These include livestock wealth, husband's birth order, wife's father's age-set membership, and, reflecting possible heirship strategies, the number of surviving male heirs from the first marriage. The first two measures represent traditional livestock-based measures of wealth in Rendille culture. The first, termed Livestock Wealth, divided wealthy from poor families based on household livestock holdings before the 1984 Ethiopian drought, using the 1990 sample's median value of 27.8 tropical livestock units, or, TLUs, per household, as reconstructed for predrought holdings. TLUs represent a standardizing measure taking into account different-livestock. In the scheme used here and adopted from the Food and Agricultural Organization (1967), weights given different species are one camel = 1.0 TLU, one cow or bull = 0.8 TLU, and one sheep or goat = 0.1 TLU.

The second independent variable, Birth Order, pertains to husbands' parity order and distinguishes first-born from latter-born sons. As with the Livestock Wealth variable, this distinction has economic ramifications, with first-born sons inheriting most, if not all, of the household herd by means of primogeniture, whereas latter-born sons must rely on gifts of livestock from kin at the time of their circumcision and marriage. Thus, it is hypothesized that first-born sons would be far better situated to enter into polygynous marital unions because they would be able to raise

Table 2.3. *Results of main effects logistic regression analysis*

Independent variable	Max. likelihood coeff.	χ^2	Coeff. × Antilog
Livestock wealth	−0.3987	3.25+	0.671
Birth order	+0.1937	0.74*	1.214
Father's age set	−0.4219	3.63*	0.525
Male heirs	−1.0805	20.24***	2.946

* $p > 0.05$; *** $p < 0.001$.
Note: The analysis uses polygynous versus monogamous marital types as the dependent variable.
Source: Table is after Roth (1993:608).

the necessary livestock for bridewealth more easily than their latter-born counterparts.

The final two independent variables, Father's Age Set and Male Heirs, were included to further test for the presence of heirship strategies. Father's Age Set defines teeria from nonteeria age sets, and hence sepaade from nonsepaade women. Under the hypothesis of an indirect heirship strategy by which men attempt to "add children by adding wives," the low fertility levels of sepaade females should translate into higher polygyny levels, as men enter into subsequent marriages to avoid being disinherited. Similarly, the variable of Male Heirs divides first marriages producing two or more surviving males by the end of the wife's reproductive period from those with fewer than two. If heirship strategies intended to secure male heirs are present, marriages producing fewer than two surviving males should be differentially associated with polygyny.

Table 2.3 presents the results of a main effects logistic regression model, that is, one with no interaction between independent variables for the 152 household sample. For all independent variables, the antilog of the maximum likelihood coefficients denotes the odds of falling into the categories of poor households, first-born sons, nonsepaade first wives, and fewer than two surviving male offspring. As predicted, a positive coefficient was recorded for first-born males, who benefit from primogeniture and thus should be in a better position relative to their latter-born sibs to afford the livestock necessary for brideprice. This suggestion is supported by the negative coefficient for livestock wealth, indicating poorer households negatively associated with polygyny. A negative coefficient was also recorded for women born to a nonteeria age set. The only statistically significant variable was that designated Male Heirs, with a positive coefficient linking polygyny with households producing fewer than two surviving males by the end of the first wife's reproductive career. Multiplying this coefficient by its antilog, as shown in the final column of Table 2.3, reveals that men in these cases would be almost three (2.946) times more likely to enter into a polygynous marriage.

In this analysis, the most important variable was concern with producing a male heir. The only statistically significant variable, the fear of being disinherited, transcends Rendille measures of wealth, livestock holdings, and birth order, all of which ease the additional bridewealth payments associated with polygyny. This suggests that ideational concern with disinheritance, rather than economic constraints arising from ecologically limited resources, appears to be the primary determinant of polygyny. Delineation of an heirship strategy provides a good working example of considering both social and biological consequences of culture-specific inheritance from a life history perspective. In a similar study of inheritance among Gabbra camel pastoralists of southern Ethiopia, Mace (1996a) also found that the probability of remarriage was strongly dependent on the number of children the first wife had, particularly the number of sons. Whereas I choose to interpret the Rendille pattern largely with regard to Goody's (1976) original concept of socially motivated heirship patterns, Mace (1996b:272) pointed out that, in both the Rendille and Gabbra cases, a strategy for securing a male heir would also be consistent with an evolutionary interpretation. In doing so she notes, "in a patrilineal inheritance system a man without sons would be more likely to have his camels inherited by a brother's sons, who are obviously less related to him than his own son would be (and unrelated to his wife). The consequences of dying without a male heir would be a reduced inclusive fitness for virtually all families" (Mace 1996b:272).

Instead of entering into a debate about which interpretation is correct, that is, anthropological demography's version stressing social concomitants or human evolutionary ecology's emphasis on the biological fitness consequences of not producing a male heir, I argue that both views are practicable and that we should focus on the interaction among the symbolic concept of patrilines, socioeconomic property, and concern with biological success evident in this example. Doing so allows us to ask further questions about the data, and more importantly about the underlying motivation. For example, what is the demographic fate of families who are disinherited relative to those who manage intergenerational livestock transfers by means of a male heir? By asking this type of question, we could test if the Rendille emic, or internally constructed, view associating poverty with disinheritance has basis in etic, or externally imposed, analysis. In a similar way, we can ask who, if anyone, would help a family that was disinherited? Would such help, if it came at all, arise from families sharing genetic links, thereby supporting Mace's (1996b) concern with inclusive fitness, working along patrilines, as a practicable, emically recognized variable? Alternatively, we could focus on those families that successfully produced male heirs, asking if they transformed their resources into improving their mating or parental success by using the inherited livestock to pay bridewealth for themselves and their sons.

Last, but certainly by no means least, we can ask why a Rendille man would marry a sepaade woman, knowing as they do that these women have low fertility and thus would lower the probability of producing a surviving male heir. We look at this question more closely in the following section. For now it is enough to stress that we can only conceive of asking such fruitful questions if we adopt the notion of an "evolutionarily informed demography" (Voland 1995) that emphasizes the interaction between cultural and biological variables in group and individual strategies.

Sepaade as Male Mating Effort

If we accept that demographic strategies are complex in their motivation and combine both social and biological factors, then a logical approach to further understanding these connections lies in compartmentalizing strategies into their constituent parts. Life history theory accomplishes this by use of the principle of allocation, which states that energy used for one purpose cannot be used for another. Because of this constraint, organisms must make reproductive decisions or strategies that often entail trade-offs, with organisms often having to choose between diverting energy into either mating or parenting efforts (see Betzig, Borgerhoff Mulder, and Turke 1988).

In Rendille culture, the bridewealth demanded for a sepaade wife is the same as for a nonsepaade wife. However, both men and women realize that sepaade women have on average far lower completed fertility. Furthermore, as just demonstrated, a widespread concern among Rendille men is not producing surviving male heirs and thus being disinherited. From this evidence, the question that logically arises is this: Why marry a sepaade in the first place? We may posit that men marry sepaade first wives for their labor contribution and then take a second wife to maximize their LRS.

An alternative hypothesis, that men marry sepaade and accordingly reduce their reproductive success for the good of the group, reflects the older view of cultural group population regulation by means of cultural group selection. This position was espoused by cultural ecologists and cultural materialists (see Douglas 1966; Sato 1980; Harris and Ross 1987), who interpreted Rendille demographic features, including age-set rules and the sepaade tradition, as attempts to achieve resource–environment homeostasis. This view is summarized by Sato (1980:68):

> The strict control of human population and inheritance of camels by primogeniture are clearly related to the reproductivity of the camels. Were the Rendille to divide their camels among sons in inheritance and unable to place controls on their own population it is conceivable that the entire population might die out if they continued to rely on animals with such a low rate of increase. This is certainly why the Rendille strictly control their population by means of rigorous social norms as well as rules pertaining to the age-system.

Evolutionary ecologists (see Smith and Winterhalder 1992b) critique this interpretation by pointing to the problem of "free riders" and the model of Tragedy of the Commons (Harding 1967). In the first case, noncooperators, or cheaters, are rewarded as they reproductively outcompete those who voluntarily reduce their fertility. The Tragedy of the Commons model provides a rational motivation for such selfish behavior. Based on the metaphor of herdsmen privately owning herds that graze on commonly owned land, cheaters who place more animals on the commons individually accrue all the benefits (+1) while only sharing the group costs ($-1/N$, where N is the size of the group), for example, range land deterioration brought on by overgrazing. Applying the metaphor to the problem of overpopulation as Hardin intended, cheaters would prosper, as they would produce more offspring. Assuming genetic selection for cheating or cooperating, cheaters' higher differential fertility would quickly result in their genes swamping those of cooperators.

Anthropologists have debated the universal veracity of the Tragedy of the Commons model, finding examples of ecologically based cooperation in small East African pastoral populations (see McCabe 1990). However, there is no need to enter this debate, because both Rendille men and women are united in ascribing its origin to specific past periods of warfare, rather than a general attempt to regulate their demography. The question now is this: Why has the tradition continued despite the cessation of intertribal warfare? With the group benefits ascribed to the origin of the tradition no longer practicable, the question should be thus rearranged: Who benefits? or, more precisely, What is the individual advantage to marrying a sepaade women as a first wife, within the Rendille cultural context?

In an attempt to elicit an emic answer to this question, in 1994–1995 I undertook a survey of fifty Rendille men who married a sepaade as a first wife. The survey featured open-ended questions, including "Why would a man marry a sepaade woman, because so many sepaade were old at the time of marriage?" Responses to this question (multiple responses were permitted so that the total number of responses was 59) ranged from the practical to the romantic. The latter was represented by the category "love" (17/59 = 28%) and concerned unmarried men who gave sepaade girls gifts of beads. As detailed in Chapter 5, acceptance of the beads by both the girl and her parents marks consent for premarital sexual relationships, with the understanding that no progeny are to result from these alliances and that men are not bound to marry the girls they bead (Roth et al. 2001).

In those cases reporting "love" as the rationale for marriage, mutual attraction led to the decision to marry beaded sepaade girls, often in spite of parental protests. Turning to the practical, seven men (12%) stated that they valued sepaade wives for their help herding livestock. The herding capabilities of sepaade, who spend their time in distant *fora* camps while married nonsepaade live in *gobs*, are highly valued throughout Rendille culture. In this regard, one respondent stated that "in most cases sepaade are married as first wives because they were looked upon as very active and hardworking."

The most frequently given reason for marrying sepaade was associated with familial wealth. Seven men (12%) responded that, because their families were wealthy, they could afford to marry a sepaade first wife and then take another, nonsepaade mate later. These men stressed the *productive* over *reproductive* potential of sepaade spouses. This choice does not contrast with the fear of disinheritance discussed earlier, as wealthy men are confident they can raise the bridewealth necessary to marry an additional, younger, nonsepaade wife. One respondent who explicitly stated this sentiment said that "it is permissible if one has enough wealth to pay the brideprice for a sepaade, then he can marry a nonsepaade if he has no children."

In a similar vein, another man stated the following:

> Many wealthy men marry sepaade as first wives and then later they could marry non-sepaade if the woman does not give birth to a child. This sepaade woman will be responsible for managing the livestock and doing other domestic work in the home.

The single most frequent response, given by over one-third of men (23/59 = 39%), was that men from poor families took a sepaade wife because they could not provide bridewealth. Instead the groom offers bride service by herding his bride's parents livestock. In return, his in-laws give the couple livestock to begin a household herd. Livestock thus flows from the bride's family to the groom's, reversing the flow of bridewealth payments. The desire to transmit the resulting family estate to a male heir is still found in these cases, as one respondent stated the following:

In cases where one has no property he will go and take care of his in-laws' livestock and later on his in-laws will give him this sepaade woman and some livestock. After a period of time when his herd increases if he is not blessed with children he will use the livestock given to him by his in-laws to marry another, non-sepaade woman.

By this arrangement the wealth of sepaade families provides for poor males who otherwise would migrate to Ariaal or Samburu groups. Rather than dampening population numbers, the tradition actually increases the de facto population by stemming the flow of poor, mainly latter-born sons outside Rendille society.

Above all, these context-specific responses delineate individual strategies underlying the maintenance of the groupwide sepaade tradition. Although all Rendille men value the productive potential of sepaade because of their livestock management experience, only in two specific circumstances did respondents perceived this to override their reproductive disadvantage. Both centered on the groom's familial wealth, suggesting an advantage for wealthy and poor men taking sepaade first wives. Overall, these findings suggest specific strategies, defined earlier as decision rules, that can be stated as an if–then statement: "If wealthy, or poor, then marry a sepaade woman as your first wife." The reasoning behind these tactics is as follows. For wealthy men, a reproductive disadvantage can be overcome by taking a second wife; this is a process facilitated by having additional livestock to pay a second bridewealth. The case of poor Rendille men marrying a sepaade wife mirrors the alternative reproductive strategy labeled by human evolutionary ecologists as "making the best of a bad job" (Krebs and Davies 1978:221–242). In animal populations, this arises from genetically coded inferior phenotypes, rendering an individual unable to efficiently compete by fighting or displaying. Males in this circumstance use "sneak" tactics to breed. A poor man's strategy of marrying a sepaade first wife is a cultural analogy to the biological model of making the best of a bad job, because in both cases the alternative is not to mate and reproduce at all.

Because the survey only included men who married sepaade women, the question of why not take a sepaade wife was not directly addressed. Again set as an if–then statement, this would read as follows: "If neither rich nor poor, then do not take a sepaade first wife." Men in this situation would not be considered poor enough to substitute bride service for bridewealth, nor wealthy enough to afford two bridewealth payments.

Consequences for the full array of male mate choices are presented in Table 2.4, represented as a payoff matrix considering reproduction, brideprice, and value of wife's labor. Values assigned to each factor are estimated from Rendille emic views of marriage and inheritance and the

Table 2.4. *Rendille marriage payoff matrix*

Tactic	Fertility value	Brideprice	Labor value	Payoff
No marriage	0	0	0	0
Marry sepaade; pay brideprice	60	−20	20	60
Marry sepaade; perform brideservice	60	0	20	80
Marry nonsepaade	100	−20	10	90
Marry sepaade; pay brideprice; then marry nonsepaade	160	−40	30	150
Marry sepaade; perform brideservice; then marry nonsepaade	160	−20	30	170
Marry two nonsepaade	200	−40	20	180

Source: Table is after Roth (1999:528).

etic values derived from the previous fertility analysis. For example, a previous analysis (Roth 1999) showed that sepaade women achieve approximately 60% of the fertility of their nonsepaade counterparts. Therefore, they are assigned a fertility value of 60 points, whereas nonsepaade women rate 100 points for the identical measure. Bridewealth payments represent grooms' compensation to their bride's family for her lost labor and the labor of any future children. Because bridewealth is the same regardless of marrying a sepaade or nonsepaade woman, this is set at −20 points. Marrying a second wife thus entails a cost of −40 points. Because many men value sepaade women because of their increased time spent and experience gained managing livestock in animal camps or fora, their labor is given a value of 20 points, whereas nonsepaade labor is given a value of 10 points.

Arranged in this manner, Table 2.4 shows that not to marry at all yields no payoff. In Rendille society such strategies are actually necessities, as livestock poor, later-born sons emigrate from Rendille to Samburu or Ariaal culture. This can be directly contrasted with the third strategy, in which poor men marry sepaade women and remain in Rendille society, achieving both by substituting bride service for bridewealth. By avoiding brideprice and enjoying the higher labor value of a sepaade wife, individuals encounter a payoff that is almost as high as that received when they pay bridewealth payments to marry a nonsepaade woman (Strategy 4), that is, 80 versus 90 points. Both of these last strategies rank above paying brideprice to marry a sepaade women (Strategy 2), as her labor value does not compensate for her reproductive disadvantage, yielding a payoff of only 60 points. Together these first four strategies show the benefit of a poor man marrying a sepaade in order to make the best of a bad job, while also showing that a man who is neither wealthy nor poor should marry a nonsepaade first wife.

The last three tactics of Table 2.4 calculate average payoffs to men who take additional wives. They yield surprising results. First, note that, in this scheme, a poor man who performs bride service and then marries a nonsepaade woman can achieve a higher payoff than a wealthy man who must make bridewealth payments for both his sepaade and later his nonsepaade spouse, that is, 170 to 150. Furthermore, the latter's payoff value of 150 points ranks below that yielded by marrying two nonsepaade wives, that is, 180. Why then would wealthy men, confident that they can afford two bridewealth payments, bother to take a sepaade first wife? Three possible reasons are suggested: (1) men who marry sepaade first wives trade fertility for status, as originally proposed by Douglas (1966); (2) the labor value of sepaade women is even higher than assigned; or (3) primogeniture negates the emphasis on a large number of surviving children, leading to an emphasis on livestock management.

All are mere speculation without testing to see if Rendille men actually behave according to the survey responses. For such a test to be made, a 1996 survey was conducted with 103 male household heads from the D'fgudo age set (marriage year = 1976). This asked men to (1) state whether their family was wealthy, sufficient, or poor in terms of livestock holdings at the time of their first marriage; (2) quantify their family's livestock holdings at this time; and (3) note if their first wife was sepaade. The first two points utilize Grandin's (1983) methodology, using emic ranking of wealth to stratify pastoral Maasai households; the last borrows from Mace's (1996b) work on marriage and reproduction among the Gabbra of northern Kenya.

The first question asked of these data was whether the qualitative rankings agree with the quantitative livestock count at time of marriage. Figure 2.2 shows livestock holdings by species for groom's family, stratified by economic rank. Differences are clearly visible and statistically significant as revealed from a one-way analysis of variance for separate species ($F_{\text{cattle}} = 40.11, p < 0.001; F_{\text{camels}} = 37.07, p < 0.001; F_{\text{small stock}} = 18.74$, $p < 0.001$). The same pattern holds when overall herd size, standardized by TLUs (one camel = 1.0 TLU, one cow = 0.8 TLU, and small stock = 0.1 TLU; Food and Agricultural Organization, 1967), is considered ($F_{\text{TLUs}} = 63.71$, $p < 0.001$). With correspondence having been shown between the qualitative assessment based on the underlying quantitative holdings, the next step was to ascertain if the marriage pattern was

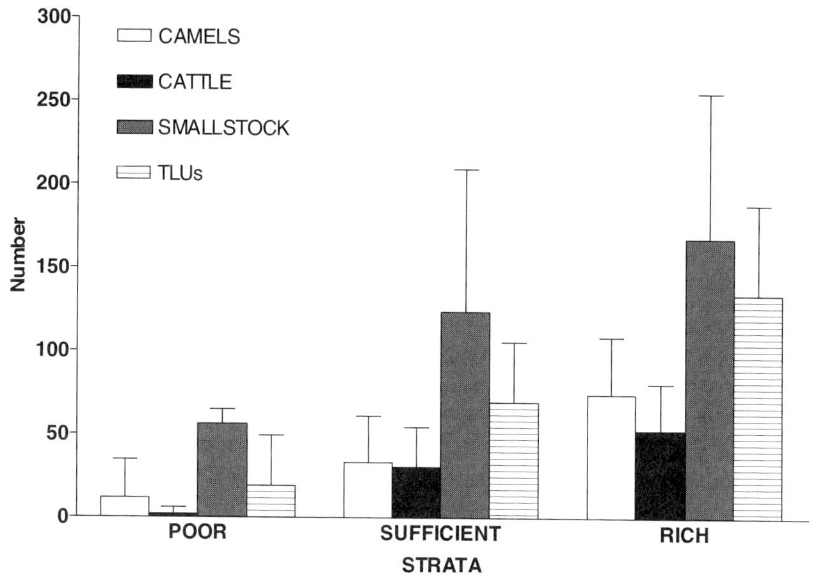

Figure 2.2. Livestock holdings by parental wealth, means, and standard deviations (after Roth 1999:530).

different for sepaade first wives. Qualitative responses to the 1992 survey lead to the hypothesis that sepaade should be disproportionately represented in the poor and rich strata. A poor man's strategy would be to marry a sepaade woman, using livestock she brings to build a herd capable of generating the necessary bridewealth to marry another, nonsepaade woman. A rich man, secure in the knowledge that his livestock wealth will allow him to acquire an additional, nonsepaade wife, can also take a sepaade first wife. As shown in Figure 2.3, these predictions are borne out, with the majority of sepaade first wives found in the rich stratum, followed by the poor. In contrast, men in the middle, the sufficient stratum, most frequently take nonsepaade wives. A likelihood chi-square analysis revealed a highly significantly different distribution of sepaade and nonsepaade first wives in the sample ($L^2 = 26.59, p < 0.001$).

Men from poor families, constitute the behavioral phenotypic variant known as making the best of a bad job, for, even considering the lowered fertility potential of a sepaade, the alternative is no marriage at all because of a lack of ability to raise bridewealth. In this case, the phenotypic variant has a clear cultural, rather than biological, pathway, as poor men substitute brideservice for bridewealth. In contrast, wealthy men take sepaade first wives with the confidence that they will be able to afford

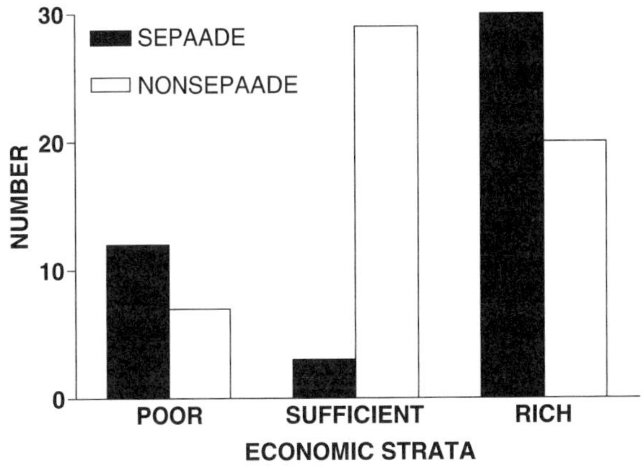

Figure 2.3. Marriage distributions by economic strata: 1996 D'fgudo sample (after Roth 1999:530).

bridewealth payments necessary to secure a subsequent, nonsepaade bride. These men value sepaade women's productive value, specifically her expertise in livestock management, over their depressed reproductive value. Taken together, both behaviors are clear examples of demographic strategies focusing on mating effort.

Rendille Primogeniture as a Parenting Strategy

No matter whether taking a sepaade or a nonsepaade wife, Rendille are concerned with producing surviving first-born males. This arises from the Rendille practice of primogeniture, by which first-born sons inherit family herds. Symbolic evidence for the high status of this particular male begins at birth (Spencer 1973:42):

> A hairstyle in the form of an elegant crest (*doko*) is proudly worn by all Rendille women whose first-born is a son. This draws attention to the importance of the first born in so many contexts in Rendille life. The *doko* is finally shaved off on the death of the husband (or the son).

Related to this concern with first-born sons is the earlier mentioned Rendille pattern of infanticide, which is aimed at males who could cause potential inheritance disputes arising from conflicting interpretation of birth order and hence property rights. As previously shown, this concern with birth order extends to and influences marriage patterns. Without the inheritance of sufficient livestock to initiate and maintain a viable household herd, latter-born sons are frequently forced to leave Rendille society and marry into either Ariaal or Samburu populations, where they herd livestock for distant kin. As we have seen for those who remain within Rendille society, the most significant determinant of polygyny is lack of surviving male heirs at the end of the first wife's reproductive period (Roth 1993), reflecting Rendille men's fear of being disinherited (i.e., dying without a male heir to inherit their herds). This concern with the special status of first-born males extends to the general Rendille age-set system, in which one age-set line, the teeria (synonymous with first born), is accorded special, higher status.

As already mentioned, the origin of Rendille primogeniture is frequently linked to the slow growth rates of their camel herds (Sato 1980). Although camels are highly adapted to the Rendille Kaisut Desert homeland, camel herds grow far more slowly than herds of cattle and small stock (Wilson, Diallo, and Wagenaar 1985). In this uncertain environment, periodic droughts can quickly decimate herds that take a lifetime to build (Roth 1996). Given these biological and environmental constraints, it is understandable that Rendille choose to concentrate family herds in the hands of one heir rather than divide them among many.

The importance of Rendille primogeniture led to the construction of three straightforward predictions to test for possible biased parental effort. These are as follows. First, first-born sons will convert the differential livestock wealth represented by primogeniture into greater numbers of offspring. Second, offspring of first-born sons will benefit from richer parental resources, resulting in greater survival relative to offspring of latter-born sons. Third, male offspring with surviving elder male sibs will be at greater risk of infant and child mortality, because of unequal parental investment favoring the eldest surviving son.

For the first two predictions to be tasted, data from a 1996 survey of 217 households headed by men from the D'fgudo age set (marriage year = 1976) were analyzed. This survey contained questions about the household head's birth order, time of marriage, fertility, and offspring mortality, and a request to provide the same information about all his sibs. Familial wealth differences were held constant by comparing reproductive success within male sibships belonging to the same age set, because the great majority of males marry en masse. Sibs belonging to different age set were deleted from this sample, as were the few men who reported having married earlier or later than age-set rules prescribed. This left a total of 212 sibships featuring 417 paired comparisons of male sibs within the D'fgudo age set.

A comparison of differences for number of children born and children surviving, based on one-tailed Student's t tests for paired variates, is presented in Table 2.5. The corresponding t values for children ever born

Table 2.5. *Calculation of one-tailed Student's t test for paired samples: 1996 D'fgudo male sib data*

Children	Mean diff. (*D*)	*SD*	*n*	*t*
Ever born	0.840	2.844	212	4.29***
Surviving	0.788	2.746	212	4.17***

*** $p < 0.001$.
Note: For paired sample, $t = D/(S_D/pn - 1)$.
Source: Table is after Roth (2000:270).

($t = 4.29$) and children surviving ($t = 4.17$) are highly significant ($p < 0.001$). These statistical differences strongly support the first two predictions: first-born sons convert their unequal share of resources, represented by livestock, into both higher fertility and lower offspring mortality compared with their relatively impoverished sibs.

A second test of demographic equality, addressing the third question, comes from an examination of Rendille male offspring survival. Data pertaining to the survival of 607 male offspring from birth to age five from a Rendille age-set line composed of three age sets, Libaale (marriage year = 1948), Irbaand'f (marriage year = 1962), and D'fgudo (marriage year = 1976), were examined by survival analysis using the LIFETEST computer program (Statistical Analysis System 2000). The total data set was stratified according to the presence or absence of one or more living male sibs. Arranged in this manner, the data distinguish between births in families with and without a living male heir. Survival was then examined during infancy (zero to one year of age) and childhood (one to four years of age) for each birth. Figure 2.4 presents the estimated survival function generated for each group by the Kaplan–Meier product limit methodology (Kleinbaum 1996:50–58). Equality of the resulting curves was tested by the Wilcoxon rank test, revealing highly significant differences between the two ($L^2 = 25.75$, $p < 0.001$). As with the previous fertility data, mortality data highlight demographic inequality within families. Offspring born to families with surviving male heir(s) are significantly more likely to die in infancy or childhood.

These results point to differential parental investment by Rendille parents as the underlying mechanism of such strong mortality differentials. While Cronk (1991a, 1991b) and Borgerhoff-Mulder (1999) draw attention to differential parental investment between offspring sexes among agropastoralists, in the Rendille case, differences focus on the male offspring's place in family life cycles, distinguishing between potential male heirs and latter-born male sibs. As in the case of Rendille mating effort,

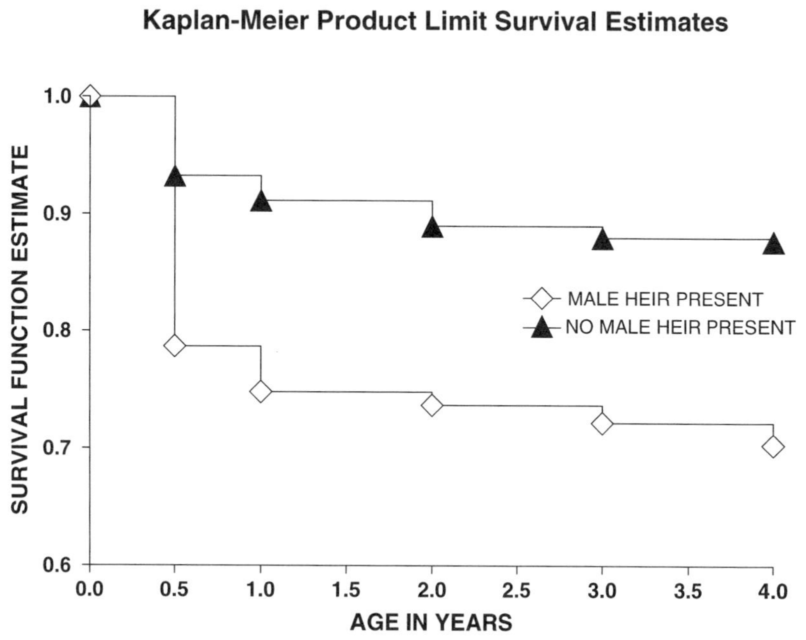

Figure 2.4. Survival analysis for Rendille males, distinguishing between those with and without a surviving male heir already in the family (after Roth 2000:270).

analysis highlights the interaction between biological and cultural factors and their effects on basic demographic parameters.

In a recent review article, Salzman (1999) argued for universal political egalitarianism among pastoralists. In his argument he did not consider inequalities arising from gender relationships. The present Rendille example strongly shows inegalitarian parental effort, or what Daly and Wilson (1988) term "discriminative parental solicitude," in this case favoring first-born males. The result is a large demographic differential, expressed biologically in terms of survival curves but arising from a cultural factor – the presence and approval of primogeniture in Rendille culture.

Summary: Demographic Strategies as Links Between Biology and Culture

In summary, this chapter outlined the potential for initiating a dialogue between human evolutionary ecology and anthropological demography by first presenting areas of shared, but generally unrecognized, common ground between anthropological demographers and human evolutionary ecologists. These include the perspective of culture as ideation, the role of human agency within the opportunities and constraints provided by specific cultural contexts, and a historical use of the concept of strategies. Defined here simply as a decision rule, the delineation of demographic strategies offers one opportunity to assess the role of both culture and biology in human demographic motivation. To explore this opportunity, I have rearranged Alexander's (1987) model of human reproductive interests so that its component parts, life effort and social interaction, now refer to evolutionary biology and culture, respectively. We can potentially gauge the costs and benefits of different strategies by incorporating natural selection as the currency to assess the adaptiveness of both cultural and biological processes and patterns. However, as demonstrated by the example of pharaonic infibulation in the Sudan detailed in Chapter 1, I am not restricting natural selection to biological phenomena. Rather, I am arguing for the application of a concept of natural selection that recognizes both cultural and biological selection as well as group and individual selection. In this regard I favor Boyd and Richerson's (1985) Dual Inheritance Theory framework, which assumes two parallel systems of inheritance, cultural and biological.

In the latter part of this chapter I attempted to illustrate this approach by using my data on Rendille pastoralists of northern Kenya and presenting examples of both mating and parental efforts in Rendille society. The next test of this approach comes in subsequent chapters, where I attempt to further outline common ground between anthropological demography and human evolutionary ecology outside my own work, but within the context of demographic strategies.

3 Mating Effort and Demographic Strategies

Mating Effort as Demographic Strategies

Evolutionary ecology's separation of mating and parenting effort is to some extent based on classificatory ease. In reality, it is much more difficult to separate the two "efforts" of mating and parenting, particularly when parental strategies focus on the twin goals of keeping resources within a familial line as well as passing sufficient amounts of genetic material to ensure the perpetuation of that family line. In addition, whereas transmitting genetic material across generations is central to the very definition of evolutionary ecology, the material aspects referred to as "resources" seem far removed from the symbolic definition of culture stressed in the preceding chapter by both cultural and evolutionary anthropologists. In fact, many anthropologists make a clear distinction between the symbolic nature of culture and the economic necessities of making a living, exemplified by Hammel's (1995) analysis of historic Balkan fertility data that is wonderfully titled, "Economics 1, Culture 0." Yet there clearly is a linkage, as cultural ideologies underlie and motivate economic behavior. Furthermore, ideologies vary between cultures with regard to the value of specific resources, as shown in Irons' (1979:257) quotation concerning variation in emic, or internally constructed, cultural measures of success:

> The Nuer value cattle and strive to increase the sizes of their herds, and a man with many cattle is judged successful. Tiwi men strive to acquire large numbers of wives, and, preferring a single quantitative measure of a man's success, measure it in terms of his wife list which includes all the living and deceased wives he has ever had, much as academics measure success in terms of the number of citations in an individual's bibliography.

The goal in this chapter is to assess how different cultures attempt to ensure the successful transfer of two currencies, one biologically coded genetic material, the second culturally defined valued resources, to future generations. I begin by looking at broad patterns of mating behaviors, analyzed by means of cross-cultural comparisons. These are by definition very coarse comparisons that run the risk of making the type of errors outlined by Hammel (1990) in the previous sections. Specifically, they do not allow us to see individual actors exercising agency within culture-specific contexts. We can see patterns, but not the important individual variation in demographic behavior. Because of these limitations, cross-cultural comparisons are followed by more in-depth, specific anthropological case studies.

Cross-Cultural Mating Strategies: Polygyny and Bridewealth; Monogamy and Dowry

I begin with Hartung's (1982) classic work on polygyny and the inheritance of wealth that revolves around the hypothesis that humans tend to transmit wealth to male descendents when polygyny is possible, reflecting the difference in variance of reproductive success between men and women. Different variances originate from biologically determined differential parental effort, with females of course contributing disproportionately more time and energy to offspring from conception to birth. This variance is heightened in mating systems featuring polygyny, because in these situations men with sufficient resources can increase within- as well as between sex reproductive differences by affording repeated bridewealth payments. Men who can afford multiple bridewealth payments obtain sexual access to multiple women and potentially improve their reproductive success by siring children with different women. Under these conditions, parents, both male and female, would benefit from a faculative male bias in offspring inheritance, because this would improve wealthy families sons' chances of maximizing their own reproductive success in the following generation.

To illustrate these hypothesized relationships between female and male reproductive variance, inheritance patterns, and reproductive success in subsequent generations, Hartung constructed the simplified model shown in Table 3.1. Imagine a population in which the standard deviation in offspring for males is three and for females one, while the mean number of offspring for both sexes is five, and each of the three couples shown in Table 3.1 favors a different inheritance strategy. Couple 1 leaves all the family wealth to their son, Couple 2 divides wealth evenly between sons and daughters, and Couple 3 leaves all their wealth to their daughter. Next assume that inheriting familial wealth translates into an increase of one positive standard deviation in offspring over others of the same sex, whereas not inheriting results in a decrease of one standard deviation. Under these conditions, the expected number of grandchildren for each couple is shown at the far right, revealing that the parental strategy of

Table 3.1. *A simplified model of the relationships between female and male reproductive inheritance, inheritance patterns, and fitness*

Couple 1: Leave all wealth to son	
♀ − 1 *SD* = 4	
♂ + 1 *SD* = 8	
TOTAL = 12	
Couple 2: Split wealth equality	
♀ = 5	
♂ = 5	
TOTAL = 10	
Couple 3: Leave all wealth to daughter	
♀ + 1 *SD* = 6	
♂ − 1 *SD* = 2	
TOTAL = 8	

Source: Table is adapted from Hartung (1982:2).

leaving all resources to a son yields the highest number of grandchildren as a result of the higher male reproductive variance and the increased fertility achieved through differential access to resources.

From this simple model, Hartung derived two further hypotheses: first, obtaining multiple wives requires substantial economic outlay; second, because of the advantages accruing to sons, polygynous societies should be strongly associated with a male bias in terms of inheritance. To assess whether these hypotheses are supported on a global basis, Hartung examined three cross-cultural collections of ethnographic data. The first was the *Ethnographic Atlas* composed of 1,170 societies (Murdock 1967). The second was the standard cross-cultural sample (Murdock and White 1969), consisting of a subset of 186 societies drawn from the larger *Atlas*, each representing one of the world's major culture areas. The final was a sample based on language families within the entire *Atlas*. The second and third subsamples were attempts to correct for "Galton's problem," or the possibility that the separate cases were not truly independent but in fact were correlated because they shared a common cultural ancestor. Tables 3.2 and 3.3 show the results of cross-cultural tabulations for both hypotheses, based on language group samples.

For Table 3.2, criteria used were coded in the Atlas as either (1) bride-price or bridewealth or (2) absence of any significant consideration of bridal gifts only. For Table 3.3, the criteria were more complicated, with inheritance patterns for real property (land or house) and movable property (livestock or money) coded in the following seven categories: (0) no information; (1) no land rights, no inherited movable property,

Table 3.2. *Mode of marriage by polygyny for the Atlas, corrected by language family*

Polygyny	Mode of marriage	
	No cost %	Bride price %
None	81.5	18.5
Limited (20%)	60.0	40.0
General (>20%)	35.7	64.3

Note: $\chi^2 = 9.68$; $p < 0.008$.
Source: Table is adapted from Hartung (1982:6).

or no rule governing the transmission of same; (2) matrilineal inheritance to a sister's son or sons; (3) inheritance by matrilineal heirs who take precedence over sister's son (e.g., younger brother); (4) inheritance by children, but with daughters receiving less than sons; (5) inheritance by children of either sex or both; (6) inheritance by patrilineal heirs who take precedence over younger sons (e.g., younger brother); and (7) patrilineal inheritance to son or sons.

In Table 3.3, the category of high bias; males only was composed of Codes 2 or 7 for both types of wealth, or one of these for each type, and for one of these in combination with Category 1. In contrast, the category of low or no bias consisted of societies coded 5 for both types of property, 5 for one and 4 for the other, and 5 for one and 1 for the other. For both hypotheses and for all samples, chi-square statistics were statistically significant at the 0.05 level.

Results from this model can be critiqued both in terms of method and theory. In the first regard, analysis used the standard cross-culture sample

Table 3.3. *Inheritance bias by polygyny for the Atlas, corrected by language family*

Polygyny	Male bias in inheritance	
	Low or none %	High; males only %
None	48.7	51.3
Limited (20%)	17.4	82.6
General (>20%)	10.7	89.3

Note: $\chi^2 = 7.35$; $p < 0.026$.
Source: Table is adapted from Hartung (1982:8).

before it was corrected for coding errors (Schegel and Eloul 1987; White 1988) and before the development of phyletic approaches to better deal with Galton's problem (Cowlishaw and Mace 1996). Theoretically, this cross-cultural model does not consider either the social structure within which marriage transactions transpire (see Goody 1973) or their symbolic content (see Comoroff 1980). Nevertheless, these results have several important interpretations. First of all, they confirm Goody's (1973) earlier assumption that bridewealth is a form of investment in sons, evidenced by the widespread custom in which parents pay the bridewealth for their sons' first wife. Second they support a linkage between mating and inheritance systems that simultaneously considers both cultural resources and reproductive success. What is equally important is that they can easily generate other hypotheses. Two that immediately come to mind are (1) if wealthy parents invest in sons, then relatively poorer families should invest in daughters; (2) if polygyny is associated with bridewealth, then monogamy should be associated with dowry.

Dowry is not the mirror image of bridewealth. In contrast to bridewealth, Bell (1998:197) does not even consider dowry a marriage payment, noting that dowry represents a transfer of consumption goods whereas bridewealth cements alliances between groups. Rao (1998:217) defines dowry as "immediate or deferred pre-mortem female inheritance in the form of movable and/or immovable material capital, e.g. livestock, cash, ornaments and land." By these terms, it is sometimes lumped with, and sometimes separated from, the concept of indirect dowry, which Rao (1998:218) defines as

> a phenomenon in which a certain fraction of the value of the bridewealth is given to the bride by her parents in addition to her eventual share of premortem inheritance.

Dowry is also not as widespread as bridewealth, occurring in only 3% of the total cultural sample of the *Ethnographic Atlas* and 6% of the standard cross-cultural sample. Geographically it is relegated to circum-Mediterranean and East Asian societies (Gaulin and Boster 1990). This circumscribed distribution negates the simple hypothesis that dowry should be prominent in monogamous societies. Rather, an examination of societies featuring dowry leads to a revised hypothesis stating that dowry should be associated with social stratified societies featuring unequal distributions of wealth and low female contributions to subsistence. To these factors must be added the condition of *socially imposed monogamy* (Alexander 1974), specifying that polygyny is not a socially acceptable option even though unequal wealth distributions result in wealthy families who could afford multiple bridewealth payments.

Traits associated with dowry are interpreted in different ways by various scholars. The economist Esther Bosserup (1970) links the geographical distribution of dowry to social conditions, arguing that the region's dependence on plow-based agriculture meant that subsistence labor was the exclusive realm of the larger, stronger male sex. Dowry is seen then as a means of guaranteeing a woman's economic contribution to her marital household, operating as an intergenerational payment securing support for women and their children in subsistence systems in which their economic contributions are small.

In contrast, the evolutionary ecologists Gaulin and Boster (1990) view dowry as female competition for male spouses, with dowry arising from faculative male–female strategies to marry daughters to wealthy males. Because polygyny is not culturally acceptable in populations with socially imposed monogamy, females compete with other females to mate with wealthy men, thereby securing exclusive rights to male familial resources. As first pointed out by Dickemann (1979a), this strategy shifts the initial payoff forward by one generation, as parents are really competing to have their daughters' sons born into wealthy families, compared with the polygynous strategy of competing to have their sons marry multiple women.

To ascertain the predictive value of the two contrasting theories, one concerned with female economic contributions, the other rooted in evolutionary theory, Gaulin and Boster (1990) constructed a multivariate model testing both against data in the corrected version of the *Ethnographic Atlas* (Murdock 1986). In both models the dependent variable was the presence of dowry, separated from the previously mentioned practice of indirect dowry, and treated as a dichotomous variable (present or absent). For the evolutionary model, termed *female competition*, independent variables were social stratification, with stratification coded in the *Atlas* as "elite," "complex," or "dual," versus nonstratified, and marital form, coded as either "monogamous" or "polygynous." This use of the *Atlas* operationalized the female competition model to test for the presence of dowry in stratified, monogamous societies, and its absence in nonstratified, polygynous societies.

Bosserup's model, termed *labor value*, uses the *Atlas*' codes for mode of subsistence and relative labor input of women and men to subsistence as independent variables. This theory predicts dowry in societies featuring both a significant dependence on agriculture and little female contribution to agricultural activities. Societies with $>45\%$ of their subsistence derived from agriculture were considered agriculturally dependent, whereas those $\leq 45\%$ were considered relatively nonagricultural. Likewise, women's contribution to subsistence economics was viewed as

Table 3.4. *Discriminant analysis results for models of dowry*

	Dowry		
Model	Absent	Present	Total
Apparently correct predictions (%) for the world			
Labor value			
Female labor	76.6	63.0	76.2
n	(907)	(27)	(934)
Plow	88.7	77.4	88.4
n	(1,136)	(31)	(1,167)
Female competition	95.3	74.2	94.7
n	(1,035)	(31)	(1,066)
Apparently correct predictions for the circum-Mediterranean and East Asia			
Labor value			
Female Labor	62.9	60.0	62.5
n	(175)	(25)	(200)
Plow	64.0	82.8	66.1
n	(1,136)	(31)	(1,167)
Female competition	83.6	78.3	83.1
n	(1,035)	(31)	(1,066)

Source: Table is after Gaulin and Boster (1990:999).

substantial unless coded as carried out by males "alone or almost alone" or "appreciably more" than females.

A third test, best viewed as a derivative of Bosserup's labor-value model, was termed the *plow version*. In this model, agricultural dependence was coded as already described, but the independent variable denoting female economic contribution was dropped in favor of type of agriculture, dichotomized as plow based (the plow was coded as "aboriginal" or "well established") or not plow based.

All models were tested by means of jackknife discriminant function analysis, using independent variables to generate an equation predicting the absence or presence of a single dependent variable, in this case dowry. An interaction term was computed as the product of the two independent variables for all models. Results of all three models are shown in Table 3.4, based first on the global *Atlas* sample, followed by a separate analysis based on the circum-Mediterranean and East Asian regions where dowry is predominant. This table shows the percentage of "apparently correct" predictions for all models, divided between absent and present. The "apparently correct" terminology refers to the fact that the tests were run on the *uncorrected* version of the standard cross-cultural Sample

Table 3.5. *Ability of dowry models to find errors in the standard cross-cultural sample*

Model	Total[a]	Data-error "hits"[b]	p value
Labor value			
Male biased labor	47	5	0.026
Plow	30	7	0.00011
Female competition	13	6	0.00000085

[a]Number of apparently correct predictions regarding the presence or absence of dowry, out of a possible 186.
[b]Number of apparently incorrect predictions that were actually correct as a result of data errors previously uncovered by Schlegel and Eloul (1987).
Source: Table is after Gaulin and Boster (1990:1001).

of the *Atlas*, before the coding corrections made by Schlegel and Eloul (1987). Tests on the uncorrected codes permitted Gaulin and Boster to examine the ability of the models to detect the eight errors in the standard cross-cultural sample, as shown with corresponding p values in Table 3.5.

An examination of Tables 3.4 and 3.5 clearly indicates that all three versions modeled generate fits to empirical data far in excess of chance expectations. Table 3.5 is particularly important, as it shows the relative probabilities of each model "finding" the errors originally coded into the *Atlas*. Results indicate that Gaulin and Boster's female competition performs far better in this regard than do the two versions of Bosserup's labor-value model. The authors correctly stress this finding as indicative that theirs is the strongest model. However, an equally workable interpretation of all the results, and one that I certainly favor, is that an analysis reveals that both models have statistically significant explanatory power. In this interpretation the results can be seen as compatible, rather than mutually exclusive. Viewed in this light, results support both a cultural model, with the economic status and autonomy of women largely derived from their contribution to subsistence bases, as well as an evolutionary model.

Like Hartung's model linking polygny with patrilineal inheritance, Gualin and Boster's model of dowry as female competition received criticism. Putting aside the usual disputes about coding keys, we can see that two arguments emerge as particularly pertinent to our subject of demographic strategies. First, Schlegel (1993) argued that dowry actually represents men's competing over "affinal alliances and the social, political and sometimes economic benefits to be gained through them" (Schlegel 1993:156). The second criticism, put forward by Dickemann

(1991), is that dowry does not constitute female–female competition. Because bride's parents provide dowry, Dickemann argues that the Gaulin and Boster model does not present a true picture of female autonomy in cultures featuring dowry. Both criticisms deal with issues central to anthropological demography and human evolutionary ecology, that is, gender and agency, with the latter in the forms of power and autonomy. Therefore it behooves us to examine particular case studies of bridewealth and dowry in order to assess who is actually making decisions about bridewealth and dowry in specific cultural contexts.

Bridewealth and the Matter of Choice

I begin this assessment by looking at evolutionary reasoning concerning polygyny and bridewealth. Polygny is by far the most widely spread human marital form, and, in contrast to the regionally limited distribution of dowry, bridewealth occurs in 52% of the 1,987 societies in the standard cross-cultural sample and in 66% of the total *Ethnographic Atlas* (Gaulin and Boster 1990:994). The predominance of polygny and its association with bridewealth suggest that it is males who choose female mates, using bridewealth to secure rights to sexual access to a woman, to compensate her natal family or lineage for her lost labor and that of her children, as well as making alliances with other groups.

However, human evolutionary ecologists have constructed and tested "female choice" models of polygyny. As with Hartung's model of polygyny and male bias in inheritance, these begin with the assumption that males and females have different reproductive interests caused by their biologically inherent reproductive variance. In the presence of these different biological parameters, why then is polygyny, in which men disproportionately control resources, so widespread? One possible answer is that, in some cases, women may also benefit from a polygynous mating system.

This possibility is raised in Orians' (1969) "polygyny threshold" model, also known in zoology as a "resource-defense polygyny" model; it pertains to any situation in which males provision or control resources that can enhance female reproductive success. In this situation, the optimal female strategy is to mate with the wealthiest available male; in sequence, the first female choosing should mate with the wealthiest male, the second choosing with the next wealthiest male, and so on. The critical factor, determining whether monogamy or polygyny predominates, is the amount of variation in the distribution of these resources under male control. Under conditions of little or no resource variation, females should choose any male who does not have a mate. Monogamy would be the best mating strategy from a female perspective, because she has exclusive claim to resources under her mate's control. However, if male-controlled resources are varied, polygyny is the optimal female strategy. This strategy is explained by the concept of a polygyny threshold, that is, a point when a female considers the *n*th wealthiest unmated male and sees a superior option in mating with a wealthier, already mated, male because one-half of the total resources he controls exceed the total resources controlled by unmated poorer males. Once this threshold is reached, it is better for females to mate polygynously rather than monogamously. The final product of female choice models is an *ideal free polygyny* distribution of mates, such that female economic choices results in a perfect correlation between a male's wealth and his number of mates. Ironically, the end result of this distribution is the cancellation of male differential attractiveness, because a male with five times the average wealth would now have five times as many mates.

Orians' model was derived for both birds and mammals, but it has been most commonly applied to passerine birds. Does it hold for humans? This simple question forms a major point of contention for anthropological demographers and human evolutionary ecologists; do models developed on nonhuman populations pertain to human populations? Certainly the underlying logic of the female choice model is captured in the George Bernard Shaw quip that "the maternal instinct leads a woman to prefer a tenth share in a first-rate man to the exclusive possession of a third-rate one." However, there are few tests of the female choice model. One of the earliest, and still among the best methodologically, is Monique Borgerhoff Mulder's (1990) analysis of female choice among Kipsigi agropastoralists of the Kericho District, southwest Kenya.

Kipsigi are highly polygynous, with some men marrying as many as twelve wives. From Borgerhoff Mulder's (1988a, 1988b) investigation of the historic relationship between polygyny and male Kipsigi reproductive success, she saw the opportunity to test the female choice model of polygyny arising from two related events in Kipsigi Colonial history. The first was the British confiscation of half the Kipsigi territory for the founding of dairy operations and tea and flax farms. The second was the concomitant establishment of Native Reserves. Kipsigi families uprooted from the confiscated land were placed within these Reserves and encouraged to participate in market-centered activities, particularly maize cultivation. The move from seminomadic pastoralism to sedentary agropastoralism led to the Kipsigi adoption of Western notions of individual land ownership. In the small Native Reserve areas, this resulted in land shortages, forcing several Kipsigi families to leave the Native Reserve areas and establish new plots in territory held by their traditional enemies, the Maasai.

From Kipsigi female fertility histories, Borgerhoff Mulder reconstructed the mating and subsequent fertility histories of twenty-five Kipsigi "pioneer" men, that is, men who established farms in the new territory. Using a Cox (1972) stratified life table analysis that allowed for varying annual risk sets, she calculated the effects of breeding opportunity on the probability of a man marrying. Breeding opportunity was linked to the plot size a pioneering man possessed, because this factor was significantly correlated with the number of wives married during the "Pioneer Period" (1930–1949) and total wives, but not with the number of previous wives. Thus plot size appears to be a cause, rather than a consequence, of a man's marital history. Two measures of polygyny calculated were marital status (e.g., monogamous vs. polygynous) and number of co-wives. As a way to designate the resources available to a new wife, the quantity "breeding opportunity" for a pioneering man at any one time was formalized as the number of acres divided by the total number of his wives plus one.

Results showed statistically significant ($p < 0.01$) associations of two independent covariates on the dependent variable of marriage. Men offering better breeding opportunities were more likely to marry, as were men married to fewer wives. Together these results support the female choice or polygyny threshold models, confirming the hypothesis that women choose a mate with an eye to the resource quality and quantity he controls.

However, although Kipsigi historical events are recognized as a unique opportunity to test female choice models as well as the positive results, there are reasons to doubt whether the Kipsigi case actually constitutes female choice. These reasons lie in ethnographic and demographic factors considered by Borgerhoff Mulder in this and her earlier (1988a, 1988b) publications. The ethnographic record raises the question of who *really* makes the decision to choose a mate. Rather than representing either male or female choice, ethnographic data suggest that mate choice is the faculative result of both the bride and groom's *parents*. Borgerhoff Mulder (1990:256) describes the actual choice of mates as this: "The parents of the young woman choose from among competing suitors a potential son-in-law, by ascertaining the young man's character, wealth and social connections." On the same page, Borgerhoff Mulder also states the following:

> Kipsigi women are not technically "free" to choose their own mates. The role of a girl's parents in choosing a son-in-law suggests that the unwieldy term "bride's parent choice" is more appropriate. Does this undermine the assumption of free female choice?

The answer to the question posed is yes. In terms of decision making, the unit of analysis is the bride's parents. Borgerhoff Mulder reports that Kipsigi girls are rarely forced into marriages they do not agree to, because of parental fear that such daughters will desert the marriage and have to be supported, along with any children, with parental resources. Yet I agree with Cronk (1991a:35–36), who states that mate choice models in general

> may be inadequate with respect to many human societies due to the influence of kin on marriage decisions. The preferences of kin are often expressed in the form of prohibitions, prescriptions and preferences about sexual and marriage partners, including incest taboos and cousin preferences.

Although negating claims for female choice mating models, this observation opens the potential for examining the role of coalitions in marriage decisions. As stressed originally by Alexander (1974) and reemphasized recently by Low (2000), human coalitions likely originated as reproductive strategies and now represent a form of *social selection* not at odds with the principles of *biological natural selection*; that is, the unit of measurement includes the persistence of genes and groups. Within the Kipsigi there are at least two coalitions dictating marriage choices, a male–female parental coalition and a larger male–male coalition representing clans and patrilines. A Kipsigi bride's agreement to enter into a marriage must be viewed as the final step in a process begun and ultimately sanctioned by these higher coalitions rather than independent female choice.

Another problem with the female choice model, clearly recognized and operationalized by Borgerhoff Mulder in her analysis of Kipsigi bridewealth, concerns the "costs of polygyny." That is, polygynously married women have to share resources controlled by men with co-wives, which may lead to increased offspring mortality or decreased fertility. The former has been found for highly polygynous West African populations (Isaac and Feinberg 1982; Strassman 2000). Possible pathways for such costs include increased exposure to human and animal disease vectors caused by shared group living conditions, resource dilution among co-wives, co-wife competition, or varying levels of parental and nepotistic investment in offspring. Findings of reduced fertility in polygynous marriages have been linked to the large spousal age differences and long postpartum sex taboos associated with African polygyny, which may reduce coital frequency, or to the presence of multiple female sexual partners, which increases the transmission of sexually transmitted diseases (Roth and Kurup 1988). For the Kipsigi, Borgerhoff Mulder's consideration of these costs revealed that the number of surviving offspring to

Table 3.6. *The costs of polygyny in Kipsigi marriages*

		Husband's acres[a]				
Marital status	Full sample	0–14	15–29	30–58	59–300	Total *n*
0 Co-wife	7.05	7.27	6.75	7.86	7.33	
	(60)	(33)	(12)	(7)	(3)	(55)
1 Co-wife	6.82	5.96	6.54	8.00	8.80	
	(102)	(27)	(24)	(31)	(10)	(92)
2 Co-wives	5.58	3.00	5.18	5.24	6.46	
	(60)	(4)	(11)	(25)	(15)	(55)
3 Co-wives	5.81	4.00	5.00	5.25	6.32	
or more	(58)	(2)	(1)	(16)	(37)	(56)
TOTAL *n*	(280)	(66)	(48)	(79)	(65)	(258)

[a] A slightly smaller sample with known ownership of husband's acres. Difference between groups, $F_{3,276} = 4.37$, $p < 0.005$; 0–14 acres, $F_{3,62} = 5.00$, $p < 0.005$; 15–29 acres, $F_{3,44} = 0.93$, *ns*; 30–58 acres, $F_{3,75} = 6.54$, $p < 0.001$; 59–300 acres, $F_{3,61} = 2.16$, $0.05 < p < 0.10$.

Note: Costs of polygyny are measured as number of surviving offspring by marital status and husband's acres to postreproductive Kipsigi women.

Source: Table is after Borgerhoff Mulder (1990:260).

postreproductive women was negatively affected by the number of co-wives in three of four classes based on husbands' land holdings, as shown in Table 3.6. Overall, the number of co-wives negatively affected LRS ($p < 0.001$) after husbands' land holdings were controlled for. Such findings do not support the female choice model in which women minimize fitness differentials. Instead, Borgerhoff Mulder (1990:26) notes that "in this population there are costs associated with polygyny for which careful marriage choices do not entirely compensate."

More recent studies of the female choice model among East African agropastoralists (Sellen, Borgerhoff Mulder, and Sieff 2000) and West African agrarian cultures (Strassman 2000) also find very high female reproductive costs associated with polygyny. Specific rationale given for deviations from the minimization of fitness predicted by female choice range from incomplete female information on groom's future economic success to the volatile nature of wealth controlled by males, which in the East African case is livestock lost in drought. In addition, both studies recognized the role of kin-based coalitions in arranging marriages. Noting the lack of fit with the female choice model and their analysis of Tanzanian Datoga pastoralists, Sellen, Borgerhoff Mulder, and Sieff (2000:109) noted the following:

> Very few women, irrespective of whether or not it is their first marriage, enter the marriage market entirely free of set constraints by kin, clan, and household. Men show considerable concern over their sisters, classificatory sisters' and daughters' marital arrangements and often try to restrict or encourage particular marriages or even extramarital affairs. We have observed many incidents where tensions arise over marital choices and alliances. Conflicts of interest within pastoral households are endemic, and they interfere with any simple optimality model, including the polygyny threshold model.

This quote exemplifies both the positive and negative aspects of the evolutionary ecology approach to human demography. On the negative side, it has a history of slighting, or even ignoring, the role of culture. This is most obvious in attempts to adopt whole cloth evolutionary models developed for nonhuman animals. The best fit for the female choice model does not even come from mammals but rather is best supported by studies of passerine birds. Yet people are not passerines, period. Cultural complexities negate any simple optimality model, as noted herein. However, before feeling smug about such blanket pronouncements, anthropological demographers should consider who is making this criticism. The answer is human evolutionary ecologists, practicing self-criticism. Furthermore, consider that this piece of self-criticism arose from the formulation of testable hypotheses and the reporting of negative results. These are the very strengths of the human evolutionary ecological approach, and they appeal to empirically minded positivists such as mainstream demographers.

Because of these strengths, instead of rejecting the evolutionary ecological perspective, we should try to incorporate human culture into the analytical framework. Borgerhoff Mulder certainly did this with other analyses of her Kipsigi bridewealth data. Unlike the fixed bridewealth of the Rendille, Kipsigi bridewealth varies, so that Borgerhoff Mulder (1988a, 1988b) logically asked this: What are the determinants, both biological and cultural, of Kipsigi bridewealth? On the basis of her fieldwork, Borgerhoff Mulder identified three culturally relevant factors. These concerned a bride's potential reproductive value, labor contribution, and affinal relationships. Operationalizations of these factors are outlined as follows.

Reproductive Value

The bride's reproductive potential, or in evolutionary terms, her future reproductive success (Fisher 1958), was examined by consideration of the following variables.

Age at menarche: This physiological landmark was estimated from the cultural rite of sending girls for circumcision in December following their first menses. For nulliparous, nonpregnant wives, final bridewealth decreased significantly ($r = -0.24$, $p < 0.01$, $n = 121$) with age at circumcision.

Physical condition: Kipsigi brides classified as "plump" commanded significantly higher bridewealth payments than those considered "skinny" (Fisher's Exact Test, $p < 0.05$).

Pregnancy: Borgerhoff Mulder expected already pregnant brides to fetch higher bridewealth because they have already shown their fecundity. Yet the opposite was true, as fathers' of pregnant brides were socially considered to have an inferior bargaining position, resulting in significantly lower bridewealth ($t_{24,193} = -2.34$, $p < 0.02$).

Paternity certainty: Women who bring children with them to marriages were hypothesized to also bring a lower bridewealth. This was true for women with children not sired by the prospective groom ($t_{19,99} = -2.81$, $p < 0.01$).

Labor Contributions

This reasoning springs from previous anthropological interpretations of bridewealth as compensation to the bride's kin group for labor lost as a result of patrilineal and patrilocal marriage customs. Borgerhoff Mulder utilized marital distance, expressed as distance between a bride's natal and marital home, as a proxy measure of her expected labor contribution. This recognized that Kipsigi mothers expect their daughters to return to their natal home to help with harvests and at the arrival of a new birth. The expectation that the groom's family would pay increasing bridewealth with increasing bride's marital distance was borne out in by means of a correlation analysis ($r = 0.20$, $n = 193$, $p < 0.01$), with a regression analysis revealing independence between this association and the wealth of the groom's father and brides' age at menarche.

Affinal Connections

This last factor acknowledges previous cultural anthropological studies showing that marriages serve to make new and cement old affinal relationships (see Kuper 1988). Such relationships may benefit poorer households, who may receive benefits in the form of labor or resources from wealthier households. If we recall that Kipsigi marriages are both patrilineal and patrilocal, then under this reasoning wealthy brides' families should demand higher bridewealth payments, whereas wealthy families offering grooms should pay far less to acquire a bride. Borgerhoff Mulder's data did not support this hypothesis, because (1) there was not a significant correlation between the number of acres owned by either bride or groom's family and bridewealth paid ($r = -0.00$, $n = 140$; *ns*) and (2) wealth differences between negotiating families did not affect bridewealth payments ($F_{4,80} = 0.19$; *ns*).

Amazingly, considering the amount of anthropological ink historically spilt on the subject of bridewealth payments, Borgerhoff Mulder's analysis was the first to actually quantify determinants of bridewealth. Her resulting analysis of variance showed that three factors, brides' age at circumcision, brides' marital distance, and brides' reproductive history (recall that pregnant and nonnulliparous brides commanded significantly lower payments) accounted for 21% of the total variance in bridewealth payments. Given the complex of sociocultural variables involved in negotiating and arriving at bridewealth, it is not surprising that the amount of variation explained is low. Borgerhoff Mulder suggests that this relatively low level of explained variation strengthens previous cultural anthropological statements that a quantitative approach to marriage payments will not be fruitful. I emphatically disagree with this interpretation and consider this work a model of anthropological research devoted to delineating mating strategies. Let us consider the results of this analysis in terms of both biological and cultural effects on Kipsigi bridewealth payments.

In the first regard, the significance of Borgerhoff Mulder's findings of increased bridewealth payments for earlier aged girls is aptly expressed in her wonderfully titled article, "Early Maturing Kipsigi Women Have Higher Reproductive Success than Later Maturing Women, and Cost More to Marry" (Borgerhoff Mulder 1988b). As the title states, Kipsigi girls who reach menarche early (ages twelve to fourteen) experience on average three additional surviving offspring, relative to late-maturing females (menarche between sixteen and eighteen years). Because Kipsigi men have no way of knowing the exact age of potential brides (nor their age at menarche), they appear to gauge female reproductive potential on physical characteristics. In particular, there is an emic Kipsigi view associating female "plumpness" with high fecundity. This immediately puts one in mind of Frisch's (1975) "critical fat hypothesis," linking the onset of female fecundity to an age-independent attainment of a minimum ratio of lean body weight to subcutaneous fat. Bongaarts' (1980) cross-cultural analysis of maternal nutrition, lactation, and birth spacing showed female physical status to be a far weaker determinant of female fecundity than lactational duration in Third World populations. Yet Frisch's (2002) recent work clearly shows that female body fat is strongly linked to the onset of fecundity in a number of populations. Kipsigi men hold by the linkage of female fat to fertility, and in this data set they are rewarded for doing so by the three extra surviving offspring.

The other biological factor, pregnancy and women with surviving children associated with decreasing bridewealth, was contrary to Borgerhoff Mulder's prediction that men should pay more for brides of proven fecundity. Uncertain paternity may be why they do not. Life history theory hypothesizes a tradeoff for men who raise children not their own between investing resources in finding mates who will bear children and investing in children already born (Lancaster and Kaplan 2000; although let us not forget our previous example of partible fatherhood from Chapter 1). For the Kipsigi, the latter can lead to familial divisiveness in terms of inheriting land, apparently tipping the balance toward investing in women who will bear children in the future.

Turning to sociocultural factors associated with brideprice, one sees that bride's marital distance has a significant effect, whereas affinal relationships do not. Borgerhoff Mulder explained the second finding as being due to the existence of other familial support mechanisms in Kipsigi society, including the lineage, the age-set system, and until recently a regimental organization for warfare, that were present to take care of families. Under these circumstances, making and maintaining affinal relationships is not such a pressing matter. Finally, the findings that Kipsigi bridewealth payments respond positively to increasing marital distance while responding negatively to bridal age suggest that the Kipsigi value both women's labor contribution and reproductive value.

All these findings are important from both a broad evolutionary and a particular culture perspective, even if they do not account for a statistically significant amount of variation. Furthermore, without a quantitative approach, it would be impossible to delineate their separate and relative effects as determinants of Kipsigi bridewealth payments. A last benefit of this type of analysis is that it provides a benchmark for future cultural and demographic change.

Demographic and Cultural Change: Values and Morals

One important assessment of any theoretical orientation in anthropology and evolution is how effectively it can explain change. Of course biological evolution is defined by change, with microevolution defined as changes in gene frequency over time. Although neither so well defined nor limited to the four neo-Darwinian mechanisms of microevolution (mutation, natural selection, random genetic drift, and gene flow), cultural systems are assumed to be inherently dynamic and changing; the inability to explain such change in large part spelled the death knell for structural functionalism and its North American offspring, neofunctionalism or cultural ecology. In this section, I examine three case studies of demographic change and assess evolutionary and cultural explanations of change.

I begin by continuing with Borgerhoff Mulder's studies of Kipsigi agropastoralists of southwestern Kenya. Following her fieldwork in 1982–1983, Borgerhoff Mulder (1995, 1996) initiated a second phase of research in 1991. In the intervening nine years there was considerable socioeconomic change in Kenya in general, and for the Kipsigi specifically. For the country as a whole, the middle to late 1980s were marked by economic stagnation, manifest in a slowing gross domestic product, weakening international investment, and rising interest rates. On local levels, these national changes, linked in turn to international economic changes, resulted in increasing poverty and differentiation of wealth; that is, the poor got poorer and the rich got richer.

In the Kipsigi land in Ambosi Location, Kericho District, Kenya, household economics shifted from a previous emphasis on maize production to milk marketing. This resulted in a larger market involvement for men, who retained their traditional first rights to the morning milking. With better access to transportation, in this case bicycles, men soon outcompeted women for market sales of milk. Recognizing the increasing profits from milk commoditization gained by older men, younger men joined the market economy through the sales of vegetables, eggs, and chickens, heightening male cash contributions to household economies.

Simultaneously, Kipsigi society showed signs of joining the incipient fertility decline occurring throughout Kenya during this period (Robinson 1992). Completed family size fell from 8.2 during the period from 1973 to 1977 to 6.7 for the period from 1984 to 1988. In addition, daughters and sons were increasingly sent to school by their parents. Both changes were attributed to the internal conceptualization that land was becoming scarcer, and that not all children could be guaranteed a living from their parental land holdings.

Economic differentiation, increased male economic involvement, incipient fertility control, and increased education for both sexes culminated in structural changes in bridewealth payments and marriage patterns. In two recent marriages, small plots of land replaced the traditional currency of livestock. In two other cases, wealthy families paid for their daughters' grooms' secondary education, in essence a form of dowry rather than bridewealth. The spread of education among young people resulted in educational isogamous marriage patterns, featuring marriages between educated grooms and educated brides. Finally, there were changes in male marital strategies, as two strong correlations from the previous analysis, one showing increasing bridewealth payments with increasing marital distance, another linking decreasing payments with increasing age, both disappeared.

Borgerhoff Mulder uses evolutionary theory to explain changing patterns of Kipsigi male marriage strategies, offering the following explanations. New diversity in bridewealth payment arrangements mirrors the diversity in new economic opportunities, as well as a changing cognitive view that land is scarce and under pressure. Changing patterns of bridewealth reflect cultural adjustments to new environmental conditions, particularly adjustments to the value of females, measured both in terms of their reproduction and labor production. Women's reproductive value fell because of incipient fertility reduction while their productive value decreased because of male market activities. As a result, bridewealth is depressed, as males no longer pay high costs for young fecund women or for the lost production of women from distant communities. Male mating strategies quickly track recent environmental change, an interpretation supporting human behavioral ecology's claim that human behavior's innate plasticity permits rapid behavioral adjustment to environmental change. This interpretation is in contrast with evolutionary psychology's basic tenet that human behavioral patterns arose by means of natural selection during the temporally unspecified Era of Evolutionary Adaptiveness (EEA), resulting in a maladaptive culture stretch or culture lag with respect to today's novel environments.

The rapid flexibility of Kipsigi mating strategies strongly supports the predictions of human behavioral ecology, but Borgerhoff Mulder is quick to point out that it does not yield any information concerning the actual decision-making rules responsible for disrupting the historic linkage among bridewealth payments, age at menses, and brides' marital distance. Kipsigi men never knew the exact age of potential brides, but instead they used the emic notion of "plumpness" as a proxy measure for early sexual maturity. In the more recent fieldwork, female age estimation became even more difficult, as young women put off circumcision until they finished primary schooling, regardless of the timing of menarche. However, in an incredibly short period, Kipsigi men no longer select for plumpness or early age at menarche. How did they accomplish this?

Borgerhoff Mulder (1996:217) also notes that her study does not shed any light on whether "by modifying their mating effort allocations in this way, Kipsigi men are in fact increasing their fitness (conventionally measured as number of descendents)." Tests for this vital question would entail an examination of LRS for both Kipsigi men to determine if producing fewer offspring actually increases LRS, perhaps as a result of improving offspring survival.

Although the limitations of her most recent fieldwork are acknowledged, Borgerhoff Mulder's research is very important, in that it clearly demonstrates the incredible flexibility of human demographic behavior's ability to track social change. In doing so it supports the human behavioral ecology view that human demographic behavior consists of adaptive response patterns, represented by phenotypes generally referred to as reaction norms (Hill and Hurtado 1996:13). Phenotypic variation, between and within populations, is considered the result of individual reactions to environmental and cultural constraints. This last point is important for a number of reasons, not the least of which is that phenotypic variation per se is not considered heritable. Rather, it is the ability to exhibit a range of flexible, or in biological terms, plastic, reaction norms that is selected for and heritable in humans. Borgerhoff Mulder's latest Kipsigi research is an important example of phenotypic plasticity,exemplifying human behavioral ecology's emphasis on decision rules or conditional strategies; these are glossed as "in context X, do α, in context Y, switch to ß" (Winterhalder and Smith 2000:54).

While beautifully exemplifying this type of behavioral plasticity in the face of changing social conditions, Borgerhoff Mulder also draws our attention to two present shortcomings in the evolutionary approach to explaining demographic change. First of all, there is at present no clear understanding of the cues by which Kipsigi men "switch to ß," that is, change their mating strategies in accordance with environmental or cultural change. Second, we cannot tell now if these changes are adaptive, in the sense that they will leave more descendents. To determine if the switch in strategies is adaptive or maladaptive necessitates the passage of time so that we can measure LRS for Kipsigi males.

Can anthropological demography do a better job of explaining demographic change? To address this question I present a case study from one of the leading anthropological demographers, Thomas Fricke, who has studied the demography of Tamang agropastoralists located in the middle Himalayan community of Timling on the Nepal–Tibet border (Fricke 1990, 1994, 1997a, 1997b). In explaining demographic change among the Tamang, Fricke grounds his theory in the belief of culture-based motivation, referring to cognitive anthropologists such as D'Andrade (1992) and Strauss (1992), who posit that cultural beliefs are directly translated into action. Fricke follows fellow anthropological demographer Sherry Ortner (1984), who sees each culture presenting and maintaining a set of "key elements" linking culture, individual motivation, and behavior through "the orientation of conceptual experience and the provision of cultural *strategies* for behaviour" (Fricke 1997b:192; italics added). The good news for anthropological fieldworkers is that these key elements are repeated in many different cultural contexts, so that they may be identified by "even the most insensitive fieldworker" (Ortner 1973:1339).

Certainly a highly sensitive field worker, Fricke has long identified one key Tamang cultural element, reciprocity, that he believes is crucial in explaining changing Tamang marriage patterns and the incipient acceptance of modern Western contraceptive techniques. Fricke argues that reciprocity arising out of an *ethos of exchange* permeates Tamang culture in daily activities, mythology, rituals, and, what is most important for our purposes, marriage. Unlike the Kipsigi for whom affinal relationships are relatively unimportant because of the presence of other mitigating social structures, such as age-set system and lineage, the Tamang can be classified as an alliance culture, that is, one in which affinity is as important as descent (Kuper 1988). For the Tamang, Fricke sees alliance, exchange, and reciprocity linked together as a vital moral system, and that demographic change comes only from moral change. Although Fricke does not define morals, we can use the two-part definition given by Irons (1991:49): the first is the near-universal propensity of individual human beings to make judgments of right and wrong; the second is the rules or systems of rules that codify and clarify these judgements. Note that this definition is relevant to the concept of *normative ethics*, which are concerned with right and wrong, rather than *descriptive ethics*, which merely describe morality as a cultural phenomenon (see Sober and Wilson 2000:204).

Fricke argues that Tamang marriage systems are demographic, cultural, and moral systems because "marriage practice is tied to a whole array of culture-laden conceptualizations that embed it within distinct forms of kinship and systems of meaning" (Fricke 1997b:187). Because marriage entails a lifetime of exchange and reciprocity between two kin groups, Tamang ideals of morality are reflected in the qualities a man should look for in a bride, as Fricke (1997b:194) records from a taped interview:

> For me, I want a girl who has good habits and character . . . and these are: when other people come to visit she has to give them some food and other things, or when children or people from this village need something like liquor or beer, then she should roast some corn and give it to them. Or if there isn't any liquor or beer, then she should roast some corn and give it. That sort of habit is what I mean by good.

In this example, Fricke notes that what is considered good or moral in everyday life translates into what is considered worthy in a marriage partner. Thus the reciprocity that dominates visiting, as shown in this example, is also sought when groups exchange brides. This cultural ideal of giving is also reinforced, both positively and negatively. In the former regard, it is emphasized in a Tamang myth in which two hunters who shared a tiny hummingbird catch were rewarded by a divine multiplication of meat so that it was necessary to carry the final load on a pole slung between two people. Inversely, sanctions against those who violate this sharing ethic are found throughout Tamang culture and include accusations of witchcraft and breaks in previously established social networks.

This emphasis on reciprocity found in marriage alliances extends to parentage. For example, Tamang believe that children are formed from the two houses represented in the marriage. Mothers provide flesh, while the father contributes bone. In his research, Fricke shows how these symbolic themes are realized as practice, with 69% of married women in Timling reporting that their husbands provided free labor to the brides' natal families; of 55 households who reported building their own home, two-thirds reported receiving help from their affinal kin in doing so.

Fricke stresses that Tamang marriage systems constitute cultural means of linking individuals to larger kin groups. Nowhere is this linkage more evident than in the process of making the marriage match. As noted for the Kipsigi and Datoga in the previous section, marriages are not usually the product of individual choice. Rather they are arranged by differing constellations of kin. Fricke (1997b:197–198) shows that, along with cultural ideals of what "good" traits a man looks for in a bride, there is also the notion that a "good" marriage involves discussions and presentations to a woman's parents as well as to her father's brothers. Other aspects of the "good" surrounding Tamang marriage include the following: (1) the exchange of ritual flasks of alcohol called *pong*; (2) indirect dowry, whereby the groom or his immediate family present money or gifts to a bride's parents, who in turn pass a portion of these presents to their daughter; (3) a form of female inheritance termed *djo*, characterized by the movement of property from mother to daughter shortly after marriage; (4) cross-cousin or first-cousin marriage; and (5) brideservice, in which a groom provides labor or service gratis to his wife's kin group. The inverse of these "good" aspects of marriage is divorce, which severs ties between kin groups.

A final variable considered by Fricke is the bride's visits to her natal home. These act as confirmation that women maintain ties and identities with natal families and clans following marriage, further symbolizing the dual nature of Tamang descent and alliance concerns. The frequency of these behaviors associated with marriage varies, depending on how the marriage was arranged. Table 3.7 presents frequencies of Tamang marriage practices, arranged by spousal choice among ever-married women in Timling. Choice of spouse represents three patterns: The first is

Table 3.7. *Frequency of first marriage practice by choice of spouse among ever-married Timling women (%)*

Spouse choice	Senior	Joint	Self	Total
No. of women	73	56	56	185
Pong exchange	92	39	18	54
Cross-cousin marriage	84	71	52	70
First-cousin marriage	38	34	4	26
Indirect dowry	68	38	29	47
Receipt of djo	60	36	50	50
Natal visits	25	46	59	42
Brideservice	70	64	73	69
Divorce	30	25	25	27

Source: Table is after Fricke (1997b:199).

"senior," that is, husbands chosen entirely by senior members of a woman's family; the second is joint, meaning chosen by a daughter with help from her senior male kin; the third is *self*, which is a husband chosen by a woman. From Table 3.7 it is clear that certain key elements of a "good" Tamang marriage decrease as one goes from the senior to the self category. Included here are pong exchange, cross- and first-cousin marriages, and indirect dowry. Going in the same direction, divorce does not increase, but natal visits do. An analysis by birth cohort for Timling ever-married women reveals the same general pattern over time, as shown in Table 3.8. Over time, pong exchange, indirect dowry, and brideservice decline, now joined by receipt of djo, as well as group ("senior" and "together" classifications). What is equally important is that divorce increases over time, as do natal visits.

Fricke interprets Table 3.8 as denoting not only changing Tamang marital patterns but also changing morals. For example, the growing number of bridal natal visitations and the growing number of divorces are interpreted as a deemphasis of the alliance factors previous ratifying the Tamang moral code centering on reciprocity. The resulting increase in familial nucleation is matched by the similar increase in individual selection of spouses, interpretable as increasing personal autonomy at the expense of the culturally generated perception concept of group (kinship) membership.

Fricke's notion that changes in group morals initiate both cultural and demographic change fits well with previous demographic thinking that cites *values* as causal factors in demographic change (Bulatao and Lee 1983; Leete 1997). However, Fricke's stress on *morals* is far more closely related to Caldwell's (1982) use of the term in his Wealth Flows Theory

Table 3.8. *Marriage cohort changes in first marriage practices among ever-married Timling women (%)*

Birth cohort	<1946	1946–1965	1966–1975	Total
No. of women	76	82	27	185
Who chose spouse				
Entirely senior	50	34	26	40
Together	32	29	30	30
Respondent alone	18	37	44	30
Pong exchange	63	48	44	54
Cross-cousin marriage	72	69	67	70
First-cousin marriage	32	21	30	26
Indirect dowry	57	43	33	47
Receipt of djo	54	49	41	50
Natal visits	33	46	52	42
Brideservice	82	63	52	69
Divorce	14	38	30	27

Source: Table is after Fricke (1997b:201).

when he describes changes in "familial morality" as underlying the trend toward familial nucleation in place of earlier versions of family based on extended kinship patterns.

Of course, anthropology has a long tradition of dealing with the concept of group morals; this is best exemplified in the concept of *cultural relativism*. This expressly stated that any particular culture's moral code must be judged within its own context. In modern anthropological texts, it is defined as meaning "not to pass judgement on the moral worth of other peoples' culture," or "disavowing any absolute, universal moral standards that can be used to rank cultural beliefs and practices as good or evil" (Harris 1995:9–10). Originally developed to escape the racist overtones of cultural evolutionary typologies and social Darwinism, cultural relativism in the strict sense means the acceptance of social behavior ranging from infanticide through slavery to female foot binding and genital mutilation. The reasoning underlying this position was anthropological functionalism, which posited that all established beliefs and practices perform specific functions in human societies. The notion of cultural relativism spread quickly within anthropology, so that the noted anthropologist Clyde Kluckhorn (1939:342) would pronounce it "probably the most meaningful contribution which anthropological studies have made to general knowledge."

Recent times have not been so kind to the concept of cultural relativism. In his text, *Sick Societies*, Edgerton (1992:22–39) notes its partial eclipse as a result of two related recent streams of anthropological thought. The first is that not all cultural practices or beliefs contain a hidden function that the anthropologist should uncover. The second is the postmodernist perspective that no culture can be understood by anyone not born into it; therefore cultures cannot even be compared, let alone evaluated (see Geertz 1973). To this I would add that cultural relativism today has run head on into anthropological concerns with the incompatibility of cultural diversity and universal human rights (Cowan, Dembour, and Wilson 2001).

Concern with morals is on the ascendancy today in evolutionary ecology. For example, reciprocity, which Fricke identifies as one of Ortner's key elements of Tamang culture, has been intensively studied as a special form of cooperation that can affect fitness levels (Trivers 1972). Cooperation between conspecifics was long a problem in evolutionary theory, which stressed competition, summarized forever in Darwin's phrase "the survival of the fittest." It was not until Axelrod's (1984) groundbreaking work entitled *The Evolution of Cooperation* that biologists could understand the selection of cooperation on an individualistic level.

Axelrod based his approach on the mathematical field of game theory, focusing on a simple model termed the Prisoner's Dilemma. This takes its name from a metaphor revolving around two prisoners, each suspected of taking part in a common crime. Separately, authorities ask each whether the other committed the crime, with the level of punishment dependent on whether one implicates the other. This situation can be best appreciated as a game, with each prisoner awarded points as a result of his or her behavior toward the other. In a true dilemma, they have two options: Cooperate (C) or Defect (D). If they both Cooperate by not informing on the other, they each earn 3 points as their *Reward*. Alternatively, if they both Defect and inform on each other, their *Punishment* is 1 point apiece. However, rewards and punishments are uncoupled if they each choose different tactics. If one Cooperates while the other Defects, a strategy known as the *Temptation*, then the Defector receives 5 points while the trusting Cooperator gains no points, the situation termed the *Sucker's Payoff*. Figure 3.1 presents this situation as a 2×2 matrix in which the rows represent one prisoner and the columns the other.

One of the strengths of this simple model is that it can be expanded into many different circumstances and fields. The payoff, measured here in points, could be prestige or status, amounts of money, or, in evolutionary scenarios, the number of offspring. Any game set up so that Temptation (T) > Reward (R) > Punishment (P) > Sucker's Payoff is a Prisoner's Dilemma. No matter what the payoff or the number of players, the best strategy in a single game is always to Defect, because this decision rule

Column Player

	Cooperate	*Defect*
Cooperate	**R = 3, R = 3** Reward for mutual cooperation	**S = 0, T = 5** Sucker's payoff, and temptation to defect
Defect	**T = 5, S = 0** Temptation to defect and sucker's payoff	**P = 1, P = 1** Punishment for mutual defection

Row Player

Figure 3.1. The classic Prisoner's Dilemma, as used in Axelrod's tournaments. Note that row payoffs are listed first.

yields the highest points. This simple game quickly becomes far more complex if repeated, mirroring real life in which people repeatedly meet and remember past interactions. In the Repeated Prisoner's Dilemma, there is no clear-cut strategy for success, because success depends on the other player's strategy, which is never known in advance. Therefore, a strategy that is successful with one player may be a dismal failure with another who "behaves" differently.

In an attempt to delineate "robust" strategies, that is, those that do well against an array of distinct, competing strategies, Axelrod (1984) proposed a computerized round-robin tournament of Repeated Prisoner's Dilemma, and he actively sought computer programs to compete as separate strategies. To the resulting fourteen programs submitted he added a fifteenth, RANDOM, which played Cooperate and Defect on a purely random basis. In the first tournament, these fifteen strategies played against each other, and a copy of themselves, for 200 rounds, using the original point system described herein (Temptation-5 points, Reward = 3 points, Punishment = 1 point, and Sucker's Payoff = 0 points). Surprisingly, the simplest program, submitted by the Canadian game theorist Anatole Rapoport, entitled TIT FOR TAT, won the tournament.

As the name implies, TIT FOR TAT begins by cooperating in the first round, and then imitating the other player's previous move. TIT FOR TAT won the entire tournament, because it featured three characteristics. First, it was *nice*, that is, never the first to defect, although by definition TIT FOR TAT is capable of retaliation in the face of Defection. Other "nice" programs fared well, with the eight nice programs all finishing ahead of the seven "nasty" programs. Second, TIT FOR TAT was "forgiving." Although it may retaliate, it does so for only short periods. In doing so, TIT FOR TAT avoided runs of low-scoring mutual recrimination (Punishment). Third, TIT FOR TAT lacked "envy," defined as striving to win more points than its opponent. TIT FOR TAT never won a single game, because it could not defect and collect the highest score (Temptation) except in retaliation. Instead, its strategy was to achieve shared scores. This was rewarded because the Prisoner's Dilemma is a *non-zero-sum* game, that is, one in which it is possible to make points without taking them away from an opponent.

Axelrod called for a second tournament, resulting in sixty-two programs submitted, many more complicated than in the preceding round. Examples of the more complex algorithms included TRANQUILIZER, which gave the appearance of cooperation, lulling its opponent into a sense of false security, only to slip in brief runs of unpredictable defections. Another was TESTER, a variant of TIT FOR TAT that began with an initial defection to test its opponent's reaction. If the reaction was defection, TESTER cooperates by playing TIT FOR TAT for the duration of the game. If, however, the reaction was cooperation, TESTER cooperates on the second and third move, but it defects every other following move. Competing among such complex programs, the simplest, TIT FOR TAT, resubmitted by Anotole Rapaport, won again on the strengths of its characteristics, niceness, forgiveness, and lack of envy.

Axelrod then performed a further simulation, modeling the effect natural selection would have on the differing strategies submitted for the second tournament. The sixty-three strategies (the sixty-two submitted plus Axelrod's RANDOM program) were started at equal frequencies to mimic the start of an evolutionary succession. This time payoffs were not points, but rather offspring, denoting the reproductive success of each algorithm. Subsequent games simulated successive generations; each was characterized by changing frequencies of strategies, modeling changing behavioral climates over time. Allowed to run for 1,000 generations, nice strategies, led by the simple but formidable TIT FOR TAT, performed the best, whereas all nasty programs fared poorly and eventually went into extinction. Following these extinctions, all nice programs cooperated with each other, making them impossible to discern from the original TIT FOR TAT. In this manner, TIT FOR TAT mimics the concept of an *Evolutionarily Stable Strategy* (ESS), defined by Maynard Smith (1974) in his original applications of game theory to evolutionary biology as a strategy that, if adopted by a critical proportion of a population, cannot be bettered or invaded by another strategy.

Subsequent significant results based on game theory include Boyd and Richerson's (1992) examination of a hypothetical game in which players could punish each other (through subtracting points) if they made the wrong choice. This led to the immediate establishment of rules that they called *moralistic strategies*, which fast became ESSs as well as inducing the regular performance of costly acts to avoid punishment. Boyd and Richerson's results, published in the article titled "Punishment Allows for the Evolution of Cooperation (or Anything Else) in Sizeable Groups," suggest that moral sanctions found in human societies can foster behavior for "the common good," raising the topic of cultural group selection once again.

One final noteworthy result is Harms' (2000) adoption of the Prisoners' Dilemma model to an agent-based simulation model (more about these models in Chapter 5). In these models, simulated beings, designated as either Cooperators or Defectors, occupy a wrapped grid, representing geographical or social environments. Simulating a life cycle, agents move between patches, acquiring and consuming vital resources. They reproduce when they acquire a certain level of resources and die when they consume all their personal resources. Harms introduced localized extinctions into this system, simultaneously killing off all agents in a patch. Under these conditions, intermediate levels of extinction fostered cooperation over defection for two reasons. First, interactions between agents became critical for survival; without payoffs from interactions, agents cannot outrun the waves of extinction. Second, vacant patches created by the extinctions provided both colonization opportunities for colonizers and spatial insulation from defector invasions. Harms (2000:312) interpreted these effects as modeling hostile boundaries of ancestral ranges providing conditions under which cooperative behavior can evolve. In addition, extinction patterns provide a mechanism for creating correlations of like with like by keeping population densities low and insulating colonies of cooperators from invasion.

One important upshot of the findings that human cooperation can arise and spread by means of natural selection is a renaissance of the concept that morals are biologically innate in humans (see Arnhart 1998 for a history of this premise running from Aristotle through Darwin). It also sparked cross-disciplinary discussion on the evolutionary origins of morality (see Katz 2000) and reopened the debate on the unit of analysis for natural selection, such as the individual or the group (see Sober and Wilson 1998).

All these findings point to morals as another potential point of common ground for human evolutionary ecologists and anthropological demographers. Here it is worth repeating Kertzer's (1995:44) reminder that moral systems are directly linked to culture by calling attention to Kreager's (1986:136) definition of culture stressing "the application of criteria of right and wrong." Furthermore, the interaction among demography, culture, and moral systems is inherent in Kreager's (1986:131) statement that "vital processes are the true playground of moral systems."

I immediately can see three very good fits between evolutionary theory and Fricke's anthropological demographic analysis. First is the enforcement of morals, or the role of moral sanctions. Among the Tamang, nonadherence to the moral of reciprocity is enforced by sanctions and punishments, ranging from accusations of witchcraft to exclusion from previously established social networks. The presence of negative sanctions for deviations from their moral code is hardly surprising. From their survey of randomly chosen cultures coded in the Human Relation Area Files (HRAFs), Sober and Wilson (1998:165) report that "human behavior is very tightly regulated by social norms in most cultures around the world." Containing both positive (rewards) and negative (punishment) qualities, "regulated social norms" are real-world examples of the Rewards and Punishments modeled in Repeated Prisoners' Dilemma simulations.

Next, Fricke (1997b:201) at least in part explains adherence to these social norms as embodying "commitment to culture-based moral goods." This parallels the evolutionary perspective, articulated best by Frank (1988) and Cronk (1994), that *moral sentiments* are solutions to commitment problems that arise "when it is in a person's interest to make a binding commitment that will later seem contrary to self-interest" (Frank 1988:47). Frank's classic example of this situation involves the desire for revenge, epitomized by the feud between two Kentucky families, the Hatfields and the McCoys, popularized in American folk literature. A rational actor caught in the continuous cycle of violence of this blood feud would want to stop the desire for vengeance. However, an unshakable commitment to vengeance can actually deter future violence. A Hatfield who knows that killing a McCoy will surely result in a committed McCoy's killing a Hatfield in revenge will think twice about the initial act of murder. Frank notes that a better target for the McCoys would be a rational actor, who reacts to each new situation by attempting to maximize his or her personal advantage. Whereas this example views a commitment to irrationality as adaptive, Irons (1996) give examples of maladaptive behavior arising and persisting as signs of commitment. Included here are female clitoridectomy and infibulation, as well as male subincision and foot binding. In a slightly different vein, Cronk (1994) applied modern communications theory to propose that moral commitments are subject to manipulation resulting in altruistic, or selfless, behavior, exemplified by soldiers dying in wars, and religious converts tithing a portion of their income to their church.

The third and final parallel with Fricke's analysis of Tamang marriage change is the very "ethos of exchange" or the moral sentiment of reciprocity. Reciprocity in evolutionary theory is found in Alexander's (1987) concept of *indirect reciprocity*, which mirrors the TIT FOR TAT strategy by positing "be nice to those who are nice, and nasty to those who are nasty." Yet Alexander goes beyond *direct reciprocity* by envisioning a system in which one group member (A) helps another (B) in return for help from yet a third, perhaps unrelated, party (C). Indirect reciprocity therefore necessitates the human ability to deduce and remember people's reputations based on their past behavior, that is, avoid interactions with people who have poor reputations (i.e., are dishonest or "free riders") and increase interactions with those who have a reputation for honesty, fairness, and other qualities deemed morally good. This type of evaluation frees humans from cooperating solely on the basis of biological kinship, enabling cooperation among even previously unknown group members, while simultaneously discouraging free riders, who are not rewarded for their moral deviance and are encouraged to conform to social norms. Recent computer simulations incorporating reputations, coded as "image scores" that could be enhanced by repeated bouts of cooperation, show that indirect reciprocity is a winning strategy to identify cheaters within a group who could then be ostracized (Nowak and Sigmund 1998).

In my opinion, the study of culture change as moral change has great potential for future joint research by human evolutionary ecologists and anthropological demographers. For example, morals mirror anthropological demography's concern with agency, with Rottschaefer (1998) arguing that individuals act as *moral agents*, making decisions on what they consider right or wrong behavior, while at the same time either conforming to or flaunting cultural group morals. In addition, as reflected in Frank's (1988) concept of moral sentiments and commitments, moral agents need not be rational actors. Freed from the constraint of individual rationality, analysis can move in new and challenging directions.

Studying morals and moral change can also provide windows into power and gender relationships. For example, Irons (1996:19) interprets cliotoridectomy and infibulation among Sudanic African women, subincision of young men among Australian Aborigines, and historic foot binding of Chinese females as examples of costly commitment signs imposed on individuals and groups of low social status. The study of changing morals also is amenable to anthropological demography's political economic perspective linking local changes to much larger national and international processes. Fricke (1997a:264–265) exemplifies this for the

Tamang when he attributes changing morals in part to widening exposure to the outside world and its emphasis on wage labor, market involvement, and non-kin-based relationships.

Last but perhaps most important, recent research into the development of morals in children shows a strong biological–cultural interaction. Damon's (1999) review of multiple cross-cultural studies concludes that children only a few weeks old show moral emotions, including empathy, shame, guilt, and indignation; this suggests an innate biological basis for human morals. However, equally strong evidence indicates that subsequent cultural experiences can lead to moral variation within and between cultural groups. This is evident in cross-cultural variation in response to the "Ultimate Game," a scenario in which two people in separate rooms decide how to divide a set sum of money. One person makes a single offer of how to divide the sum, which the other can either reject or accept. Unlike Repeated Prisoners' Dilemma, the offer and response are one-time-only interactions, and the game is over regardless of acceptance or rejection of the offer (Sigmund, Fahr, and Nowak 2002). When presented to fifteen small-scale societies, ranging from the Au of Papua New Guinea to the Machiguena of Amazonia, a large variation in offers as well as responses emerged (Heinrich et al. 2001). Variation was explicable in terms of cultural variation; for example, strong social obligations associated with gift giving among the Au led them to reject both overly generous and miserly offers. Together this evidence points to a true coevolution of human morals, influenced by both biology and culture.

However, we gain nothing by simply substituting the words *moral change* for *culture change* without investigating the mechanisms of change. As Borgerhoff Mulder stressed, we need to know how decision rules are formed and applied. To that end, let us look at the demise of the Rendille sepaade tradition as a test case for using changing group morals as triggers for new decision rules affecting demographic change.

The End of the Sepaade Tradition: Behavioral Tracking and Moral Change

As outlined in the previous two chapters, the Rendille sepaade tradition arose in the mideighteenth century as a reaction to Borana raiding, rather than as a conscious attempt to regulate Rendille population growth in relation to their camel herds as previously suggested (Douglas 1966; Sato 1980; Harris and Ross 1987). However, the tradition does significantly reduce fertility and population growth, by delaying marriage and hence the onset of reproduction, to all daughters of one age-set line called the teeria, or first born. In the summer of 1998 the Rendille terminated the sepaade tradition. Throughout Rendille villages at that time, the daughters of the Il-Kachili age set (fathers' marriage year = 1976) inhaled incense smoke and ate honey served by elders, releasing them from their obligation to be sepaade.

I was in the field when these ceremonies were enacted, and later in 2001 I asked my long-term field assistant, Larion Aliaro, to conduct a survey of daughters of Il-Kachili men to see if they took advantage of this release to marry earlier than the previous sepaade daughters of Il-Kilako age set (fathers' marriage year = 1934). Figure 3.2 presents the results of this survey, comparing the distribution of marriage for 102 daughters of the more recent Il-Kachili age set with 110 sepaade daughters of the Il-Kachili age set by means of the SAS LIFETEST survival analysis routine. Results showed a highly significant log-rank chi-square value (46.52; $df = 1, p < 0.0001$), arising from a much lower average age of marriage for the young women released from their sepaade obligations (mean age = 19.8, $SD = 3.6$, median age = 22.0) versus the sepaade daughters of Il-Kilako (mean age = 29.2, $SD = 10.2$, median age = 26.5). The daughters of Il-Kachili, released from their sepaade obligations by the 1998 rituals, have a mean age at marriage much more in common with the other nonsepaade cohorts shown in Table 1.2.

How to explain the demise of the sepaade tradition and the role morals played in its termination? Let me take these questions one at a time, as the possible answers to the first affect the second. To address the first question, I use four different data sets, two qualitative and two quantitative. The first qualitative data come from a 1993 survey in Korr, again collected by Larion Aliaro, that asked 50 Rendille men and 50 Rendille women two questions: (1) "How did the sepaade tradition arise?" and (2) "Why maintain the sepaade tradition: What function does it serve today?" In response to the first question, all respondents agreed that the tradition arose out of intertribal warfare in the mideighteenth century. In contrast with this uniformity, there was response variation with respect to the second question, although almost all respondents again agreed that the tradition no longer served its original function and that sepaade women sacrificed their fertility to become sepaade. Thus one married woman, referring to the daughters of the Il-Kachili age set scheduled to become sepaade, said the following:

Since *D'fgudo* (Il-Kachili) children are still young there is no sepaade tradition [existing]. But what I heard from *wazee* [elders] nowadays is that it was better to do away with [the] sepaade tradition because if those children are left out [of] marriage for [a] long time just to defend the community and nowadays it is peaceful, there is no need. Sepaade are always facing some problem, such as not

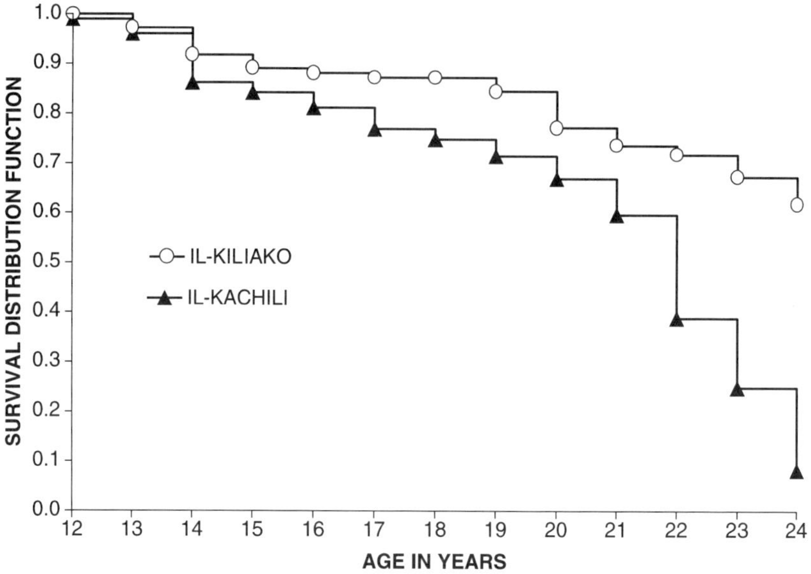

Figure 3.2. Survival curve for first marriages (two teeria lines).

bearing children, which also leads to their husbands to look for second and third wives just to have children.

This recognition of both the changing conditions and the individual plight of sepaade women is also expressed in the words of another married woman, who stated the following:

I don't think it [sepaade] will continue even in the future. Because it is now useless to make those children remain unmarried for so long until their age pass[es] and [they] face other problems such as not bearing children, which is the main reason for marrying in our society.

Likewise, yet a third married woman responded as follows:

Bad things follow the sepaade. The most important thing is that most of them are past the reproductive period and so they do not give birth to any children.

The survey showed that both men and women recognized the negative ramifications of reduced fertility for sepaade women. As shown earlier, failure to produce a living male heir by the end of a first wife's reproductive period was the most significant determinant of a man taking a second wife. Because Rendille forbid widow remarriage, a woman without sons to take care of her is among the poorest of the poor in Rendille society.

Analogous to Cain's (1988) analysis of Bangladeshi women without surviving sons, Rendille women also face a potential "downward spiral" that may entail impoverishment, increased morbidity, and premature mortality. This potential is acknowledged in the quote that "bad things follow the sepaade."

Although recognizing and acknowledging both the harmful consequences of lowered fertility and the diminished importance of intertribal warfare, many Rendille males adamantly urged continuation of the sepaade tradition. Their rationale for this was twofold. First, they argued that it was an integral part of Rendille culture, and therefore worthy of retention although it no longer served its original purpose. Second, they noted the individual benefit a man accrued by marrying a sepaade woman as a first wife. As an example of the first factor, one married man from the *Irbaales* age-set said "but it [sepaade] must be there in our future because it is our Tradition and custom of society and should be maintained." In the second regard, one married man stated the following:

> They [sepaade] work as a warrior, more or less equal to them in their work. For example, defending the community from attack, fetching water from far places, fencing the animals, watering animals, milking and doing heavy domestic work above the females' efforts.

These responses suggest that Rendille men's commitment to this tradition may reflect perceived individual-level advantages. To pursue this last point, I (Roth 2000) examined two related quantitative data sets; both pertained to livestock dynamics for men from the Il-Kachili age-set (marriage year = 1976). The first contains data collected in 1990 detailing household livestock owned before, and lost during, the 1982–1984 drought. The second data were recorded in 1996 and delineate household herds owned at the time of marriage in 1976, compared with present livestock holdings. The former is relevant to short-term advantages of marrying a sepaade wife. For these I was interested to see if sepaade women's considerable livestock management experience before marriage resulted in lower livestock loss during drought times. The latter data address the potential long-term advantages of having a sepaade wife. Focusing again on her livestock management expertise, I wanted to see if households with sepaade first wives would exhibit different herd growth from those with nonsepaade first wives.

Turning to the first data set of 98 Il-Kachili households, I found that the overall level of loss during the 1982–1984 drought was horrendous for Rendille households. On average they lost 57% of their camels and 49% of their small stock. Previous analyses of drought loss (Roth 1990,

1996; Fratkin and Roth 1996) showed that household wealth levels affect livestock loss during drought times, with wealthy households consistently faring better than poor ones. Although wealthy households suffered more losses in terms of absolute numbers, they also featured approximately equivalent *proportionate* loss. For example, a household with 100 camels losing 50% of its herd suffers greater numerical losses than a household losing the same proportion but that entered the drought time with only ten camels. Therefore wealthy households can rebuild their herds more easily following the end of the drought and the return of the rains.

Because of this, I divided the 98 households into three wealth levels, standardized again by TLUs (1.0 TLU = 1.0 camel, 0.8 cattle, and 0.1 small stock; Dahl and Hjort 1976:224). These were as follows. First, poor is $\leq$ 19 TLUs, $n = 32$; second, sufficient is 20–46.5 TLUs, $n = 33$; and third, rich is >46.5 TLUs, $n = 33$. Within each stratum, households were further divided depending on whether or not a sepaade first wife was present during the drought. Table 3.9 considers proportional household loss by species in the absence or presence of a sepaade first wife. An analysis by two-tailed Student's t tests yielded statistically nonsignificant results, negating the premise that sepaade women's livestock expertise and labor contributions reduce short-term livestock loss arising from drought. Instead, Table 3.9 reveals some occasions when proportional livestock loss is greater for households with sepaade first wives, for example, for cattle and small stock among the poor stratum.

The same pattern arises when we consider possible long-term benefits to herd growth arising from the labor contribution and herding expertise of a sepaade first wife, as shown for the 101 Il-Kachili households over the period from 1976 to 1996. Unlike the previous data that were divided on an etic or externally imposed basis, these are stratified according to Rendille internal or emic notions of wealth divisions. After completing the questionnaire, each Rendille male respondent was asked to rank his household at the time of his marriage and give his present household wealth status, choosing from the three categories of poor, sufficient, and rich. As reported in Chapter 2, a previous one-way analysis of variance (Roth 1999) on these data conducted for separate species as well as for total household TLUs confirmed the validity of these rankings. Recalling also from chapter 2 that sepaade are married far more often to emically defined poor and rich households, I limit analysis here to these two strata. Figure 3.3 depicts mean and standard deviation TLUs values for poor households measured as net change over the period 1976–1996, whereas Figure 3.4 does the same for the rich stratum. In both cases, data were divided according to the presence or absence of a sepaade first wife. In neither case do households with sepaade first wives fare

Table 3.9. *Il-Kachili households' proportional TLU losses from the 1982–1984 drought, stratified by wealth and first wife*

Proportion lost	Sepaade	Nonsepaade	*T* score
Rich			
Camels	$x = 55.5$	$x = 55.8$	
	$SD = 28.5$	$SD = 17.6$	0.034*
	(17)	(14)	
Cattle	$x = 54.3$	$x = 62.3$	0.860*
	$SD = 27.7$	$SD = 25.2$	
	(18)	(15)	
Small stock	$x = 26.1$	$x = 24.0$	
	$SD = 27.7$	$SD = 28.5$	0.229*
	(18)	(16)	
Sufficient			
Camels	$x = 50.0$	$x = 57.8$	
	$SD = 26.9$	$SD = 23.3$	0.893*
	(15)	(18)	
Cattle	$x = 63.4$	$x = 73.8$	
	$SD = 30.0$	$SD = 21.3$	1.162*
	(14)	(19)	
Small stock	$x = 53.7$	$x = 61.1$	
	$SD = 31.5$	$SD = 23.9$	0.777*
	(16)	(18)	
Poor			
Camels	$x = 65.3$	$x = 57.8$	
	$SD = 19.3$	$SD = 29.4$	0.450*
	(12)	(16)	
Cattle	$x = 82.1$	$x = 76.2$	
	$SD = 15.7$	$SD = 23.7$	0.538*
	(8)	(14)	
Small stock	$x = 67.1$	$x = 63.5$	
	$SD = 20.0$	$SD = 28.4$	0.402*
	(13)	(18)	

* $p > 0.05$.
Note: Sample sizes are given in parentheses.

better; in fact, they fare worse. For poor households with a sepaade first wife, Figure 3.4 shows that average TLU difference was a mean loss (mean $= -7.4$ TLUs, $SD = 17.4$, $n = 15$). In contrast, households without a sepaade first wife recorded a small net gain (mean $= 5.40$, $SD = 16.7$, $n = 7$). The same relationship holds for the rich stratum shown in Figure 3.4, revealing another average net loss for men with a sepaade first wife (mean $= -2.0$, $SD = 36.4$, $n = 30$) and a much larger positive value for men married to nonsepaade first wives (mean $= 14.9$, $SD = 43.0$,

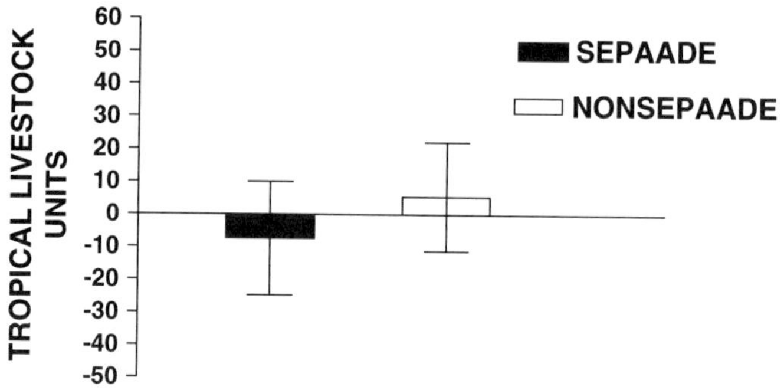

Figure 3.3. TLU difference from 1982 to 1996 by first wife; poor stratum (mean and standard deviation; after Roth 2001:1019).

$n = 20$). Student's t tests performed on each stratum yielded nonsignificant values ($t_{\text{poor}} = 1.513$, $t_{\text{rich}} = 1.6.26$; both $p < 0.05$).

An overall analysis found no evidence of either short- or long-term benefits of marrying a sepaade first wife. These etic findings contradict male Rendille emic models extolling the advantages of sepaade wives. The disparity between what Rendille men perceive and what my data point to casts doubt on the interpretation that Rendille males reap individual benefits with regard to herd management in either the short or long term as a result of taking a sepaade first wife.

These results led us to undertake another survey. This was conducted in 2000 in Korr, and it incorporated a question on the role of women in the demise of the sepaade tradition: "What role did women play in the decision to end the sepaade?" Inclusion of this question sprang from the

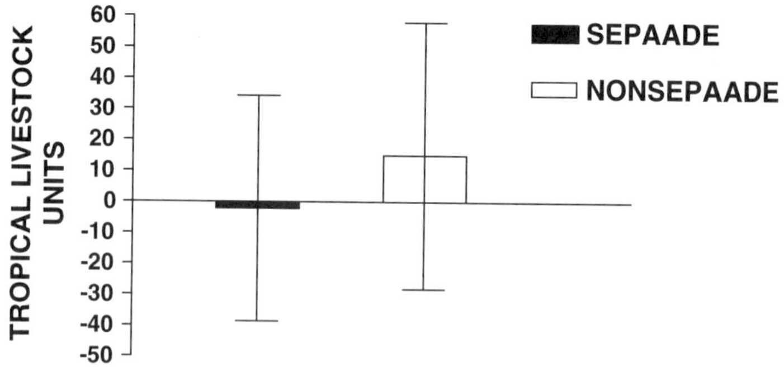

Figure 3.4. TLU difference from 1982 to 1996 by first wife; rich stratum (mean and standard deviation; after Roth 2001:1019).

1990 survey in which women consistently argued against the continuation of the sepaade tradition and its imposition on the daughters of the Il-Kachili age set. On the basis of these qualitative data, I hypothesized that the end of the sepaade tradition represented a change in gender relationships within the patriarchal Rendille culture, with women taking more control and autonomy over their reproduction. However, survey results appeared to prove me wrong. Men and women replied that only male elders made and enforced the decision to terminate the sepaade tradition. Here is a reply to the question from a male elder of the Il-Kachili age set, who stated the following:

It was the role of elders to make decisions in any given community of the Rendille people. Women did not take part in any decision making.

This was mirrored in the words of a married woman who is a daughter of the Il-Mekuri age set:

It was the Rendille elders who played a major role in coming up with this decision of dismissing this practice. Women did not take part in decision making.

Although these responses did not support my hypothesis, the main question on the survey sheet, which read, "Why did the Rendille recently decide to end the sepaade?," consistently yielded one very interesting result with respect to gender relationships. This was that elders could not stop the daughters of the Il-Kachili destined to become sepaade from leaving and marrying into other groups, particularly the highly polygynous neighboring Samburu or Ariaal populations. One Il-Kilako elder stated the following:

The Rendille people decided to end sepaade practices due to the reason that the sepaade girls ran away from their own homes to other neighboring tribes and later they help those other tribes during war in order to protect those tribes.

Elders' inability to stop young women destined to be sepaade from leaving Rendille communities was also expressed in video-recorded interviews of Rendille elders by my colleague, Dr. Merwan Engineer, Department of Economics, University of Victoria. Here Rendille elders quite unabashedly state that "all the girls will run away if the tradition is continued." This fear of female mass migration appears to be the main determinant of the elders' decision to end the sepaade tradition.

Of course, there is historical precedence for leaving the Rendille and joining either the Samburu or Ariaal. In Spencer's (1973) reconstructed genealogies of Samburu families, approximately one-third of all families claimed Rendille ancestry. On the basis of these data, Kreager (1982:256) refers to Rendille migration as a "societal escape clause," by which "disinherited sons and extra daughters may migrate and become Samburu." Ironically, it is young unmarried women who are freer of the elders' influence than their unmarried brothers. The latter can be cursed by elders, and threatened with disinheritance if they do not shoulder their livestock labors, whereas no such sanctions or threats exist for unmarried women.

Turning to our second question concerning the role of morals in the cultural and demographic change entailed in the termination of the sepaade tradition, I propose that instead of one single factor there are multiple strands of causation. These converge on one particular Rendille "key cultural element," to use Ortner's (1973) terminology. Just as Fricke cites an ethos of reciprocity as constituting the moral good in Tamang culture, I argue that the key cultural element in Rendille culture is that of the first-born male. In the Rendille patrilocal, patrilineal society practicing primogeniture, this person holds a special status in an otherwise egalitarian society, and Rendille culture is permeated with its symbolic and real connotations. The crest of hair, or doko, proudly worn by Rendille mothers with first-born sons exemplifies the former, whereas the previous analysis of differential infant and childhood mortality presented in Chapter 2 shows that this category elicits differential parental solicitude, resulting in significant, real, demographic differentials. Rendille extend this special status from the individual to the group with the naming of one age-set line as teeria, or first born. Sepaade, as daughters of teeria men, add a fertility differential to the mortality differential evident in the earlier examination of infant or child mortality patterns. This ascribed, rather than achieved, status of first-born males also plays a significant role in Rendille migration patterns, with latter-born males leaving for Ariaal or Samburu populations.

From its inception, Rendille have used this concept of moral good as represented by first-born males to achieve group and individual goals. In the beginning the sepaade, designated as daughters of the teeria, were treated as honorary males. Symbolic high status associated with this treatment was realized by granting sepaade their own circumcision ceremony en masse one year after their brothers' own ceremony. Several researchers (e.g., Douglas 1966; Sato 1980) have noted that sepaade effectively traded their fertility for the special status bestowed on them in Rendille culture.

Granting high status represented the carrot, but there was also a stick; noncompliance meant expulsion from one's natal ethic group. Subsequent intermarriage with either Samburu or Ariaal always entailed loss of Rendille membership for women in the patrilineal world of northern Kenyan pastoralists. Because of this, women designated sepaade were forced to make a choice, within the constraints of Rendille culture. Their choice was an act of moral agency with clearly defined consequences, that is, high status honorary man and later valued first wife in Rendille society, or junior wife and perpetual outsider in either a Samburu or Ariaal group. This was a daunting choice; consequences meant residence in a familiar yet distinctive cultural setting. Sepaade epitomizes the hard-to-fake commitment problems that Irons (1996) and Cronk (1994) see as one vital aspect of human group morals. It is impossible to fake being a sepaade; either one delays her marriage and takes on the role of honorary *moran* in Rendille culture before finally marrying, or one is no longer a Rendille.

Rather than being lured with the carrot of special status, or threatened with the stick of group expulsion, the young women designated as the next sepaade simply resolved to leave Rendille culture. This constitutes a perfectly successful strategy as evidenced in the elders' decision to terminate the tradition because they could no longer enforce it through moral sanctions. In this context, sepaade can be seen as cooperation maintained by punishment, as modeled by Boyd and Richerson (1992) in their Reiterated Prisoners' Dilemma.

Schlee (1989:50) described Rendille culture as "a society easy to leave, difficult to join." Sepaade, as well as latter-born sons who will not inherit the family herds because of the Rendille practice of primogeniture, are the subgroups that most frequently leave. Rendille were able to successfully reproduce biologically and culturally without these outmigrants. However, it was the fear of mass migration by the daughters of the Il-Kachili age set destined to become sepaade that made Rendille elders decide to abandon the tradition. Survey data showed that male elders exclusively made the decision to terminate the tradition, yet in reality elders were reacting to threats, either implicit or explicit, made by unmarried women.

Termination of the sepaade tradition also meant withdrawal of the women's special status equating them with the Rendille key cultural symbol of first-born male. Demise of the sepaade tradition stems not from changes to the underlying group moral emphasizing the cultural good embodied in first-born males per se, but rather from its changing application within Rendille culture.

This examination of the termination of the sepaade tradition offers some support to both anthropological demographers and human evolutionary ecologists considering demographic change as moral change, if we expand this to include changing applications of the concept of moral good and the loss of effective moral sanctions. This specific case also parallels the broader main point repeated throughout this chapter, that it is necessary to include both culture and evolutionary biology in the analyses of mating strategies. This is true whether we consider broad cross-cultural patterns of mating, exemplified by Gaulin and Boster's (1990) analysis of the determinants of dowry, or in microdemographic studies presented here for the Kipsigi, Tamang, and Rendille. This interdependence of evolutionary biology and culture runs throughout the following chapter, which examines parenting effort.

4 Demographic Strategies as Parenting Effort

Parenting Effort and the Theory of Allocation

In this chapter I begin the search for strategies relating to parenting effort by examining links between the high parity, Pre-Transitional demographic behavior of rural Gambian populations already referenced in Chapter 1 (Bledsoe and Hill 1998; Bledsoe, Banja, and Hill 1995, 1998; Bledsoe 2002) and evolutionary ecology's Theory of Allocation. This is followed by a discussion of parental strategies predicted by the Trivers – Willard Theory of Sex-Biased Parental Investment (Trivers and Willard 1972, 1973). Subsequent sections focus on parental effort as inheritance strategies, beginning with consideration of the demographic and larger social effects of primogeniture in historic Europe. The concluding section presents the culture–biology debate surrounding infanticide and child abandonment, utilizing historic European and contemporary Asian data.

In Chapter 1, I described Bledsoe and Hill's (1998) study of the resumption of postpartum sexual relationships among Gambian populations as an example of anthropological demography's concern with individual strategies operating within the context of both local and international cultures. Working with data from the same populations, Bledsoe (2002; also see Bledsoe et al. 1998) discovered a small sample of women using Western contraceptives (in this case Depo-Provera injections) immediately following miscarriages or stillbirths. In a population where high fertility is intensely desired, such behavior is highly unusual, clashing with Western concepts of high fertility, natural fertility, or parity-independent populations commonly applied to Pre-Transitional fertility regimes. It also appears paradoxical in the specific context of West African pronatalist culture, where children are highly valued and a woman's inability to produce children constitutes strong grounds for divorce or abandonment (see Caldwell and Caldwell 1989).

This behavior is illustrated by one woman's maternal history, which consisted of four pregnancies that resulted in two child deaths and two stillbirths. As a consequence, her first marriage ended, and she was forced to remarry as the "marginal second wife" (Bledsoe et al. 1998:15) of a man already married to a younger woman who had borne him three children. This unfortunate woman's comment to researchers was, "I am suffering in my marriage" (Bledsoe, Banja, and Hill 1998:15). Yet immediately following the loss of her last pregnancy, this thirty-year-old woman began using Western contraceptives.

To understand why, the authors tried to delineate the emic view of Gambian fertility. They uncovered an indigenous model linking maternal health and fertility histories. The key factor in this perspective was of a mother's physical endowment, termed *hapo*, a term signifying a number or amount, as routinely applied to mangos or kilograms of rice. When applied to fecundity, the term denotes the number of reproductive outcomes God has allotted a woman throughout her reproductive career. This essence embraces both live births and aborted or stillbirth fetuses, and it is independent of the number of pregnancies required for a woman to meet this intrinsic, divinely ordained, "quota" of reproductive outcomes. A twenty-four-year-old woman aptly summarizes this perspective (Bledsoe, Banja, and Hill 1998:33):

> I would have any number [of children] that God gives me. The number of children that everyone will have since when He created us and whatever the case may be, everyone will get that number.

Because a woman's reproductive endowment is divinely determined, no human can ever know how many pregnancies, stillbirths, or surviving live births a woman will produce throughout her reproductive career. A woman can only continue childbearing until her endowment is extinguished. However, men and women know some facts about fertility. One is that there is great variation in a woman's intrinsic endowment. Some women will never produce any children; others will have many, some or all of whom survive the rigors of infancy and childhood. It is also "known" that although a woman cannot exceed her reproductive endowment, she can bear fewer than allotted. This is because reproductive senescence is linked to a woman's physical reproductive capacity, represented by the three important bodily resources of muscles, strength or energy, and blood.

Muscle is used as a gloss for muscle tone, which decreases with each delivery. One woman who had undergone three deliveries stated (Bledsoe, Banja, and Hill 1998:34) the following:

> Concerning muscle reduction, after each pregnancy it is true, because of the severe pain and muscle contraction. During this contraction all muscles opened wide in order to give enough space for the baby to pass through. The space from womb to the birth canal is very tight and it needs to be widened for the baby to pass.

When women experience childbirth their muscles wear out, translated here as *koto*. A woman with many childbearing experiences is denoted as *muso koto*, or "old worn out woman." Women whose maternal history features many long and difficult pregnancies, exacerbated by their closeness, become worn out more rapidly than others whose reproductive histories feature easier pregnancies with long interbirth intervals. This is because muscle is a fixed but unknown quality varying among women.

Arduous pregnancies also decrease a woman's strength, or energy, known in the local language as *sembo*. Unlike muscle, strength or energy can be replenished with rest and proper foods. Women commonly referred to strength or energy relative to muscle, because the former determines how a woman will be able to use her muscles.

The final characteristic is blood, or *yelo*. Blood is considered vital for producing a baby, but women recognize that substantial amounts of blood are lost during childbirth. Being weak and pale from hard labor, illness, or malnutrition is interpreted as a sign that a woman is not ready for the physical demands of a pregnancy.

Together these three vital resources, that is, muscle, strength or energy, and blood, determine how fast a woman spends her reproductive endowment. They also influence the fate of her children, that is, spontaneous abortions or stillbirths when resources are depleted or healthy live births when a mother is strong and rested. A woman's childbearing potential is seen as a finite but unknown resource rather than as a time period (i.e., her reproductive period). This perspective substitutes the Western time and age-dependent demographic model of female fecundity with an indigenous health model in which intrinsic aspects of maternal health are linked directly to the health and well-being of her pregnancies and deliveries. Recognizing this explains why some young women described themselves as "old" in surveys and open-ended interviews. Their age is not linked to the passage of time but rather to the expenditure of their bodily resources, muscle, strength or energy, and blood through difficult and closely spaced pregnancies and deliveries.

This emic view of female fecundity also explains why women immediately following what Bledsoe, Banja, and Hill (1998:18) term "reproductive mishaps," that is, miscarriages and stillbirths, begin contraceptive measures. Working from the rural Gambian health model of female fecundity, these women pursue individual strategies to ensure the maximum utilization of their divinely granted, humanly unknowable, but fixed reproductive endowment. Bledsoe, Banja, and Hill (1998:49–51) find evidence for this emic model linking the depletion of bodily resources to the wear and tear of reproduction throughout sub-Saharan Africa. World Fertility Survey data collected in 1977–1980 drawn from Kenya, Ghana, Lesotho, Senegal, and Sudan all show a group of ever-married women with no formal education using Western contraceptives following a non-surviving pregnancy, as predicted by the Bledsoe, Banja, and Hill (1998) body expenditure thesis.

Finding a possible sub-Saharan African indigenous health model based on maternal resources parallels the long-debated phenomenon of "maternal depletion" (see Miller, Rodriguez, and Pebley 1994; McDade and Worthman 1998), linking maternal nutritional status to reproductive infant health. The Gambian models also provides an indigenous, empirical model of life history theory's principle of allocation, which states that energy, in this case maternal energy, used for one purpose cannot be used for another. Evolutionary ecologists (Kaplan and Lancaster 2000, 2003) argue that this principle provides a bridge between Pre-Transitional and Post-Transitional demographic regimes. In the former, somatic resources form the primary currency; in the latter, extrasomatic resources are viewed as crucial. Kaplan and Lancaster's (2000, 2003) Theory of Fertility and Parental Investment is firmly based on the Theory of Allocation. The model has two stages, a high fertility phase representing Pre-Transitional high populations and a second phase denoting Post-Transitional low fertility populations. In the former, factors regulating fertility are linked to female physiology, specifically maternal energy demands relating to pregnancy, breastfeeding, and childcare. These bear a striking resemblance to the Bledsoe (2002; also see Bledsoe, Banja, and Hill 1998) model of reproductive endowment, because in both models these factors are assumed to depreciate with time and maternal effort.

Unlike the Pre-Transitional Gambian case, Kaplan and Lancaster's analysis of parental investment among contemporary Albuquerque men combines biological and economic currencies, treating parental fertility decisions as trade-offs between quantity and quality of offspring. Their theory begins with the concept of *human capital* (Kaplan and Lancaster 2000:285):

> This is the stock of attributes embodied in an individual, such as skills, and education, that affect the value of time allocated to labor, and hence affect both earnings and the utility of time spent outside the labor market.

This utilizes biological fitness as the currency to measure optimal allocation of what Kaplan terms *embodied capital*, which is defined to two manners. In a physical sense, it denotes organized somatic tissue; in a functional sense, it includes strength, immune competence, coordination, skill, and knowledge, all qualities that must be allocated among a myriad of biological and social tasks (Kaplan 1996:95).

This last factor leads to the concept of *lifetime income*, defined as the total value of time allocated to alternative activities, such as resource allocation, childcare, maternal rest, and so on. Income can be invested directly in reproductive effort, or in embodied capital, which in turn can be divided into "stocks affecting the ability to acquire the resources for reproduction and stocks affecting the probability of survival" (Kaplan and Lancaster 2000:285).

For Pre-Transitional demographic regimes, these two models, one based on culture and the other grounded in evolutionary biology, share the common view of a finite reproductive endowment, represented in various factors (e.g., strength, blood, net energy). Although fertility appears at first glance to be the overriding focus of both models, the real underlying concern is with maternal health, which determines the probability of a successful birth, or, inversely in the words of Bledsoe, Banja, and Hill (1998), a "reproductive mishap." Together these models point to future research focusing on the allocation of maternal somatic resources. From the cultural anthropological side, a body of theory concerned with "the anthropology of the body" with specific reference to reproductive health could be combined fruitfully with biological work focusing on maternal depletion. Applying this approach to specific cultural and ecological settings would permit the assessment of culturally grounded strategies, operationalized by measures of maternal fitness and evaluated as LRS. This has the potential to determine if emic strategies of maternal reproductive health actually realize their goal of maximizing maternal reproductive success.

All these models assume that all children, regardless of sex or parity, are accorded equal parental investment. In the following sections I examine this assumption by using models that predict differential parental solicitude depending on offspring sex or parity.

The Trivers–Willard Model and Parenting Strategies

In 1973, Robert Trivers and Dan Willard hypothesized that, under certain conditions centering on the health of the mother and the reproductive potential of her offspring, natural selection should favor unequal parental investment between daughters and sons. As the health, or, as specifically stated in the model, the "condition," of the mother changed, so too should the reproductive opportunities of her sons and daughters. Parental investment should track these environmental changes so that unequal parental investment adapts to specific environments. This situational perspective is detailed by Hrdy (1990:33), who identifies three scenarios under which parents should invest in favor of females: (1) when variance in female reproductive success exceeds that of males, (2) when female reproductive success is variable in females and maternal condition affects the reproductive career of daughters more strongly than that

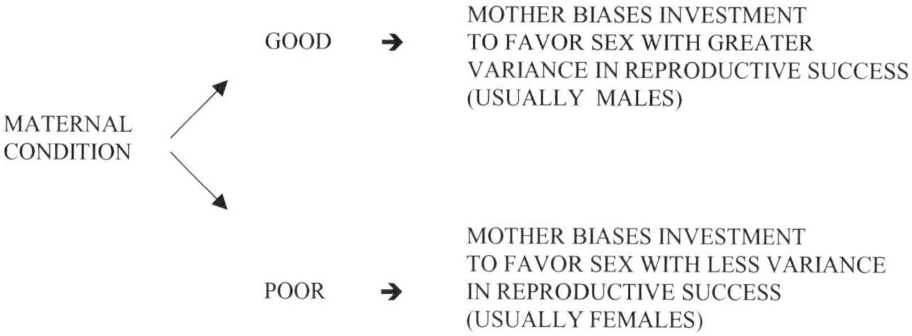

Figure 4.1. Specifications of the Willard–Trivers model (after Hrdy 1999:332).

of sons, and (3) when variance in male reproductive success exceeds that of females but parents have relatively poor prospects of producing a son who will be reproductively successful. Figure 4.1 depicts these different conditions specified by the Willard–Trivers model.

The Willard–Trivers model was originally designed for and applied to nonhuman populations, raising the question of whether the model is applicable to human cultures. Trivers and Willard (1973:91) thought so:

> [T]he model can be applied to humans differentiated on a socioeconomic scale, as long as the RS (reproductive success) of a male at the upper end exceeds his sister's, while that of a female on the lower end of the scale exceeds her brothers'.

One of the best applications of the Trivers–Willard hypothesis comes from Cronk's (1989a, 1989b, 1991a, 1991b, 1993, 1999) study of Mukogodo pastoralists of Kenya. As recently as the early part of the twentieth century, the Mukogodo lived in caves, subsisting on collected honey and by hunting–gathering. They were last to adopt livestock keeping and the pastoral way of life in their region. Along with the adoption of livestock, Mukogodo learned the Maa language of the dominant ethnic group, the Samburu, and entered the East African cultural tradition featuring livestock as bridewealth. Here Mukogodo labored under both materialistic and ideational handicaps. In the latter regard, Cronk (1991a) showed that Mukogodo households suffered the dual disadvantage of having far lower livestock per capita than neighboring groups while simultaneously Mukogodo men paid higher amounts of livestock to marry non-Mukogodo women than non-Mukogodo men did to marry Mukogodo women.

The ideational bias against the Mukogodo comes from their status in the East African pastoralist hierarchy of Maa speakers. To these populations, social status is determined by the possession of livestock, which is associated in the Maa-speaking universe (which also includes the Ariaal and Maasai) with a diverse list of positive attributes, including honor, wealth, prestige, and maleness (Cronk 1989b:418). In contrast, peoples without livestock are referred to as *Il-torrobo* (anglicized as "Dorobo"); this term is associated with offensiveness, meanness, poverty, cowardice, imperfection, and degeneration (see Galaty 1979). In the creation myth of Maa speakers, Il-torrobo are associated with the original fall from grace. In this myth an Il-torrobo severs the cord by which God had been sending cattle to the earth. Given all these negative connotations, it is no wonder that Cronk (1993:275) glosses the term Il-torrobo as "pond-scum."

On the basis of Mukogodo low status in the Maa-speaking universe, the Trivers–Willard hypothesis predicts that girls should receive more parental investment, as their reproductive potential should be greater than that of their brothers, who have material and ideological handicaps to overcome before they marry. Cronk's data support these predictions with respect to marriage opportunities and realized fertility. Of 422 Mukogodo marriages recorded, 173 were between Mukogodo men and women, 152 were between Mukogodo women and non-Mukogodo men, and only 97 were completed between Mukogodo men and non-Mukogodo women (Cronk 1989b:419). As a result, many Mukogodo men never marry, and Mukogodo women produce on average almost one additional child than Mukogodo men, even though the latter have the advantage of polygynous marriages and the potential for producing significantly higher male fertility.

Do these demographic disadvantages lead Mukogodo to favor female offspring? In a series of articles reflecting two different periods of fieldwork (1986 and 1993), Cronk (1989a,b, 1991a, 1991b, 1993, 2000) delineated pathways by which Mukogodo parents favor daughters over sons. In his original 1986 fieldwork, Cronk found that Mukogodo parents took their young daughters (ages newborn through four years) to a medical dispensary far more often than their sons. A trip to the clinic represents a substantial investment in both time and money; it takes from one-half to three days, and the dispensary charges a fee of five shillings (about thirty cents in U.S. currency in 1986) for each visit. Even more telling, Cronk's examination of the clinics dispensary's records revealed that all non-Mukogodo groups using the facility had a higher frequency of male visits. Cronk attributes this parental bias in seeking medical help in favor of daughters as the cause of a pronounced mortality differential in childhood deaths (deaths per 1,000 known live births, aged newborn through four years) favoring females.

In his 1993 revisit, Cronk initiated a study based on three measures of caregiver solicitude: mean distance between caregiver and child, proportion of time the caregiver held the child, and the proportion of time the child nursed. A partial correlation analysis revealed that all measures favored females. The result of such differences was not in differential mortality, but rather in differential growth patterns, with three anthropometric measurements, height for age, weight for age, and weight for height, all favoring females (Cronk 1999).

Cronk's analysis remains one, if not the, most rigorous successful test of the Willard–Trivers hypothesis to date for a number of reasons. Perhaps the most obvious is that the pattern he found in 1986 was replicated in 1993, suggesting a continued behavioral path. In addition, unlike the authors of many other studies, he actively pursued alternative explanations. For example, as an alternative to Trivers–Willard predictions, Mukogodo parents could be interested in female survival because the costs of raising daughters are compensated by the brideprice payments grown women bring to their natal households. However, using male marital success as a proxy for reproductive success in this polygynous culture, Cronk (2000:206–207) reports a low and statistically insignificant Pearson correlation coefficient between a man's daughters who survived to age fifteen from his first marriage and the number of wives a man has. Furthermore, the mean number of wives with one or more daughters who survived to the same age is actually lower than that for men with no daughters.

This attention to alternative explanations also strengthened Cronk's responses to critics of his findings. Sieff (1990) suggested that the overrepresentation of Mukogodo females at the dispensary actually constituted female bias *against* daughters, who necessitated more health interventions as a result of a parental bias in food allocation favoring boys, as long reported for Southern Asia (see Basu 1997). Yet Cronk's anthropometric data argue strongly against this criticism, as do his data on breastfeeding. In another criticism of his work, Fix (1990:36) argued that Cronk's results could not be construed as evolutionary:

> [W]hat has evolved? Mukogodo parents of females might have more grandchildren than those with male offspring, but a hereditary bias for producing females could not increase through natural selection because there is no consistency across generations.

This criticism reveals a basic misunderstanding of the Willard–Trivers hypothesis. Rather than representing a fixed, obligate trait, the Trivers–Willard model views parental investment as faculative, changing frequently and rapidly to achieve adaptation with environmental conditions.

Finally, Cronk's research is notable for the effort made to understand the rationale for parental behavior. Faced with the findings of female sex bias, Cronk (1993, 2000) interviewed Mukogodo mothers about their ideal family size and composition. In both 1986 and 1993, more mothers stated a preference for "more boys" (1986 = 12%; 1993 = 25%) than "more girls," (1986 = 7%; 1993 = 5%). Cronk (1993, 1995, 1999) interpreted these conflicting results, with parents stating specific intentions and yet behaving differently, as arising from culture, which he succinctly defines as "socially transmitted information." He notes that the predominant Samburu–Maasai culture is very androcentric, so that both Samburu and Maasai express strong preferences for male offspring. Cronk posits that, in mimicking this behavior, Mukogodo parents are using culture as a means of signaling, in this case signaling that they are Maa-speaking pastoralists and not lowly Il-torrobo.

Outside Cronk's work, applications of the Trivers–Willard hypothesis are mixed. In a study of another East African pastoralist society, Borgerhoff Mulder (1999) could not find evidence of parental bias through a sophisticated analysis of Kipsigi agropastoralist socioeconomic strata. Conflicting results were uncovered from analyses of wills in contemporary and historic Western populations. Smith, Kish, and Crawford (1987) found that, in their sample of 1,000 Canadian wills, wealthier decedents favored male kin, whereas poorer decedents were biased in favor of female relatives, supporting Trivers–Willard predictions. However, Judge and Hrdy (1992) found no evidence of sex bias in the inheritance records of California dating from 1890 to 1984. Gaulin and Robbins (1991) found support for the Trivers–Willard hypothesis in their analysis of 900 contemporary American women, whereas Keller, Nesse, and Hofferth (2001) found no such supportive evidence by using multivariate analyses on large representative data sets.

Parity-Specific Parental Strategies: The Case of Primogeniture

The Trivers–Willard hypothesis is concerned with unequal parental investment on the basis of reproductive opportunities for the different sexes, yet a broad range of societies discriminate within the same sex on the basis of birth order. This is exemplified by the practice of primogeniture described in Chapter 2 for Rendille pastoralists. It is this last practice that I wish to focus on in this section.

In their review of primogeniture, Hrdy and Judge (1993:2) noted that Darwin was opposed to a practice that featured an arbitrary, predestined choice of heir, rather than relying on natural selection to guide the choice. "Suppose the first-born bull was necessary made by each farmer the begetter of his stock," Darwin wrote scornfully to a colleague. Today anthropologists, demographers, and evolutionary ecologists agree that

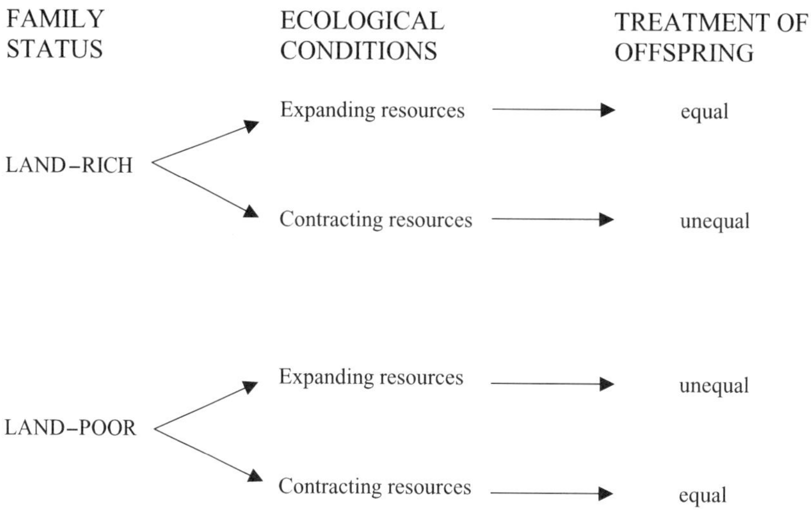

Figure 4.2. Effects of ecological conditions and family status on treatment of offspring (inheritance; after Hrdy and Judge 1993:10).

patterns of divisible or partible versus indivisible or impartible inheritance strategies represent the ends of a continuum of parental inheritance strategies grounded in ecological and economical conditions.

With respect to partible inheritance, Hrdy and Judge (1993:3) cite the British social historian Cicely Howell (1976 :117):

> [P]artible inheritance is found where there was enough land for all sons, or where land was not especially significant and the distinction between land and chattels not vital to the survival of the family.

Demographers will of course recognize these conditions in Hajnal's (1965) classic distinction of non-European marriage patterns featuring early and almost universal marriage as distinct from non-European marital patterns characterized by late marriage and high levels of celibacy. Both systems exhibited different marital eligibility rules based on sufficient land holdings to start a new family.

Considering ecological conditions and household economic status, Hrdy and Judge (1993:10) suggest unequal treatment of offspring should arise among both land-poor and land-rich families with contracting resources, and partible inheritance should be the rule for both land-rich and land-poor families under conditions of expanding resources, as shown in Figure 4.2. These predictions stem from an analysis of North American historical patterns, contrasting settled New England inheritance patterns (Ditz 1990) with those from the American frontier (Newell 1986). In both cases, analysis showed that land-rich parents were generous in estate division during expansion times, whereas they resorted to impartible inheritance to consolidate family wealth during difficult economic times. When unable to bequeath enough land to support even one son, land-poor families divided their assets equally. Hrdy and Judge (1993:12) note that this last pattern echoes Dickemann's (1979b:318) interpretation of Eurasian strategies for poor families as placing "equal bets on a series of equally uncertain outcomes." Under more favorable ecological conditions, land-poor families concentrated land holdings in one heir.

Whether rich or poor, heir or excluded from inheriting, impartible inheritance has great potential for determining demographic rates, as seen in the earlier analysis of infant or child mortality for Rendille sons. Impartible inheritance systems may do so either directly through differential parental investment, realized perhaps in amount of food or care given certain sibs, or indirectly through unequal survival and mating opportunities associated with unequal distribution of resources among sibs. One of the most thorough examinations of how primogeniture affects demographic parameters is provided by Boone's (1983, 1986, 1988) analysis of historic Portuguese family structure. His data were drawn from the *Peditura Lusitana*, an eleven-volume manuscript containing several hundred Medieval and Early Modern noble lineages. Within these records, four distinct groups are identified. In descending order of status, these were (1) royal lineages, including the royal family, dukes,counts viscounts, and barons; (2) the royal bureaucracy, represented by largely hereditary offices; (3) the landed aristocracy, holding hereditary titles to lands and associated labor; and (4) *Cavaleiros*, or members of religious military orders.

Higher status families featured higher reproductive success, yet Boone (1988:210) notes that the paradoxical results of biological success were often cultural failure in the form of downward social mobility caused by the dissipation of the lineage or "house" as a result of multiple marriages, particularly through the male line and the continuing division of lineage wealth over time. Sons' multiple marriages reflected high offspring mortality, so that large families were necessary to ensure intergenerational transfers of familial resources. The Portuguese strategy in the face of the biological necessity of large families countered by resource dissemination arising from multiple male marriages was to adopt primogeniture. Boone (1988:210) observes that the Medieval Portuguese were ripe for such an adjustment in inheritance strategies in an area where wealth was dependable and stable over time:

> Such would be the case where wealth is in the form of rights to the surplus produced by a subject agrarian infrastructure already in place, and where these rights are a matter of inheritance of a title.

Table 4.1. *Reproductive performance of men grouped by birth order*

	All men in sample			Ever-married men only		
Birth order	Men (*n*)	Children (*n*)	Mean	Men (*n*)	Children (*n*)	Mean
1	504	1,561	3.10	376	1547	4.11
2	366	843	2.30	223	785	3.52
3	240	447	1.86	111	422	3.80
4	261	434	1.66	102	386	3.78
TOTAL	1,371	3,285	2.40	812	3,140	3.87

Note: Table uses the Kruskal–Wallis test. For all men in the sample, $p < 0.001$; for ever-married men only, $p < 0.09$.
Source: Table is after Boone (1988:212).

Boone details how the cultural adoption of primogeniture affected demographic rates including marriage, reproduction, migration, and mortality. The first of these variables is shown in Table 4.1,which clearly shows declining reproductive performance of men by birth order. Effects of migration and mortality are shown in Figure 4.3, depicting the proportion of males who lived to adulthood only to subsequently die in warfare, grouped both by birth order and place of death. Boone (1988:210) interprets the lower rates of survival for latter-born sons relative to their first-born sib as reflecting the former's longer exposure to risk. In addition, as shown in this figure, latter-born sons served in campaigns farther from home, with the increase in birth order correlated with rising proportions of deaths from warfare in Portuguese territories in India rather than in nearby Morocco.

The association of young, latter-born sons with military campaigns led Boone (1983, 1986) to argue that the adoption of primogeniture had a large impact on European cultural history, beginning in medieval France, where the dissolution of the Carolingian Empire led to increased social differentiation and land disputes by rival parties claiming descent from Charlemagne. One result of this situation was the process of subinfeudation, with noble lineages claiming hereditary rights over lands, or *fiefs*. These claims were often established through strength of arms, as noble families raised and maintained standing armies to ward off the military threat to their lands posed by other noble lineages.

The social historian Duby (1977) studied the linkage between noble family structure and the origin of knighthood through an analysis of the adoption of primogeniture in the region of Macon during the tenth to twelth centuries. His book, *The Chivalrous Society* (1977), details how de facto primogeniture was first the rule of inheritance, as only the eldest

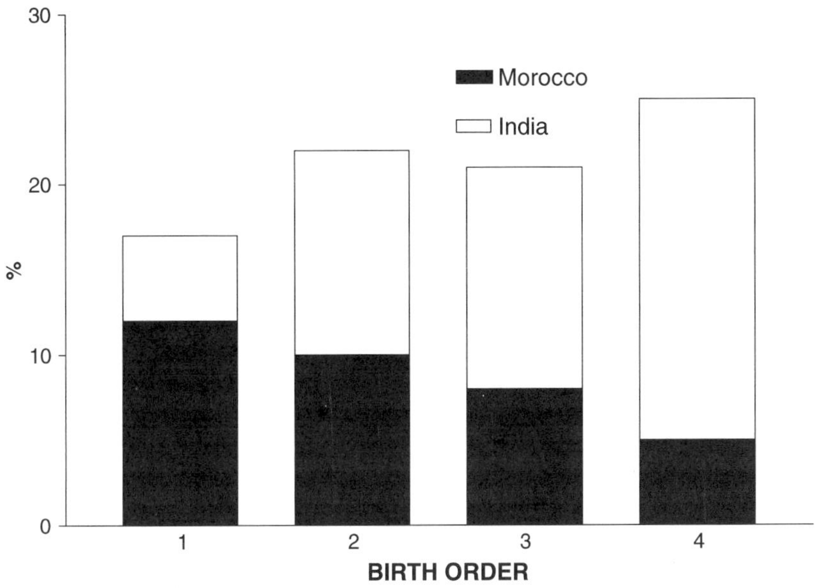

Figure 4.3. Proportion of males who lived to adulthood, who subsequently died in warfare, grouped by birth order and place of warfare death (after Boone 1988:211).

son was permitted to marry. This restriction led to the formation of a group of unmarried men, or youths, termed *juvenis*. Drawing on their family estates to arm and horse themselves, these youth banded and traveled together in the prescribed tradition of *vagabondage*. Keen (1976:43) describes these youths who traveled the countryside as an armed troupe with poor prospects for their individual futures:

> The second and third born sons, and others, who by the custom of the land have little or no portion in the inheritance of their fathers, and who by poverty are often constrained to follow wars that are unjust and tyrannical so as to sustain their estate of *nobelesse*, since they know no other calling but arms; and therein they commit so much ill that it would be frightening to tell of all the pillaging and crimes with which they oppress the poor people.

Noble families, now faced with a strong internal disruptive force created by means of primogeniture, turned to the Church for a solution. In an attempt to nullify the youth who now represented the "spearhead of feudal aggression" (Duby 1977:115), the Church launched the Peace of God (*paix de Dieu*) movement in the tenth and eleventh century. This movement had as its goals the transformation of the ideology of warfare, which until then was viewed as a means of personal gain, into an institution for the glorification of Christianity (Boone 1983:90). It did so by initiating religious military orders under the control of the Church and deploying them outside their natal lands in the Crusades. Thus Duby (1977:12) states the following:

It is obvious that it was the bands of "youths" excluded by so many social prohibitions from the main body of settled men, fathers of families and head of houses, with their prolonged spells of turbulent behaviour making them an unstable fringe of society, who created and sustained the crusades.

Boone (1983) argues that this pattern was repeated in the thirteenth-century Portuguese extension of the *Reconquista*, the reconquest from the Moors of land in the Iberian Peninsula to northern Africa. By the time the source of new territory represented by Iberian lands taken by the sword was exhausted, an intensified competition within the state led to the establishment of entitled estates (*morgados*) transferred across generations by means of primogeniture. As in the earlier French context, these events resulted in the creation of a large group of latter-born sons, the *cavalaria*, who became men-at-arms to powerful lineages, joined the Church, or entered into commerce. In the first option, these *cadets* turned also to piracy, robbery, and looting to support themselves. Boone (1983:94) quotes the historian Malowist (1964:15–16), who wrote of this time, the following:

[I]t was above all the *cadets* who lacked land and other sources of revenue within the county (who) desired war, which would permit them to accede to a situation of social and material independence.

Taking a page from the previous Crusading tradition to rid their homeland of this dangerous, disruptive internal force, the reigning Portuguese monarch King Joaz obtained Papal consent to attack Islamic territory in Morocco.

Boone's analysis is unique in considering both the individual and the larger societal ramifications of primogeniture. His results stress that, although individually latter-born sons were selected against with respect to LRS, they were nevertheless an important factor in society. In addition, a repeated pattern of European ruling elites dealing with dispossessed latter-born sons through expansionist warfare suggests a coalition strategy to nullify what must have been an important degree of parent–offspring conflict arising from the cultural concept and social practice of primogeniture.

This source of conflict and tension extends beyond historic Europe and is also evident in East African pastoralists. Here the presence of age sets delays marriage of young men, leading to the establishment of groups of men-at-arms comparable with the young juvenis of France and the cadets of Portugal. In the Maasai and related groups such as the Samburu and Ariaal, these unmarried groups are known as *Il-Murran*, or *moran*, glossed as "warriors." They all share an extended time before marriage, analogous to the vagabondage of the French juvenis, during which they represent a formidable force for intertribal warfare and livestock raiding (Fukui and Turton 1979) as well as a constant source of parent–offspring tension and conflict (see Spencer 1988).

Among the Rendille, this same situation holds. Because each man is expected to marry the prescribed three age sets from his father's age set, and because age sets span fourteen years, a first-born male may be forty-two years of age (i.e., 3 × 14 years) at the time of his marriage. However, despite this culturally imposed "wastage" of a first-born male's reproductive span, first-born males still feature significantly higher fertility levels than their sibs, when wealth and age-set membership are controlled for (Roth 1999). As previously described, this is because a first-born male will inherit all his parents' livestock and thus be able to quickly pay brideprice and set up a practicable household. By comparison, his latter-born sibs may have to migrate to Ariaal or Samburu groups where they can work for kin in order to raise the necessary resources for brideprice, marry, and have children. This is a clear case of culture overriding biology, in this case through the materialistic pathway of unequal access to resources.

Latter-born sons in all these cases represent what Boone (1983, 1988) calls "floaters," that is, individuals dispersing as a result of subordination effects. In nonhuman biological models, such individuals feature lower reproductive and higher mortality rates (Brown 1975:98). Boone's data suggest that cultural processes in the form of primogeniture translate into the same effect. The difference between the cultural and biological models is that the former is initiated culturally and maintained socially, by the imposition of primogeniture, whereas the latter is usually the result of physical factors such as size, strength, and aggression.

Parental Investment: The Local Resource Competition Model

Primogeniture, or any other sex- or parity-biased form of inheritance, constitutes differential parenting effort. In the case of the Willard–Trivers hypothesis, the underlying assumption is that such behavior is adaptive, in this case to the parents' goals of effecting intergenerational transfers of familial wealth, status, or genetic material. Another example of parental strategies as demographically adaptive behavior is a specialized form of the Trivers–Willard model, called the Local Resource Competition

Model. The best test of this model comes from the historical demographic work of Voland (1989, 1990, 1995; 2000; also see Voland and Dunbar 1995), which concentrates on the Krummhorn region of northwest Germany and is based on family reconstitution. Church registers from 32 parishes permitted complete family reconstruction for the eighteenth- and nineteenth-century Krummhorn population, beginning in 1720. From this time until the end of the nineteenth century, population was stable at approximately 14,000, spread across an area of 153 km^2. The region's soil was quite fertile and supported intensive agriculture. Economic produce from farming and dairy production permitted development of a capital and market economy earlier than in other parts of Germany. Accumulation of wealth, represented by both land holdings and capital, permitted the establishment of lineages as well as the creation of socioeconomic classes.

Voland and colleagues combined data from church registers with tax roles to delineate social classes, such as farmers versus laborers. Tax roll information quantifying the amount of land owned allowed further classification of landowners as either farmers (i.e., all those with more than 75 Grasen of land, where, 1 Grasen = 0.37 ha), small holders (fewer than 75 Grasen), and laborers or tradespeople. Results supported evolutionary ecological predictions; wealthier men had higher overall reproductive success relative to poorer social groups, achieved by marrying younger wives (Voland 1990) and producing more children over their lifetime than the population mean (6.58 vs. 4.59, $p < 0.001$; Voland 1990). Wealthy farmers managed greater reproductive success in spite of having higher infant and child mortality rates than the population mean (infant mortality farmers = 0.195, infant mortality population mean = 0.134; $p < 0.001$). However, when put into a familial context, results dramatically deviated from Trivers–Willard predictions, with wealthy families exhibiting a strong parental investment bias against males (Voland et al. 1997).

Subsequent consideration of these results yielded two highly interrelated possible explanations, one cultural and one biological in nature. In the first, Voland's (1995) analysis of male mortality within families showed increasing male infant mortality among wealthy farmers, but not for landless families, with increasing same-sex sibs. This pattern is reminiscent of the data presented for Rendille sons in Chapter 2, suggesting a parental investment strategy arising from an impartible pattern of inheritance with one son inheriting the lion's share of the familial wealth. Indeed, Krummhorn society practiced unogeniture, with the last-born male (ultimogeniture) inheriting the family estate. Impartible inheritance was linked to ecological conditions in the Krummhorn during this period. Surrounded by the North Sea on three sides and flanked on the fourth by moorlands unsuitable for agriculture, the population had little or no opportunity for geographical, and hence population, expansion. This resulted in social stability, with half of wealthy farmers' sons retaining the same status as that of their fathers. These were, on the whole, sons who inherited family land holdings. Under the prevailing system of ultimogeniture, other sons were forced to either migrate or remain celibate (Voland and Dunbar 1995:43).

Placing this cultural interpretation within an evolutionary context, Voland and Dunbar (1995) stress that differences in male and female infant mortality reflect different underlying parental "production costs" such that males with limited reproductive opportunities within the same social stratum relative to females are more expensive to raise. This exemplifies the evolutionary Local Resource Competition Model, in which parental sex bias toward offspring depends on differences in the production costs of offspring and differences in offspring reproductive potential (Voland and Dunbar 1995; Voland et al. 1997). Population growth or stability influences offspring reproductive potential and hence alters parental investment patterns. When population growth is low, natural selection operates by displacement competition as a result of high levels of local resource competition. When population growth is high, natural selection favors genetic expansion and expansion competition. Applying this logic to the Krummhorn case, we see that, in the low-growth scenario, high-ranking families should favor daughters, because male economic and reproductive opportunities would be limited. However, in cases of rapid population growth, parents should favor males, because they will have disproportionately more economic opportunities than daughters, who at this time were excluded from commerce.

To test these predictions, Voland and Dunbar (1995) expanded their Krummhorn study to include five additional areas, described in Table 4.2. Recording data spanning the time period from 1820 to 1869, Voland et al. (1997) calculated separate sex-specific measures of infant mortality (${}_1q_0$ males and ${}_1q_0$ females), population growth rates, and an index of Trivers–Willard (TW). This last quantity was determined for each of the five regions as follows:

$$[({}_1q_0 \text{ females}/{}_1q_0 \text{ males})]_{\text{upper class}}/[({}_1q_0 \text{ females}/{}_1q_0 \text{ males})]_{\text{lower class}}. \quad (1)$$

Quotients above 1.0 indicate excess mortality to girls, whereas those below 1.0 point to excess male infant mortality. Table 4.3 shows the results of this analysis. In interpreting these results, the authors first stress

Table 4.2. *Socioeconomic characteristics of six historic German regions*

Region	Socioeconomic characteristics
Krummhorn	Fertile soils gave rise to early market and capital-oriented agriculture, leading to the accumulation of great wealth in some land-holding lineages. Population remained stable during the eighteenth and nineteenth century as a result of geographical circumscription between the North Sea and moorlands.
Geest	Less fertile soils cultivated by colonizing small holders, leading to a modest increase in farms. Similar to Krummhorn, unigeniture in the form of ultimogeniture kept land within lineages and stopped fragmentation.
Moor	This sample consist of two moor parishes first colonized in the eighteenth century. Over time the economic situation deteriorated, as small plot size could not support families and there was little opportunity for wage labor. The resulting population pressure was relieved by emigration to North America.
Leda	Leda is represented by five parishes whose economies centered on intensive agriculture along river marshes. Unlike Krummhorn, these communities expanded into adjacent moors.
Leezen	A single parish, Leezen, like Krummhorn, had wealthy farmers, small holders, and landless laborers. It established early links to major markets in Hamburg and Lubeck, which partially alleviated its poor agricultural productivity stemming from mediocre soils, as well as buffering the population from economic downturns.
Ditfurt	Unlike the other populations, Ditfurt was dependent on the local aristocracy, to whom it rendered feudal services. It also suffered economically more from the local wars of the seventeenth and eighteenth century.

Source: The six regions were studied by Voland and Dunbar (1995).

that upper-class ${}_1q_0$ females/${}_1q_0$ males values are consistently higher than the lower classes, that is, $[({}_1q_0 \text{ females}/ {}_1q_0 \text{ males})]_{\text{lower class}} = 0.763$, mean $[({}_1q_0\text{females}/ {}_1q_0\text{males})]_{\text{upper class}} = 0.910$, indicating that lower-class families tend to favor daughters, as predicted by Trivers–Willard. At the same time, however, three of the six upper-class samples (Krummhorn, Geest, and Moor) feature ${}_1q_0$ males values higher than their female counterparts, whereas two others (Leda and Ditfurt) have almost identical male and female values. The second point that Voland and Dunbar (1995) stress is the significant positive correlation between the six resulting TW values and rates of population increase (Pearson one-tailed correlation coefficient $= 0.829$, $p < 0.05$). These findings support the Local Resource Competition Model's prediction that, in populations characterized by

Table 4.3. *Infant mortality by sex and social group, TW, and r*

Group	Krummhorn	Geest	Moor	Leda	Leezen	Ditfurt
Upper class						
Sample size	307	106	118	143	1,156	376
$_1q_0$ males	0.091	0.250	0.080	0.070	0.126	0.170
$_1q_0$ females	0.070	0.220	0.059	0.069	0.146	0.171
$_1q_f/_1q_m$	0.769	0.880	0.738	0.986	1.079	1.006
Lower class						
Sample size	667	451	535	430	763	1,605
$_1q_0$ males	0.110	0.105	0.102	0.109	0.136	0.220
$_1q_0$ females	0.078	0.072	0.059	0.096	0.118	0.188
$_1q_f/_1q_m$	0.709	0.686	0.578	0.881	0.868	0.855
TW index	1.085	1.283	1.277	1.119	1.243	1.177
Population growth rate, *r* (%)	0.415	0.939	0.769	0.713	0.757	0.327

Note: Infant mortality by sex and social group is for the years from 1820 to 1869; TW denotes differential parental investment; and mean annual population increase, *r*, is for the years from 1821 to 1871.
Source: Table is after Voland and Dunbar (1995:131).

high growth levels, parental investment should favor sons, who should find more economic opportunities, whereas in a stagnant environment, parents should favor daughters.

As a final test of whether parents are responding to differing periods of population growth, the authors focus on within-group variation by examining regions that had reliable long-term data through the eighteenth century, Krummhorn and Ditfurt. These data allowed delineation of parental investment patterns in the face of changing population growth rates. Neither sample yielded a significant correlation between population growth rate by thirty-year cohorts and corresponding TW indices. However, when the variables were lagged by one generation, a significant correlation between *r* and TW was found for both regions. Voland and Dunbar interpreted these results as reflecting both parents' childhood experiences of economic conditions as well as grandparental influences on current childbearing conditions. They point out that the latter interpretation was also advanced as an explanation of the twentieth-century baby boom. However, their explanation differs significantly in terms of mechanisms; parents in the twentieth-century had access to modern fertility control, whereas parents in Voland and Dunbar's historical data were achieving family composition by means of mortality control, represented by what must have been differential parenting effort. Overall, this suite of studies provides specific tests of parental effort strategies varying over time, as well as further empirical examples of culture–biology interactions.

Infanticide and Child Abandonment: Accentuating the Negative

The preceding sections considered differential parental effort with respect to offspring sex. The most drastic results of differential parenting effort, also called discriminative parental solicitude (Daly and Wilson 1994), are of course infanticide or child abandonment, which are legally and morally different but biologically identical (Hrdy 1999:297). Today there is a voluminous literature on infanticide and child abandonment, including perspectives ranging from evolutionary ecology to culture theory (see Hausfater and Hrdy 1984; Boswell 1988; Daly and Wilson 1984, 1994; Kertzer 1993; Fuchs 1984; Panter-Brick and Smith 2001; van Schaik and Janson 2001). In this section I examine two aspects of infanticide or abandonment. The first focuses on infanticide as an adaptive strategy; the second examines child abandonment from the perspectives of cultural constructionism. In the following section I look at recent studies dealing with the inverse of infanticide, which is adoption.

For infanticide, there have been several attempts to classify motivational causation or context-specific situations for the act (Alexander 1974; Scrimshaw 1983, 1984; Dickemann 1984; Hill and Hurtado 1996:433–434; Hrdy 1997, 1999). An abbreviated list of cultural and evolutionary rationale includes (1) ecological limitations on raising the child, (2) congenital defects that limit the child's societal potential or reproductive potential, (3) unwanted sex of the child, (4) pathological behavior arising from atypical conditions, (5) uncertain paternity of the child, and (6) a sex-specific, usually male, adaptive strategy to enhance reproductive success.

Although the last three factors form the main controversy today, we can look quickly at the others. Ecological limitations on raising children are exemplified by the killing of twins; among the Dobe !Kung hunter–gatherers of Botswana studied by Howell (1979, 2000), no pairs of twins were ever observed. The second factor, killing the child with congenital defects, is also found among the !Kung, where it is the mother giving birth alone in the bush who has the prerogative to decide if the child would live or die, and who killed children born with congenital defects. For the third factor, we have already seen some of the concomitants of unwanted sex of the child in the original infant or child mortality differential Cronk (1991b) found for the Mukogodo. In today's technological world, offspring sex can be manipulated by prenatal sex determination followed by sex-selective abortion, as seen throughout Asia (Miller 2001).

Today, the most heated debate concerns the last three factors, with uncertain paternity of child and sex-specific adaptive strategies to enhance reproductive success linked to form what is known as the sexual selection hypothesis. At its root is the concept that infanticide is an *evolved behavior*, arising and maintained by sexual selection. The idea originated with Hrdy's (1977, 1979) work with Indian languars, during which she repeatedly observed that adult males stalk and kill unrelated infants. The cessation of lactation following this event sped up the mother's return to sexual receptivity. In this manner, the male gained sexual access to the infant's mother while simultaneously reducing the genetic contribution of rival males to the troop. The resulting interpretation that male infanticide represented an adaptive reproductive strategy led to what Sommer (2001) termed "holy wars" within primatology. In one camp, primatologists and ethologists who abhorred the notion of conspecific homicide retorted that Hrdy's results were the results of either biological or ecological pathologies (the fourth cause in our list), exemplified by "abnormal," "deviant," or "maladaptive" pathological consequences of overcrowding (Curtin and Dolhinow 1979; Bartlett, Sussman, and Cheverud 1993; Sussman, Cheverud, and Barlett 1995).

The debate only intensified when the evolutionary psychologists Martin Daly and Margo Wilson (1980, 1984, 1985, 1994, 1996) examined human infanticide from the viewpoint of evolutionary biology. Their work centered on the fifth factor associated with infanticide, parental uncertainty. Their argument was that discriminative parental solicitude, a suite of behaviors spanning benign neglect to outright physical abuse, was an evolved psychological human trait. They predicted that stepparents would discriminate in favor of children who share biological material and against those who do not. Consequently, they predicted that stepchildren would feature significantly higher levels of abuse than children living with both biological parents, or with only one biological parent. Controlling for income and examining samples drawn from population-at-large surveys, a child abuse registry, and a police data set for juvenile offenders, Daly and Wilson (1985) found significantly elevated risk of parental abuse for children living with stepparents in the overtly benign Anglophone society of southern Ontario, Canada. Their results now have been reproduced for a diverse group of cultures (for reviews, see Daly and Wilson 1994). Historical demographic studies also found empirical support for the worldwide folklore proclaiming the danger of stepparents, such as the story of Cinderella. In the Ditfurt, Germany data discussed previously, Stephen (1992, cited in Voland and Stephan 2001) found that living with stepmothers reduced a person's average life expectancy during the seventeenth to nineteenth century by about seven years.

A final human deviation from the nonhuman primate patterns of infanticide by males to improve their reproductive success is reported by Voland and Stephan (2001), who used historic data from nineteen parishes in Krummhorn, Germany. These data permitted examination of the consequences of an early death for an illegitimate child on the mother's chances of marriage and final reproductive success, or, as they succinctly phrased it, "does it pay to abandon the bastard" (Voland and Stephan 2001:457). For the time period from 1720 to 1874, a small sample of 79 women met the following criteria: (1) they did not marry the named father of the child, or their marriage did not occur within eleven months of the birth of a child; (2) their children were born in the parishes, and the mother died there; (3) they were in an unmarried, not widowed marital state at the time of the illegitimate birth; and (4) mothers survived at least five years after the birth of the child. Results showed that if an illegitimate child died before his or her fifteenth birthday, the mothers' chances of marrying ($19/24 = 0.79$) were significantly ($p < 0.01$) higher than if the child survived past his or her fifteenth birthday ($25/55 = 0.45$). In addition, the nineteen mothers who wed after the loss of their child before the age of fifteen produced a subsequent total of thirty-seven children. This average of 1.9 children exceeds the average cost of 1.0 children lost, increasing a woman's lifetime reproductive success following an initial offspring loss. This counterintuitive result is important because it points to an essential difference in parental investment in human versus nonhuman primate societies; only in human societies does sexually selected *maternal* neglect of one's own offspring make evolutionary sense, because of fathers' time and resource investment featured in human cooperative relationships (Voland and Stephan 2001:462). The lack of paternal resource and time contribution to offspring survival in nonhuman primate society explains the total lack of evidence for maternal infanticide.

However, considering only simple fitness gains and losses removes parental emotions from consideration, making parents appear to operate as soulless, fitness-calculating autonomons. In particular, it omits consideration of the bond that mothers, who perform the bulk of child-raising duties in prehistoric, historic, and contemporary societies, form with their young offspring. A recent debate centering on maternal behavior in historic and current patterns of infanticide and child abandonment seemingly revives the age-old biology versus culture dichotomy.

On one side of this debate, the evolutionary ecologist Sarah Blaffer Hrdy (1997, 1999) argues for the existence of a maternal instinct, or "mother love," grounded in biology. Hrdy (1999:378) states that "throughout human evolution, the mother has been her infant's niche," because human infants are so vulnerable and dependent for so long a time, that the level of commitment to them by the close relative on the spot at birth, primed to care, and lactating, is the single most important component of infant well-being.

Hrdy's quote of the mother as her infant's niche follows from the evolutionary psychologist John Bowlby's (1988) conceptualization of human infant maternal attachment behavior as an evolved biological system allowing infants to form a unique bond with one caretaker, their mother. This bond is formed and strengthened by the onset of lactation, which releases what Hrdy terms a "hormonal storm" eliciting maternal emotions. In particular, two maternal hormones related to breastfeeding and milk letdown, oxytocin and prolactin, have been linked to the onset of mother–infant bonding (for a review of the pros and cons of hormonal control of maternal behavior, see Ball and Panter-Brick 2001).

Bowlby's Attachment Theory looks at the evolution of infant–mother bonding from the perspective of the infant, yet there are also evolutionary theories of parent–child conflict. Assuming that parents attempt to allocate investments in offspring to maximize the number surviving, Robert Trivers (1974) introduced the concept of unequal parental investment. Trivers noted that mothers are equally genetically related to all children, but that children share 50% of their genetic makeup with their sibs and less (25%) if they have different fathers. Given these genetic inequities, it only follows that parent–offspring relationships should feature a large degree of cooperation as well as competition. Thus Trivers (1974:249) states the following:

In particular, parent and offspring are expected to disagree over how long the period of parental investment should last, over the amount of parental investment that should be given and over the altruistic and egoistic tendencies of the offspring as these tendencies affect other relatives.

If optimal parental investment is indeed inequitable, then the principle of allocation comes into play once again, as resources, such as time, energy, and food, given to one child cannot be allocated to another. Examples of discriminative parental solicitude ranging from the Mukogodo to historic German parishes and Portuguese lineages show that unequal parental investment inevitably translates into differential fertility, mortality, and migration parameters. From an evolutionary perspective, parent–offspring relationships consist of a never-ending series of compromises and fitness trade-offs. Hrdy (1990) reviews reports of human infanticide and concludes that in all instances infanticide involves fitness trade-offs, with mothers sacrificing current reproduction in the hopes of improving the value of future reproduction. Seen from an evolutionary vantage point, a mother's biological commitment to her offspring, although rooted in evolutionary biology, is, as Hrdy (1999:315) notes, a contingent commitment, with maternal decision making influenced by historical and ecologically produced circumstances. Maternal instincts are *faculative, not obligate*, and they derive from "complicated interactions among genes, tissue, glands, past experiences and environmental cues, including sensory cues provided by infants themselves and other individuals in the vicinity" (Hrdy 1999:174).

This definition of maternal instinct entirely omits any mention of culture. Yet a strong tradition in Western history, sociology, and anthropology holds that maternal instinct, and its expression as maternal love, are only historical and cultural constructs. The social historian Phillipe Aries' (1962) book, *Centuries of Childhood*, asserted that, in the European Middle Ages, infants and children were not considered to have the same degree of humanity as adults; mothers' relationships with infants and the young could best be described as "maternal indifference." This reflected the historic context of high infant or child mortality; children were seen as arriving and departing at the Will of God, and not particularly deserving of adult care or empathy while on this mortal coil. Likewise, Edward Shorter's (1977) tome, *The Making of the Modern Family*, argued that, throughout most of European history, children were so numerous and so prone to mortality that parents did not bother to invest in them. Shorter (1977:179) argued the following:

> Good mothering is an invention of modernization. In traditional society mothers viewed the development and happiness of infants younger than two years of age with indifference. In modern society they place the welfare of their small children above all else.

Kertzer (1997:147) cites historical demographic research supporting this claim, including Sussman's (1982) history of French wet nursing and Knodel's (1988) studies of nineteenth-century German mothers who neglected to breastfeed their infants, whereas Panter-Brick (2001:4) reviewed the historical concept of childhood and declared that "childhood has been shown to be a social construct that can have no universal validity." Her research suggested that the modern, Western concept of childhood arose during the Industrial Revolution in North America and Europe, a time when children were withdrawn from labor pools and moved into parental homes. As a result, the Western concept of childhood stresses *domesticity*, expressed by Ennew (1995:202) as "the place for childhood to take place is *inside* – inside a society, inside a family, inside a private dwelling." In contrast, non-Western settings exhibit different concepts of childhood, each reflecting distinctive socioeconomic, class, and kinship milieus (see Scheper-Hughes and Hoffman 1998). For example, instead of the Western model stressing that a child needs one stable pair of parents, other societies believe that multiple sets of temporary parents provide for the best childhood. Bledsoe's (1990) anthropological work on child fosterage among the Mende of Sierra Leone found that a child not fostered outside his or her natal family was considered "unworthy or dull."

If the concept of childhood is a cultural construct, then can the same be true of maternal love of her child (ren)? The best known response to this question is found in the anthropological demographer Nancy Scheper-Hughes' (1992) book, *Death Without Weeping*. In the chapter titled, "(M)other Love," Scheper-Hughes (1992:401) states that "mother love is anything other than natural and instead represents a matrix of images, meanings, sentiments and practices that are everywhere socially and culturally produced." Working with poor women in northeast Brazil, Scheper-Hughes identifies mothers' strategies in response to poverty, poor health facilities, and high infant mortality. Faced with these conditions, mothers fail to bond to all their children. Instead, mothers only nurture children deemed to possess higher chances of survival. Others are deemed to have an inherent constellation of syndromes termed *crianca condenada*, or "child sickness." Analogous to a lethal congenital anomaly, children with this affliction are viewed by mothers as doomed, or "as good as dead" (Scheper-Hughes 1992:365). In these cases mothers do not "hold on" to their child, that is, try to provide care and medical health, but rather "let go," a form of benign neglect (Cassidy 1980) recognized across four generations of mothers in the study region.

Mothers hope for a swift end for children born with crianca condenada. Those who die young are referred to as "little angels" or *angelitos*, called away from the earth to sit with Jesus. Maternal attitudes mirror those of eighteenth-century French peasants (Lebrun 1971:423, cited in Shorter 1977:173):

> The death of a small child, provided it had been baptized, is considered on the religious plane as a deliverance, for the infant has had the grace of ascending directly to paradise without knowing the bitterness of this life and of risking his [spiritual] health.

Grieving for lost children is severely discouraged, for tears are thought to make the little angels' wings wet, impeding their flight to heaven.

Commenting on mothers' relationships with their children, Scheper-Hughes (1992:401) writes the following:

> The invention of mother love corresponds not only with the rise of the modern, bourgeois nuclear family but also with the demographic transition; the precipitous decline in infant mortality and female fertility. My argument is a materialistic one; mother love as defined in the psychological, social-historical, and sociological

literature is far from universal or innate and represents instead an ideological, symbolic representation grounded in the basic material conditions that define women's reproductive lives.

Taken to its extreme, this perspective views human maternal instincts, and indeed all human emotions, as purely cultural constructions, or "historical inventions" or "rhetorical strategies" (Abu-Lughod 1986), expressed differently by different cultures under varying socioeconomic conditions. Scheper-Hughes (1992:400) points out that such a position may be likened to the American General William Westmoreland's infamous 1968 quotation about the enemy during the Viet Nam War: "They do not grieve the way we do."

Scheper-Hughes' model of maternal indifference or maternal underinvestment as a major cause of infant and child mortality made an immediate and lasting impact on anthropological demography. Nations and Rebhun (1988:142) suggest that there are now two major theoretical approaches to the problem of high infant mortality: (1) a biomedical model stressing the synergism between nutrition and morbidity (for more recent manifestations of this model, see Scrimshaw, Taylor, and Gordon 1989; Pelletier 1994) and (2) a cultural model termed the "neglect school," focusing on the role and extent of cultural and individual maternal attitudes and behaviors in reaction to infant mortality. Similarly, Basu (1997) proposes an anthropological framework of the determinants of infant and child mortality stressing underinvestment as a corollary to the Mosley and Chen (1984) framework of proximate mortality variables. The resultant "underinvestment framework" can be further subdivided to include two types of neglect: (1) neglect as a defense mechanism and (2) neglect as an offensive strategy. The first would include the concept of *angelitos* and the discouragement of grieving for dead offspring; the second would include maternal choices of which infants to hold and which to let go.

The contrasting views of evolutionary ecologists such as Hrdy and cultural anthropologists such as Scheper-Hughes and Abu-Lughod have been seen as a nature–nurture dichotomy with maternal love seen as either biological instinct or as historical invention. In historical demography, Kertzer (1997:148) points to the nature–nurture dichotomy represented in the debate between Fuchs' (1984) and van der Walle and van der Walle's (1990) interpretations of parental motivation for historic European child abandonment. Fuchs' explanation is aligned with Basu's concept of maternal indifference as a defense mechanism forced on parents by dire economic circumstances. Fuchs (1984:25) makes this statement:

> Children, whether legitimate or natural, were secondary to the economic and social survival of working mothers .... Impoverished mothers could not afford to expend emotional or physical time energy on nurturing their offspring.

In rebuttal, van der Walle and van der Walle (1990:156) argue that, if so, then historic European parents must have been unique, for children among poor people today are globally valued and worthy of parental investment, emotional or otherwise.

The following section examines the history of European child abandonment with respect to parental investment. However, rather than continuing the debate on the biological or cultural roots of mother love, this overview again looks for common ground, stressing that both perspectives recognize maternal agency. In both views, mothers, and fathers, are making facultative, not obligate, decisions about parental investment in specific offspring. From this starting point, we can hypothesize that these decisions are formed by decision rules and therefore constitute strategies. Rather than argue on the basis of Hrdy's (1990, 1999) or Scheper-Hughes' (1992) data and interpretations, we search for demographic strategies in the phenomenon of historical European child abandonment, a five-century phenomenon studied by historians, anthropologists, and demographers (see Fuchs 1984; Boswell 1988; Kertzer 1992; Painter-Brick and Smith 2001).

The study of child abandonment within Western history begins with Boswell's (1988) now classic tome, *The Kindness of Strangers: The Abandonment of Children in Western Europe From Antiquity to the Renaissance.* Here Boswell first intimates the enormous scale of child abandonment in the Early Christian Period of the Roman Empire from the theological advice that men should refrain from visiting brothels in order to avoid incestuous relationships. Subsequent research led Boswell to conclude that 20% to 40% of all children born to Early Christian Romans were abandoned.

A common theme in Western mythology, religion, and literature is that of the abandoned child, who from a terrible start in life ascends to power, a la Romulus and Remus and the founding of Rome, or Moses abandoned in the bulrushes. Similarly, fictional street-smart foundlings such as Dickens' Artful Dodger or Mark Twain's Huck Finn paint a picture of roguish, yet endearingly worldly, children. Unfortunately, the grim demographic reality surrounding abandoned children in historic Europe is one of almost incomprehensibly high levels of infant and child mortality.

This is particularly true in association with foundling homes and institutes opened throughout Europe from the fifteenth to the nineteenth century. Hunecke (1994:119–124) sees distinct stages in the historic development of these homes. The earliest he terms the "Classical" pattern, beginning in the seventeenth century and limited to large Italian cities, including Florence, Milan, Venice, Rome, and Bologna. The second stage featuring the establishment of foundling institutions in other European countries in the eighteenth century can be subdivided into two contrasting systems. The first consisted of what Hunecke (1994:123) terms the "Catholic" system of support for illegitimate children, characterized by prohibition on paternity establishment, moral and material protection of the mother, and state support in raising illegitimate children. In contrast, the "Protestant" system encouraged the investigation of paternity, linked to attempts to have the father support any abandoned children. Whether initiated and supported by monarchs, private philanthropic orders, or revolutionary governments, both systems were united in the belief that foundling institutions could serve to improve the overall situation for illegitimate children, curb infanticide, and produce a pool of useful citizens for government programs.

Despite this combination of lofty and practical goals, conditions within foundling homes were not benign. Kertzer (2001:43) summarizes from the work of various historical demographers:

> Half the infants left at foundling homes in the nineteenth century typically failed to survive to their first birthday, a rate of mortality twice that prevailing in the general population.

Van der Walle and van der Walle (1990:150) argued that parents could not know the elevated risk of mortality for children left at these institutions, but instead entertained dreams that their offspring would enjoy a richer, and perhaps longer, life than they could in their natal home. However, historic specifics do not support van der Walle and van der Walle's (1990:155) contention of "a conspiracy of silence to hide this massacre of the innocents." Hrdy (1999:304) notes that the residents of Bresia proposed carving above the gate of the city's foundling institution this motto: "Here children are killed at public expense."

What is certain is that these terrible mortality rates are strongly linked to the historically increasing scale of European child abandonment. Hunecke (1994) estimates that, during the midnineteenth century, over 120,000 children were abandoned per year in continental Europe, whereas for the city of Milan alone between 1780 and 1869, over a quarter of a million children were abandoned, a number twice the size of the city in 1820. The mind-boggling increase of infant abandonment was sped along by the development of devices enabling parents to anonymously deposit children at public institutions. Called *tours* in France and the *ruota* in Italy, these featured revolving wheels or barrels connecting the institution with the outside world. Parents wishing to deposit a baby simply placed it in a shelf on the wheel, rang a bell to alert authorities inside to the child's arrival, and then departed. The effect of granting anonymity to families wishing to deposit children is seen in the huge influx

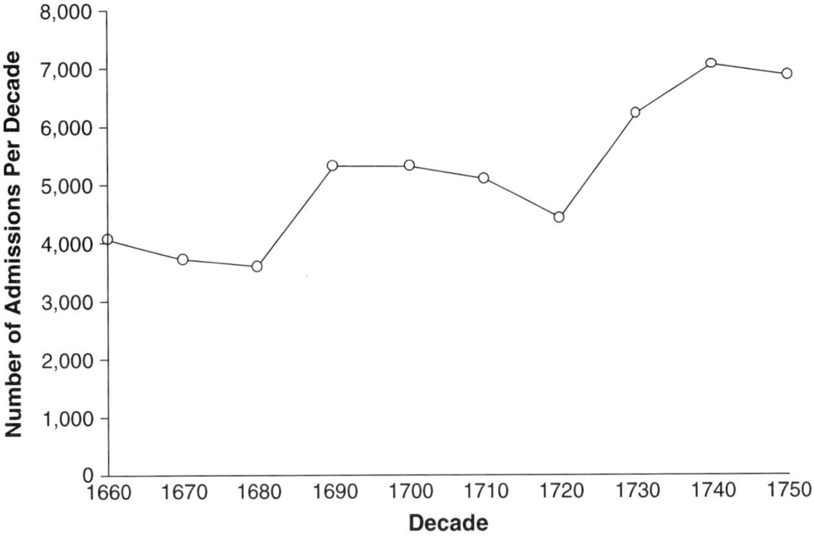

Figure 4.4. Admission to the foundling hospital in Milan, 1660–1759, with the introduction of the *ruota* in 1689 (adapted from Hunecke 1994:118).

of children left in the ruota following its installation at Florence's Innocenti in 1660. Hrdy (1999:304) reports that, by 1699, it was necessary to place a grill across the ruota to prevent parents from shoving in older children!

Viazzo, Bortolotto, and Zanotto (2001:76) present aggregate data for one of the most famous foundling institutes, the Spedale degli Innocenti, established in Florence in 1445. Their reconstruction of Innocenti data shows an initial annual intake of fewer than 100 children, which climbs to about 350 by the year 1480. By 1550 the scale had changed to thousands, rather than hundreds, with admissions peaking at over 20,000 just before 1850. Hunecke's (1994) data for the foundling hospital in Milan, opened in 1659, show a similarly rapid increase in abandonment. Figure 4.4 shows admission per decade for the century 1660–1759, a time period before and after the initiation of a *ruota*, or turning cradle, in 1689. Note the immediate jump in admissions following this date. Figure 4.5 also uses Hunecke's data, spanning the time period 1800–1890, before and after the closure of the *ruota* in 1867–1868. Here the notable event is the immediate and continued decrease of admission once the *ruota* is closed.

Faced with steady, sometimes exorbitant, increasing numbers of children, foundling institute personnel turned to wet nurses. The result was

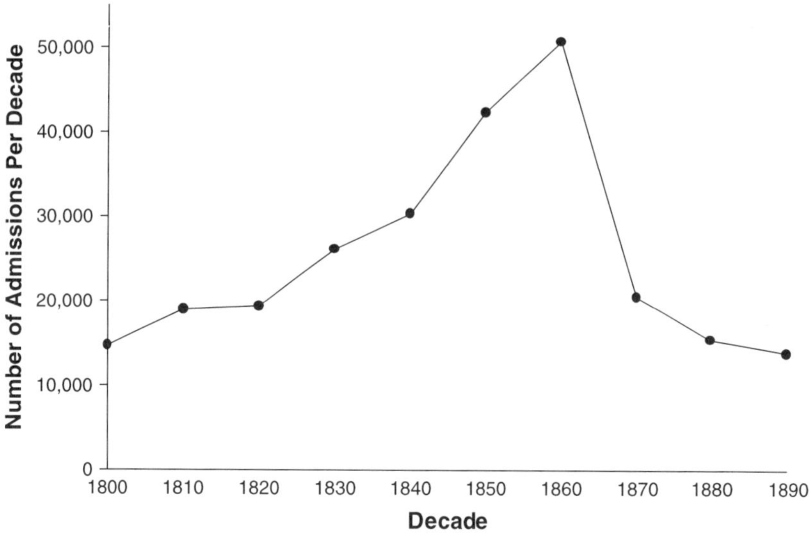

Figure 4.5. Admission to the foundling hospital in Milan, 1800–1899, with the closure of the *ruota* in 1867–1868 (adapted from Hunecke 1994:118).

a market in mothers' milk and the creation of a new economic class of wet nurses (see Sussman 1982 for a history of wet nursing in France). However, the promise of maternal milk was often compromised by unhygienic conditions within the foundling institutions' urban setting or in the rural locales to which parents sent offspring, as well as simply insufficient amounts of milk, even though wet nurses attempted to suckle multiple children. As a result, the widespread use of wet nurses apparently exacerbated child mortality rates, evidenced by referring to wet nurses as *angelmaker* in England and the German equivalent *Engelmacherin* (Kertzer 1992; Kertzer and White 1994; Hrdy 1999).

The overall expense of paying wet nurses and running the institutions also contributed to the high rates of infant or child mortality within them, simultaneously ruining private and public schemes for the population of abandoned children. As Sa (2001:35) observes, not only was child abandonment legal, it was usually highly encouraged by authorities who recognized that children had economic, reproductive, military, and legal value. Economically the sale of breast milk supported numerous poor families, and sending foundlings to rural wet nurses expanded spheres of economy and redistributed money from urban centers. Foundlings were redistributed through adoption into farming as well as noble households, where they served as additional sources of labor (see also Kertzer 2001). However, all these positive aspects were negated by high mortality rates, largely generated by the tremendous increase in child abandonment, so that the expense of caring for foundlings inevitably outstripped resources allotted for their protection.

Smith (2001) modeled the effects of increased costs associated with increased levels of child abandonment for one administrative unit in the Azores for the period 1856–1863. Based on survival data from foundling hospital admission books and estimates of expenditures for wet nurses and revenues from public taxation, his model showed that even slight changes in infant survival levels produced significant effects on the system's costs and eventual sustainability. His interpretation of these results allows the arrow of causality to run both ways: Authorities could have knowingly adjusted survival rates to stay within budget, or the increasing numbers of children could have simply exhausted all public resources, resulting in heightened mortality levels.

No matter which interpretation is correct, the important point is that the authorities running foundling homes had in mind strategies by which they could gain from abandoned children (Kertzer 2001; Sa 2001; Viazzo et al. 2001). Whether or not these strategies were ever realized does not matter for our purposes. What does matter is that even such a spiritually dreary subject as child abandonment featured strategic thinking on an institutional scale.

Also important is the fact that these studies recognize temporally and geographically changing behavioral patterns in the face of dynamic local socioeconomic conditions and cultural thought. For example, in his extensive history of child abandonment in Italy, Kertzer (1993) notes that, in the first half of the nineteenth century, only 10% to 15% of children born in Bologna were abandoned and almost all were illegitimate, whereas in Florence during the same time period, almost half of all baptized children were abandoned, and of these the great majority were born in wedlock. Similarly, in contrast with the enormous number of children left at urban institutions, rural Basque villages featured extremely low abandonment levels during this time (see Valverde 1994), and Viazzo's (1994; Viazzo et al. 2001) analysis of infant mortality over five centuries in Florence's Innocenti revealed large amounts of temporal fluctuation. Although mortality levels were always high inside institutions, Viazzo et al. (2001:88) make this argument:

> Surely it made a difference whether parents had only a slim chance of getting back a child alive or a probability of two-thirds, as was the case both in Florence and Milan in the 1840s.

These regional and temporal differences undoubtedly reflect a myriad of cultural and socioeconomic factors, including the strength of the Catholic Church and its strictures on birth within marriage, the ability of foundling institutions to arrange for wet nurses, and the availability of rural wet nurses. Indeed, child abandonment regional heterogeneity mimics variation in historic European fertility found earlier by Coale and Watkins (1986).

The literature on historic child abandonment also reveals a longstanding focus on individual strategies (see Corsini 1977; Gavitt 1990), which a new generation of scholars has continued (see Kertzer and White 1994; Sa 1994, 2001; Viazzo 1994; Kertzer 2001; Smith 2001; Viazzo et al. 2001). Focusing on the individual level allows us to see strikingly distinctive strategies for differernt segments of society, combining concepts of fitness with socioeconomic circumstances. Recall, for example, the high infant mortality for abandoned children of the poor associated with wet nurses, who were called angelmakers. Yet Fildes' (1988:98–133) study of breast feeding among the upper strata of British society showed wealthier families taking advantage of professional wet nurses to maximize fertility by minimizing time spent lactating, hence hurrying the return of ovulation. Similarly, Hrdy (1999:360–362) shows that, for wealthy families, wet nurses actually led to greatly improved infant survival. Considering eighteenth- and nineteenth-century French infants, Hrdy (1997:409) found a linear relationship between parental money spent on wet nurses and concomitant infant survival. At one extreme, poor French parents spending 10 livres for a wet nurse experienced 69% offspring infant mortality in 1751 and 86% in 1781. At the other extreme, for the period 1774–1794, wealthy parents paying over 100 livres to have their babies fed at home by wet nurses featured 18% infant mortality, a level comparable with the 16% level recorded by maternally nursed infants.

Although wealthy families took advantage of the newly created supply of wet nurses, they did under some circumstances abandon children. Gavitt's (1994) analysis of Florence's Santa Maria degli Innocenti, from 1467 to 1485 reveals that abandonment was not "exclusively, or even largely, the recourse of poverty-stricken families," and that "before 1600 strategies of inheritance resulted in as much abandonment to the Innocenti as strategies of survival" (Gavitt 1994:65). Wealthy families' inheritance strategies arose from two differing situations. In the first, wealthy family scions impregnated female servants, with resulting offspring sent to the foundling home to avoid inheritance conflicts between legitimate and illegitimate children. Between 1445 and 1466, approximately one-half of the children admitted to the Innocenti were products of such liaisons, whereas in the period from 1467 to 1485, 40% of mothers of abandoned children were servants (Gavitt 1994:74). The connection between illegitimate children and servants was so public that legislation in 1456 made the following proposal (Gavitt 1994:75):

> Given that the majority of children abandoned to this hospital are born of persons of low estate and servants who care not for their honor, it is requested that any person who places, hires, or brings into the city, environs or countryside of Florence a slave or servant should pay and be required to pay for each head to the treasurer of the hospital of the Innocenti one large florin within eight days from when she was hired.

Wealthy families also abandoned children as a result of what Gavitt (1994:65) calls the "unhappy conflict between the demography of fifteenth-century Tuscany and its prevailing system of inheritance." At that time, the average age at marriage was at least ten years greater for males than females, resulting in high rates of widows. Because of a patrilineal inheritance system, women with children from previous marriages found few prospective husbands, again because of the potential for conflicts surrounding inheritance rights for children born to different unions. Faced with poor marital, and hence economic, prospects, many wealthy women took advantage of foundling homes.

Turning our search for strategies from the wealthy to the poor, we need to consider two types of data. The first is parental, and particularly maternal, motivation for child abandonment; the second is whether any effort was made to recover children. The study of individual motivation is difficult during the period of the wheel, when parental anonymity was ensured. However, there are some data that record parental reasons for abandoning children, and in a few cases link parents with children so that the latter can be reclaimed at later dates. One example of this situation is provided by Gavitt's (1994:76–78) analysis of data for maternal causes of child abandonment in Florence for the years 1472–1480 and 1482, before the advent of the *ruota*. Here by far the greatest number of entries of maternal motivations only, 107 out of a total of 268 (40%), pertain to the mother being a slave or servant of wealthy households. As previously described, children abandoned in these cases were most likely sired by wealthy males and then abandoned to avoid inheritance problems. Maternal poverty is listed six times, far less than injury or illness of mother ($n = 36$), mother placed as wet nurse ($n = 33$), or death of mother ($n = 28$). For the 118 entries recording motives to both mothers and fathers, poverty is mentioned only ten times.

Equally important is evidence about which children were abandoned, and which were later reclaimed. In the first regard, Corsini (1977)

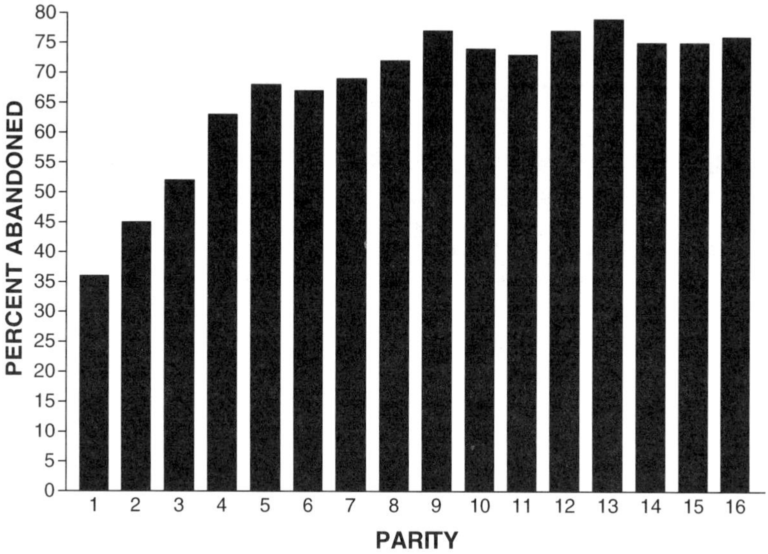

Figure 4.6. Percentage of children abandoned in Milan foundling hospitals by parity, 1842 (adapted from Hunecke 1994:129).

suggested that poor families used foundling homes as a strategy to achieve a target number and composition of children in the absence of effective family-planning methods. This is supported by Hunecke's (1994:129) Milan 1842 sample of 649 couples who abandoned at least one of their children. Based on these data, Figure 4.6 shows parity-specific percentages of abandonment. Note first that mothers who abandoned their children featured incredibly high fertility as a result of early breastfeeding termination. For this sample, Hunecke (1994) calculated female total marital fertility levels to average 12.2 children for women aged twenty to forty-four years. Figure 4.6 clearly reveals increasing abandonment with higher parities. Although the sample does not give information on number of children surviving per family, these data strongly suggest that parents used the foundling hospital as a repository of children they could not economically support. In doing so, did parents knowingly condemn children to death, or did they use these institutions as state-run allomothers?

The vital piece of information needed to address this question is the proportion of children reclaimed. Throughout Europe, children were often left at foundling homes with identifying signs, or accompanying letters, in the hopes that their parents would return for them later. How many actually did? Again, answers are historically and regionally variable,

Table 4.4. *Age of ruota children at time of parental recovery from Milan foundling hospitals, 1842*

	Children reclaimed		Children returned alive	
Year of life	No.	%[a]	No.	%
1	154	5.6	83	53.9
2	794	28.6	533	67.1
3	574	20.7	317	55.2
4–5	473	17.1	242	51.2
6–10	327	11.8	137	41.9
11–15	153	5.5	43	28.1
Later (>16)	298	10.7	106	35.6
TOTAL	2,773	100.0	1,461	55.3[b]

[a] Cumulative; [b] average value.
Source: Table is after Hunecke (1994:131).

but an important source of data comes from Milan (Hunecke 1994: 125):

> [w]here virtually everyone could abandon and later recognize and reclaim the child without any danger of punishment; if a child were still alive that child was then returned to the parents.

Table 4.4 shows two important variables for children abandoned in Milan, based on Hunecke's (1994) 1842 sample. The first is cumulative percentage of children reclaimed (regardless of survival) by age. This reveals that mothers left the majority of their children with foundling hospitals until after the age of two. This pattern is explained by historic changes in the allotment of the *allattamento gratuitio*, free breastfeeding by wet nurses in the hospital. Beginning in the seventeenth century, this favor was freely granted for a period of sixteenth months for women who could produce a certificate of poverty from their local priest. It was granted less frequently in the nineteenth century as increased numbers of foundlings strained the hospital's resources. Because of this, mothers took advantage of the *ruota*, because they could then reclaim the child at any time they wished.

Not shown in Table 4.4 is the overall average percentage of children reclaimed. Hunecke's data show that 70.1% of married mothers reclaimed all abandoned children before their fifteenth birthday (after this age they would not be returned), and that a mere 2.8% of parents did not reclaim any of their children. Explaining this pattern, Hunecke (1994:132) quotes a medical doctor who cared for poor Milanese women and described their motives in abandoning their children in the following words:

> In fact all mothers who abandoned their children, assured me that they would not leave them forever in the Pia Casa, but that they would call them back as soon as they were able to care for them themselves and when the children no longer require their unremitting attention; they act in this way in order to dedicate themselves fully to the work which brings them the earnings on which they live.

How do these figures reflect on our debate about maternal emotions? The Milan data are unique in permitting linkage between the great majority of parents and offspring using the *ruota*. They very strongly support Hrdy's (1999) claim for a biologically based maternal instinct, rather than Scheper-Hughes' (1992) claims for historically contingent or culturally constructed emotions. They also accord well with Hrdy's (1997) contention that poor European women followed a pattern of "delegated mothering," using the state-supported foundling hospitals of Southern Europe as institutionalized allomothers. They also agree with Fuchs' (1984) data from Madrid and those of Viazzo et al. (2001), all of which show a high proportion of children being reclaimed by parents, paralleling the cultural analysis of the "circulation of children" in non-Western societies (see Goody 1984; Bledsoe 1990). However, before accepting this strategy as adaptive, we must look at the second column in Table 4.4, which reports the age-specific proportion of children reclaimed who survived abandonment. These dismally low figures remind us again of the horrific mortality conditions within foundling homes. Mothers who abandoned their children must have known that they were taking a calculated risk that their children would have a better fate within these walls than they would outside with their natal families. In this way, poor mothers' (and fathers') behavior can be described in evolutionary terms as another example of making the best of a bad job.

Overall, this necessarily cursory overview of historic patterns of European child abandonment show differing strategies for different groups in differing environments and temporal periods. This behavioral plasticity is in line with evolutionary ecology's emphasis on flexible reaction norms, glossed previously as "In context X, do α, in context Y, switch to β" (Winterhalder and Smith 2000:54). This interpretation reinforces Hrdy's statement that maternal love, although based in biological factors, can be at best a "*contingent commitment*, with maternal decision-making influenced by historical and ecologically produced circumstances." Yet if we consider that these circumstances reflect varying access to resources necessary for infant survival, then Hrdy's (1999:316) statement is not so dissimilar from Scheper-Hughes' (1992:354) position that mother love is far from "innate and represents instead an ideological, symbolic representation grounded in the basic material conditions that define women's reproductive lives." What the two positions have in common is the recognition that mothers behave differently in different circumstances. In the historic European example, rich women increased their reproductive success through the use of wet nurses whereas poor women used foundling homes as allomothers, attempting to reclaim abandoned children at a later date. Although both cases support evolutionary ecology's theme of fitness enhancement, it would be ridiculous to dismiss the role of culture in maternal decision making. Such phenotypic variation must entail more than biological factors interpreting environmental cues when the cues themselves are cultural; for example, if rich, abandon and do not try to reclaim out-of-wedlock offspring, but, if poor, abandon but try to reclaim offspring. Although child abandonment was grounded in economic necessity for much of Europe's poor, in terms of culture as ideology, consider the historic increase in acceptance of the behavior of child abandonment represented by the trends shown in Figures 4.4 and 4.5.

Rather than continuing the nature–nurture false dichotomy surrounding the issue of maternal love, I find that it would be far more beneficial to consider what the two fields of evolutionary ecology and anthropological demography can each bring to the study of infanticide or child abandonment. With respect to mother–infant bonding and Attachment Theory, two factors cited are self-deception and alternative caregivers. In the first, the evolutionary biologist Robert Trivers and Huey P. Newton, the black activist founder of the Black Panthers, argued that self-deception was a human survival tactic with a long evolutionary history (Trivers and Newton 1982). Expanding on this argument in subsequent publications, Trivers (1985, 2002) notes that deception is central in animal communication, such as males bluffing or threatening other males to ensure sexual access to females, or in the case of females concealing ovulation from males. From this starting point, Trivers argued that there must have been strong selection to practice and detect deception in all organisms. The relevance of self-deception to child abandonment or infanticide is that it can act as a means of overcoming mother–infant bonding and terminate parental investment, in spite of the hormonal storm mothers elict with breastfeeding. This is exemplified in Scheper-Hughes' (1992) study of Brazilian women who believed certain children suffered from crianca condenada, or child sickness, and who were "as good as dead" (Scheper-Hughes 1992:365). Children with this disease were perceived as listless and lacking energy; this description is grounded in biology for both Third and First World children weakened by malnutrition and disease (for Chilean infants, see Valenzuela 1990; for U.S.

children, see Drotar 1991). However, the belief that those suffering from child sickness are as good as dead and the subsequent notion of dead infants as angelitos are certainly cultural constructs, not biological products. Going from the specific to the general, we see that consideration of maternal self-deception would also figure into Basu's (1997) underinvestment framework of infant and child mortality and is certainly worth pursuing in future research.

The second factor to consider is the role of culture in providing alternative caregivers. Bowlby's Attachment Theory argued that the establishment of a primary bond between infant and caregiver was an ancestral human pattern arising in an Environment of Evolutionary Adaptiveness, or EEA. This position has been criticized by cultural anthropologists and evolutionary ecologists alike (for a review of these criticisms, see Wiley and Carlin 1999), all of whom point to the role of social institutions and demographic patterns in mediating infant care. Wiley and Carlin's (1999) cross-cultural study of infant care shows that kin networks, fosterage, female work patterns, marriage systems, and maternal workloads are all important determinants of infant–caregiver bonding patterns. Drawing on previous research that considered parental investment in terms of demographic regimes (Harpending et al. 1991; Chisholm 1999), Wiley and Carlin further argued that Bowlby's hypothesized pattern of exclusive, intensive mother–infant bonding is only found with any frequency in low-fertility, low mortality populations. This combination of demographic parameters characterizes Post-Transitional populations and is limited to the past few centuries; it is a far cry from any ancestral human pattern formed in a prehistoric EEA.

Only by considering both cultural and biological patterns in relationship with prevailing demograpic regimes can we fashion models of parental investment. What is equally important is that, by doing so, we can avoid the dead-end debate over mother love as arising from nature or nurture.

Adoption in Modern China: Stressing the Positive

As the flip side of child abandonment, adoption featured prominently in early debates about sociobiology. In his text, *The Use and Abuse of Sociobiology*, the cultural anthropologist Marshall Sahlins (1976) argued that adoption of non-kin-related children is inconsistent with sociobiological theory. He specifically pointed out that, in some Pacific Island societies, the majority of households contain an adopted child, from which he concluded that adoptive practices in these countries showed the primacy of culture over biology. In rebuttal, the human evolutionary ecologist Joan Silk's (1990) examination of Oceanic societies showed that the great majority of adoptions feature shared genetic kinship between adoptive parents and children, a finding predicted by sociobiological and general evolutionary theory under the topic of inclusive fitness by means of kin selection.

Adoption of abandoned children in modern China provides a good test case for this earlier cultural–biological debate. In contemporary China, the impetus for abandoning children is completely different than the historic European situation. In the European case, exemplified by Hunecke's (1994) data from mid-nineteenth-century Milan just shown in Table 4.4, higher-parity children were most frequently abandoned, as poor families could not support large numbers of offspring. In contrast, the modern Chinese history of child abandonment is directly linked to governmental enforcement of strict family-planning measures. The forced implementation of a one-child policy in 1979 along with a long historical preference for male children (Greenhalgh 1995b; Greenhalgh and Li 1995; Riley 1997b) combined to revive the Chinese tradition of child abandonment, or "throwing away the baby" (Johnson 1993:78). Today Chinese government reports conservatively estimate between 100,000 and 160,000 abandoned children per year (Johnson, Huang, and Wang 1998: 471).

Like those in the historic European situation, Chinese abandoned children end up in foundling homes with higher infant mortality rates (Johnson et al. 1998). Chinese regional variance also mirrors historic European child abandonment patterns, with some regions featuring abandonment of disabled children and others showing both disabled and able-bodied offspring abandoned (Johnson 1993). However, what really distinguishes historic European from contemporary Chinese abandonment patterns is the latter's tremendously strong historical bias against females.

In China, males are associated with economic success, perform rituals honoring lineal ancestors, and provide old-age security for their parents. In contrast, daughters are deemed a loss to their natal family as their labor and support is lost through patrilineality and patrilocality. These unequal expectations are evident in the old Chinese adage, "many sons bring [much] happiness" whereas girls were viewed as "goods on which one loses" (Greenhalgh and Li 1995:615). As a result, Chinese history features centuries of female infanticide and abandonment of female children. Both practices were declared criminal activities in the seventeenth century, followed by the creation of foundling hospitals throughout China (Johnson, Huang, and Wang 1998). Official government histories linked this bias to "remnant feudal thoughts" (Johnson 1993:80), undoubtedly viewing entrenched male bias as an embarrassment under a Communist regime. The strength of this embedded son bias was grossly underestimated when the Chinese government brought in their original one-child policy in 1979. Originally stating that parents could have one child regardless of sex, this quickly became a "two-child, one son" policy. In rural areas, parents whose first child was a daughter simply proceeded to another parity in an effort to produce a son.

In addition to the ancient tradition of son preference, Chinese society also has an equally old tradition of adoption. The great majority of research on Chinese adoption stresses male adoption, either within or outside the adopting family's lineage as an inheritance strategy to provide an heir for the familial patriline (see Waltner 1990). However, at least two patterns of Chinese adoption favored women. The first is the "little wife" or "minor marriage" format extensively studied by Wolf and Huang (1980) for nineteenth- and twentieth-century Taiwan. In this custom, girls as young as one year, termed *sim-pua*, or "little daughters-in-law," were placed into their future husband's home and raised as a "daughter" who would later marry her "brother." A second, less fortunate tradition of adopting female children was called *ca-bo-kan*, or "servant-slaves." These were frequently offspring of poor families who sold their children into servitude, or directly into prostitution.

Johnson and colleagues (Johnson 1993; Johnson, Huang, and Wang 1998) investigated contemporary Chinese adoption patterns, focusing on adoption within China by other Chinese. During the mid-1990s, they collected information from 629 families who had adopted children and 237 families who had abandoned children. Their sample was overwhelmingly rural for both adoption and abandonment. The sample's other major distinguishing factor was sex; 90% of the abandoned children were females, as were 78% of the adopted children. Not surprisingly, one of the most important determinants of abandonment was family composition; 87% of abandoned girls had no brothers. Of these 171 girls, 69 were second daughters, 62 were third daughters, 26 were fourth daughters, and 3 were fifth daughters. Only 11 were first-born daughters, and in six of these cases there were extenuating circumstances (e.g., death of the father or infant physical disability).

This sample of abandoned children conformed closely to historic and contemporary Chinese notions of the sex-specific value of children, but the sample of adopting parents did not. Researchers found no evidence of parents adopting to obtain either a future daughter-in-law or a servant. Instead, parents stated they adopted girls for their own sake, because they wished to acquire a "child of the missing gender" or to realize the ideal family composition according the to Chinese proverb, "A son and a daughter make a complete family" (Johnson, Huang, and Wang 1998:489). Table 4.5 confirms these responses, with 130 of the total 307

Table 4.5. *Description of family composition of adopting families*

Family composition	Families: Adopting girls	Adopting boys	Total
Childless	148	47	195
Sons only	130	4	134
Daughters only	7	22	29
Sons and daughters	20	10	30
Unknown	2	2	4
TOTAL	307	85	392

Source: Table is adapted from Johnson, Huang, and Wang (1998:488).

adopting families having only sons before they adopt a girl. These data also support Riley and Greenhalgh and Li's contention that, in contemporary Chinese culture, parental bias in favor of boys exists side by side with a growing appreciation of girls. Ironically, increased daughter status apparently arises from economic reforms that freed sons to pursue private economic goals. These meant that sons were not as willing to stay in the natal village to look after their aging parents. As a result, parents interviewed by Greenhalgh and Li (1995:617) presented a new image:

> the small-hearted son and selfish daughter-in-law refusing to honor their obligations to their elders and, in their place the faithful daughter, appreciated at last, coming home to render personal services and comfort in her parents' final years.

Another important result is that 90% of the adoptions were between biologically unrelated parents and children. This goes against earlier general evolutionary interpretations of adoption, as well as the specific historic Chinese social norms forbidding the adoption of nonrelated children. Chinese prohibitions against cross-surname adoption are found in ritual texts dating to the tenth century. Later law continues these prohibitions, as shown in the following quote from Ming law (Waltner 1990:48):

> He who adopts a child of a different surname, thereby causing chaos in the lineage, is to be beaten sixty strokes. He who gives a person of a different surname as heir is to suffer the same punishment. The adoption is to be annulled.

Recognition that the great majority of adopted children in China today bear no biological relationship to their adoptive family is highlighted by their collective name as *ming-ling tzu*, or "mulberry insect children." This comes from the folktale that Wolf and Huang (1980:110) attribute to the author Lu Hsun's wonderfully titled work, "Idle Thoughts at the End of Spring," in which he recounts watching wasps taking caterpillars from nearby mulberry trees:

> The old folk informed me that the slender-waisted wasp was the sphex mentioned in the old classics, who, since all spheges are female, must adopt bollworms (*ming-ling*) to carry on her line. This wasp imprisons the green caterpillar in her nest, while she herself raps and taps outside day and night, praying: "Be like me! Be like me!" Then, after a certain number of days – I forget exactly how many, but probably seven times seven – the caterpillar turns into a slender-waisted wasp. This is why the *Book of Song* says, "The bollworm's young is carried off by the spex." The bollworm is the green caterpillar found on mulberry trees.

As Wolf and Huang (1980:111) describe, ming-ling tzu breaks all ties with their natal family and trace descent only from their adoptive parents. Johnson, Huang, and Wang (1998:485) note that this transformation in kinship allegiances totally denies the biological heredity of the adopted children, exclusively emphasizing their culturally given identity. Here then is a complete domination of biological descent by cultural means.

Summary: Culture and Biology in Inheritance Strategies

Throughout this chapter, one of the overall text's main themes, the necessity of considering biological and cultural interactions to fully understand human demographic strategies, was further illustrated. In the immediately preceding two sections I examined two contrasting aspects of parental effort, child abandonment and adoption. When combined with data showing strong parental attempts to reclaim their offspring, historic European patterns of child abandonment support evolutionary theory in terms of "delegated mothering" (Hrdy 1997). In contrast, the adoption of nonbiologically related offspring in China today favors cultural theory. However, there is little gain in casting child abandonment and reclamation or adoption in the false dichotomy of biology versus culture. Instead, it is far more productive to think of them as representing "reproductive interests" originally proposed by Alexander (1987) and enlarged here to include cultural as well as biological motivation.

Looking at historic European and contemporary Chinese patterns from this perspective, we can avoid the either–or narrow view of the evolutionary and cultural demographic debate and see that, in both cases, biology and culture are essential to understanding parental behavior. In the European context, we saw the differing uses that wealthy and poor families made of state-run institutions. Wealthy families used them to avoid conflicts of inheritance or to find a suitable mate for remarriage, whereas poor families used foundling homes and hospitals as institutionalized allomothers. What links these two diverse behavioral patterns is that, at the individual level, both represent biocultural strategies. This is also true for the contemporary Chinese case, with both abandoning and adopting parents attempting to adapt cultural ideals and social norms to their individual family biological composition. As a result, Confucian ideals about the primacy of biology, expressed in terms of patrilines, are ignored if this serves individual familial goals.

In both cases, we see physiologically based parental emotions that are the products of literally millions of years of natural selection adjusting rapidly to changing cultural conditions. Biological and cultural factors are so intertwined that it is inefficient to restrict analyses to one factor at the exclusion of the other. This points to the need for further integration of the biological and cultural aspects of human emotions, exemplified by Hinton's (1999) edited work, *Biocultural Approaches to the Emotions*. As the title promises, this contains a variety of current approaches to human emotions, including evolutionary psychology, systems theories, and biocultural synergism. Scheper-Hughes and Lock's (1998:30) quote that emotions are the "missing link... capable of bridging mind and body, individual and society" expresses the potential importance of studying emotions from a biocultural perspective. Emotions, like morals discussed in Chapter 3, have a biological origin. Controlled by the brain, they are processed and expressed by means of the central nervous system. Handwerker (2002:109) states the following:

> [O]ur central nervous system constructs culture with sensory inputs which in turn translate into the set of cognitions, emotions, and behavior that uniquely identifies each of us as individuals, reflects where we live and the web of social relationships through which we have lived our lives.

From this perspective, emotions can be viewed as proximate variables linking distal variables represented by cognition, seen as socially transmitted symbols, or culture, with behavior constituting the final realized variable. This model addresses the problem of how symbolic culture translates into concrete behavior by providing a pathway through emotion, such as culture → emotions → behavior. Emotions change in expression and incidence; consider, for example, the emotions elicited by human slavery in Western countries now and just a few centuries ago. In this way, the model is compatible with evolutionary ecology's emphasis on natural selection favoring phenotypic plasticity, as well as with cultural anthropology's view of emotions as historical artifacts. Emotions such as fear and maternal attachment simultaneously can be seen as the evolutionary product of millennia of natural selection, representing the life effort component of our expanded model of reproductive interests, and as culturally contingent, representing the social interactions component of our revised reproductive interests model. Because of these unique properties, emotions, like moral systems stressed in the previous chapter, are ideal candidates for joint research by human evolutionary ecologists and anthropological demographers.

5 Future Research Directions

The Centrality of Sex in Anthropology and Evolution

This book began by noting a chasm between anthropological demographers and human evolutionary ecologists encompassing both theoretical and methodological approaches to the study of human demography. Both approaches have much to offer, yet each has a purposeful ignorance and outright disdain of the other that threatens to harden into dogmatic stances of limited analytical value. In an attempt to open lines of discussion between these two fields, in preceding chapters I delineated areas of common ground not recognized by each field and used a framework of lifetime reproductive interests, originally developed in sociobiology (Alexander 1974), which I expanded to include cultural motivations. The revised model broke the concept of reproductive interests into two compartments: life effort pertains to evolutionary biology's life history theory, and social interactions are relevant to cultural goals. I then proposed that these could be fruitfully examined by use of the concept of demographic strategies, which has a long history in both anthropological demography and human evolutionary ecology. From these starting points, this text covered a lot of ground, presenting both cross-cultural research and case studies ranging from contemporary East and West Africa, North America, and China to historic Europe. Instead of ending with a review, I offer a short perspective on future research directions, concluding with a discussion of what anthropological demographers, human evolutionary ecologists, and demographers can learn from each field's strengths.

To begin, I believe that human evolutionary ecology and anthropological demography have slighted the importance of sex in both evolution and culture. By sex, I do not mean "gender," so prominently featured in anthropological demography; nor do I mean sex defined by chromosomes. Instead, I mean *human sexuality*, a biological drive mediated by cultural symbols, values, and socially approved norms. Human sexuality sits at the intersection between demography's interest in quantification and anthropology's emphasis on culture-specific meaning. Large-scale surveys of sexual patterns (see Carael 1997) and models of sexual networking (Morris and Kretzschmar 1997) represent the former, whereas the study of sexual cultures, defined as "a consensual model of cultural ideals about sexual behavior in a group" (Herdt 1997a:10), exemplifies the latter.

Despite early anthropological studies of human sexuality (Malinowski 1927, 1929; Mead 1927, 1935), the field then lost interest in the subject. Demography's focus on fertility and nuptuality historically ignored sexuality; thus fertility models appeared as marriage → birth with no intervening process. Today the subject is frequently obfuscated under the demographic catchall term of "reproductive health" (though for notable efforts to improve this situation, see Moore and Zeidenstein 1996). This interdisciplinary lack of attention has shown recent signs of change; this is exemplified by Shirley Lindenbaum's (1991) article, "Anthropology Rediscovers Sex." There is a veritable anthropological revival of sexual studies, with volumes on biocultural approaches to human sexuality (Abramson and Pinkerton 1995a, 1995b) and full-length ethnographies (see Herdt 1999). This research has demonstrated that sexual behavior changes over time and may even be considered a driving factor for cultural change. It has also recognized the role of nonprocreative sexual activities, which may perform specific functions, such as ritualized homosexuality in Melanesia (Herdt 1984), or be maintained simply for their pleasurable rewards. Perhaps most pertinent for our topic of strategies, this research shows that some sexual patterns may be maladaptive in today's world.

This last result points to the fact that much of anthropology, demography, and evolutionary biology's recent interest in human sexuality stem from the AIDS pandemic. This tragedy provides another area of common research interest, exemplified by the International Union for the Scientific Study of Population's Committee on Anthropological Demography's volume titled, *Sexual Cultures and Migration in the Era of AIDS* (Herdt 1997b). In the following section, I look at three sexual cultures, focusing on male sexual behavior in sub-Saharan Africa, Thailand, and gay men in North America, in relation to HIV/AIDS.

Male Sexuality, Education, and High-Risk Behavior

Lacking a vaccine, we deem education to be the most important preventative tool against HIV infection, based on the premise that, once people know the biological facts about HIV transmission, they will change their sexual behavior to reduce high-risk sexual behavior. However, although acknowledging local, community-based successful education programs, Caldwell et al. (1999; also see Caldwell, Orubuloye, and Caldwell 1992) points to the overall lack of success of education programs in changing sexual behavior in sub-Saharan Africa. For example, demographic health surveys from Tanzania in 1992 and Kenya in 1998 showed that, respectively, 98% and 99% of male respondents were aware of AIDS and its transmission by means HIV, yet the same surveys showed little or no change in sexual behavior.

Why is there resistance to sexual change in the region with the highest prevalence rates of HIV/AIDS in the world? Caldwell (1999) first approached this question by considering African fatalism arising from three deeply embedded cultural beliefs: (1) a person's time of death is preordained, negating any type of behavioral change for health reasons; (2) causes of death are multivariate, combining both biological and cultural factors, rather than a single infection; and (3) mortality can arise from witchcraft or "curses," which people are powerless to avoid. However, Caldwell and colleagues (Caldwell et al. 1992; Orubuloye, Caldwell, and Caldwell 1997) go beyond fatalism to consider African cultural views of male sexuality as an important factor negating HIV/AIDS educational programs, noting the widespread sub-Saharan African belief that the male biological sex drive is innately strong and "programmed" to need multiple partners. Young men in Nigeria repeatedly stated that the need for multiple, sometimes concurrent, sexual partners was linked not to sexual pleasure but to a biological urge (Caldwell, Orubuloye, and Caldwell 1999). This belief is linked to an indigenous model of overall male personal health in which failure to have multiple sexual partners results in general ill health. The concept of a strong, innate male sex drive finds support from other African studies. Varga (1999:24) reports in interviews with young South African women this repeated statement: "He can't control himself if he sees a woman he likes." Similarly, a young man in this study man reports that "if my penis wants it, it must have sex."

The view of a strong, biologically innate male sex drive is strongly linked to polygynous marital systems. In West Africa, polygyny features the following: (1) late age at marriage for males, (2) long postpartum abstinence periods, (3) large degree of economic independence among husband and wives, and (4) sexual imbalance favoring males (Caldwell, Orubuloye, and Caldwell 1992). Combined with the indigenous belief in the biological need for multiple sexual partners, the first factor leads to cultural acceptance of male premarital sexual activity, whereas the second means that a man in a polygynous marriage does not enjoy full-time sexual access to a wife and therefore may be tempted to engage in extramarital sexual unions. Likewise, the lack of economic and cultural constraints represented by the third and fourth factors make extramarital sexual unions easy to achieve and maintain for men.

These factors are nested within a general sub-Saharan pronatalist philosophy, what Romaniuk (1968) called "a general procreative ethos" and what Caldwell and Caldwell (1989) term "reproduction-oriented" sexual social tradition. Before HIV/AIDS, this system did not control the sexuality of males or females to the extent featured in Europe or Asia. In sub-Saharan Africa, male sexuality had a freer rein because inheritance was traced through the male line; male parental investment costs were low as a result of the economic independence of women; and more children translated into more economic and political power to a father's lineage.

For women, this meant little or no stigma attached to children born outside marriage. A far greater stigma, often the cause of divorce in sub-Saharan Africa, is female sterility, or *not bearing* children, regardless of paternity. Recognition of an innate, irresistible male sex drive also meant a lack of stigma for female sex workers. Under this system, "Young women can retire from prostitution without worrying for the rest of their life that their past life will catch up with them." (Orubuloye, Caldwell, and Caldwell 1997:1204).

Before the spread of HIV/AIDS, these behaviors provided stability to sub-Saharan African cultural regimes, facilitating the social reproduction of traditional societies. In today's post-AIDS world, they constitute a recipe for disaster, culturally condoning high-risk behavior in the form of frequent partner change, sex with commercial sex workers, and concurrent partnerships within marriage, and they largely explain why this region contains the world's highest levels of sexually transmitted infections (STIs), including HIV/AIDS. Furthermore, because of STIs and HIV/AIDS, cultural systems originally designed to maximize fertility by featuring early age of sexual debut, rapid and high rates of partner change, and polygny often actually lower fertility by facilitating the spread of STIs.

Bailey and Aunger (1995) provide an excellent example of this in their study of farming and foraging groups in the Ituri region of Central Africa. Lying within the great African infertility belt, their interview data clearly show that all groups understand the relationships between early sexual debut, increased risk of STIs, and reduced fertility, yet they maintain risky sexual cultural practices, such as early age of sexual debut, multiple partners, and extramarital partners. Bailey and Aunger (1995:217) ask this question:

> Why do people in the Ituri persist in their promiscuous attitudes and behaviour even in the face of such great loss in fertility, and by extension, in their own sense of social and psychological well-being?

Their answer is that humans are designed by evolution to actively seek sexual contact.

They point to the products of natural selection for human sexual pleasure, including large penises, permanently enlarged female breasts, and female capacity for multiple organisms, and they make this argument (Bailey and Aunger 1995:218):

> An outcome of our remarkable capacity for sexual pleasure and desire for sexual contact is an apparent inability or unwillingness to detect and avoid the pathogens transmitted by the frequent sexual contacts we seek. While we have the cognitive processes that enable us to be conscious of the risks associated with sexual contacts, the evolved psychological mechanisms driving out desires may be overcome only under extreme conditions.

This evolutionary perspective goes a long way toward explaining why educational programs stressing the voluntary changing of sexual behavior have failed to stem the tide of HIV/AIDS in sub-Saharan Africa. It also predicts that we should encounter evidence that evolved psychological mechanisms can be overcome under "extreme conditions." One strong case for this is made in Thailand, where different studies (Knodel et al. 1996; VanLandingham and Grandjean 1997) found radically different cultural views of male versus female sexuality. Similar to those in sub-Saharan Africa, Thai men are seen as "having a natural and driving need for sex that requires frequent outlet" (Knodel et al. 1996:182), whereas women are viewed as more in control of their sexual feelings, which are considered weaker than men's. Studies in northern Thailand found cultural support for male sexual impulsiveness arising from a strong innate biological sex drive. This support included a cultural history of polygyny, the taking of mistresses, and traditional patterns of prostitute visiting. Survey data from Chiang Mai found that 98% of men reported knowing about AIDS, yet 58% also reported a recent visit to a prostitute and only 59% of those visiting prostitutes consistently used condoms. Mirroring the situation in sub-Saharan Africa, VanLandingham and Grandjean (1997:128) state, "knowledge about AIDS risk has not been enough to prompt widespread behavioural change."

Because education failed to change sexual behavior in Thailand, the government intervened to provide "extreme conditions" in the form of systems of state-run penalties and moral sanctions underlying the country's enormously successful "100% Condom Program." Begun in the mid-1990s, this program introduced and enforced consistent condom use at all Thai commercial sex venues (World Bank 1999:159–160). Through government-sponsored programs, condoms were provided free to commercial sex establishments. As a result of supply and enforcement, condom use in commercial sex establishments went from fewer than 20% in 1989 to over 90% by 1992. Consequently, the number of new STI cases for men treated at government clinics dropped from 200,000 in 1989 to fewer than 20,000 in 1992, and HIV prevalence rates among Thai army conscripts declined from 4% in 1993 to less than 2% in 1996.

The program's success has been attributed to "mass media campaigns, education and skills building in workplaces and schools, and peer education" (World Bank 1999:159). An equally workable alternative explanation for the program's accomplishments is government coercion. Health officials, government workers, and police enforced condom use. Men turning up for treatment in STI clinics were reported to this bureaucratic array, who had the authority to trace sexual contacts back to possible sources of infection. Other officials posed as clients in commercial sex establishments to check on condom availability and policies. Uncovering noncondom use in sexual acts made offenders liable for fines and, in the cases of commercial sex houses, led to loss of government licensing or immediate closure. These actions recall the power of punishment or moral sanctions in enforcing cooperation, or in the words of Boyd and Richerson's (1992) article, "(or anything else) in sizeable groups." Yet these extreme conditions also led to the creation of 'invisible brothels," that is, restaurant bars and karaoke pubs where sex workers serve as waitresses, and private massage parlors (Im-Em 1999). In these establishments, "condom use is more difficult" (Im-Em 1999:168) to enforce.

Male unwillingness to wear condoms, whether driven underground in Thailand or openly maintained throughout sub-Saharan Africa in spite of massive public education campaigns, forces us to focus on the pleasurable aspects of human sexuality rather than maintain an exclusive emphasis on its procreative function. This is particularly true for male homosexual unions. Until recently, gay communities were one of the true voluntary successes of HIV/AIDS education programs. Under the rubric of "sustaining safe sex," gay groups around the world educated themselves about HIV and initiated and maintained low-risk sexual practices (see Dowsatt 1993). Their success led to an emphasis on the concept of "community" as a means of combating the spread of HIV/AIDS (Caldwell 1999:249) and the hope that this approach would be applicable to all high-risk groups, such as commercial sex workers, injecting drug users, and hemophiliacs (Dowsatt 1999). Tragically, following years of decline, recent data from the United States (Kellog, McFarland, and Katz 1999), Canada (Martindale et al. 2001), Europe (Dukers et al. 2000), and Australia (Van De Ven and French 1998) all show increasing rates of STIs and HIV/AIDS among gay and bisexual men. Explanations for this reversal include improved HIV therapy combined with "epidemic fatigue" or "safer-sex burn-out."

Table 5.1. *Application of Subjective Utility Theory to the perception of risky sexual activity*

Option	Utility	Prob. of AIDS	Expected utility
O_1 = Abstinence	U_1	p_1	$U_1 + p_1 U_A$
O_2 = Safer sex	U_2	p_2	$U_2 + p_2 U_A$
O_3 = Risky sex	U_3	p_3	$U_3 + p_3 U_A$

Source: Table is after Pinkerton and Abramson (1992:562).

This final factor acknowledges that, from gay men in developed nations to heterosexual men in developing countries, there is resistance to condom use in spite of the known risk of HIV/AIDS. Pinkerton and Abramson (1992) utilize subjective expected utility theory to explain this phenomenon. This proposes that a rational actor faced with multiple possible uncertain outcomes will choose that with the greatest subjective expected utility, that is, the greatest perceived reward. Their model, shown in Table 5.1, assumes that a person faces three greatly simplified choices, which the person tries to link to his or her perceived risk of contracting HIV, and eventually AIDS. These options are (1) abstinence (O_1), (2) safer sex (O_2) and (3) risky sex (O_3). To each option the actor assigns a utility value u_1 denoting his or her perceived pleasurable benefits and a corresponding probability value p_1 marking his or her subjective view of the risk of contracting AIDS as a result of this behavior. A final assumption is that the actor has a negative view of the utility of contracting AIDS (U_A), which, like all the other parameters, is perceived and hence subjective.

Subjective expected utility theory predicts that rational actors will choose the option O_i for which the compound utility $u_1 + p_1 U_A$ is maximal. From this expectation, Pinkerton and Abramson (1992) show that, when $u_3 + p_3 U_A > u_1 + p_1 U_A$ and $u_3 + p_3 U_A > u_2 + p_2 U_A$ (i.e., the actor prefers risky sex to no sex or safer sex), then the behavior is rational. The authors note that the connotation "rational" is limited to the theory and its model. What is important is not that risky sex is rational, *it is not*, but rather that it can be *perceived* as a reasonable gamble, given the benefits, under a certain set of assumptions and perceptions. From this starting point the next question to ask is this: "Do people (men in particular) highly value risky sex, that is unprotected sex, even though they are aware of the risks of contracting HIV/AIDS?"

Looking at the cases of sub-Saharan African and Thai heterosexual men and gay men in developed countries, the answer appears to be a resounding "yes." In sub-Saharan Africa, Caldwell (1999:247) points to the failure of social marketing condoms in a region where men seek to maximize flesh-to-flesh contact by means of vaginal tightening and drying (Brown et al. 1993). For Thai men, VanLandingham and Grandjean (1997:134) report that respondents frequent reply to questions concerning nonuse of condoms with prostitutes participants with, "Why bother going [if you have to use a condom]?" Similarly, recent AIDS incidence increases for gay men in developed countries correlate with increased episodes of unprotected anal, and oral, sex (see Van De Ven and French 1998).

In addition to the physical pleasures of high-risk sexual practices, we must consider perceived psychological benefits. These are highlighted in the Flowers, Hart, and Marriott (1999) study of gay men in Glasgow, Scotland, who seek sexual unions in public environments. In spite of high knowledge levels of HIV/AIDS transmission, this group had different social constructions of "risk." Risk was negatively associated with the threat of attack or police arrest, rather than the increased probability of contracting a sexually transmitted disease. What was equally important was that men were united on the positive aspects of risk, perceiving the danger of attack or arrest as a large portion of the pleasure of anonymous sexual encounters in public places.

Resistance to changing sexual behavior among heterosexual and gay men who are aware of the risk of HIV/AIDS means that anthropologists and demographers must consider both the perceived physical and psychological aspects of sex in the context of pleasurable, rather than solely procreative, behavior. At the same time, recognition of cultural mediation of innate biological drives constitutes a convergence of research interests for anthropological demographers and human evolutionary ecologists. To exemplify this potential, I turn again to my own work, this time detailing the interaction between the long-standing view of strong male sexual drive and the emergence of female education among the Ariaal Rendille.

The indigenous concept of a strong male sex drive was revealed to me in a 1996 survey designed to delineate Ariaal Rendille sexual culture. Conducted in collaboration with my colleague Elliot Fratkin from Smith College (Roth et al. 1999), the survey asked questions about sexual attitudes, practices and behaviors, and knowledge of HIV/AIDS and STIs. The survey took place in the Ariaal Rendille community of Karare–Nasakakwe, a settlement established by the African Inland Church as a refuge for Ariaal and Rendille families impoverished by the recurrent droughts of the 1970s (Fratkin 1998). Today the inhabitants of Karare practice agropastoralism, growing maize and sorghum and selling milk from their cattle herds in the Marsabit markets, while the adjacent community of Nasakakwe features irrigation agriculture, and likewise sells grains and fruits in Marsabit.

One initially perplexing survey result was a pronounced sexual difference in attitudes toward premarital sex, in response to this question: "Should a man or woman be a virgin at the time of his or her marriage?" When asked in the male context, agreement was high between the sexes, with 97% of men and 89% of women answering that a man should practice sex before marriage. This agreement was lost when women's virginity was the subject; a majority of women (60%) stated that a woman should be a virgin at marriage, compared with a minority (16%) of men. We attempted to clarify these sex-specific results in individual interviews with both male and female Ariaal, who interpreted the results in the following manner.

Agreement on male premarital sex arises from the belief that adult males must have regular sexual activity, before, within, and outside marriage. Because the question focused on premarital sexuality, results were explained in the context of the economic role of unmarried men. Ariaal culture is maintained and regulated by an elaborate age-set system so closely aligned with that of the Rendille system that anthropologists debate which was the originator of the system, the Rendille or the Samburu, both parent populations to the Ariaal (see Beaman 1991). Like those in the Rendille system, Ariaal age sets operate on multiples of fourteen years, although the opening and closing dates are slightly different for the two systems, and the Ariaal use Samburu names for specific age sets.

Age sets open with male circumcision ceremonies, marking the transition from boy to warrior for males. In this stage of the male life cycle, warriors provide both labor and defense of livestock for an eleven-year period before they marry en masse. During this period, warriors are not expected to remain celibate, for a man must satisfy his sexual drive. Rather, warriors, known by the Maa term, *moran*, are encouraged to participate in the premarital tradition known as *nykeri*. In this tradition, warriors present an unmarried girl's parents successive strands of beads, which are sequentially placed around the girl's neck by her mother. Once "beaded," these girls, known as *nkeryi*, initiate long-term sexual relationships with the gift-giving warrior. Warriors and *nkeryi* usually do not marry, instead taking spouses designated by their parents upon the successful completion of brideprice negotiations. Thus although warriors and *nkeryi* are expected to have full sexual intercourse, procreation is severely discouraged, because it raises biological questions of paternity and socioeconomic issues concerning inheritance.

The nykeri tradition maintains Ariaal pastoral economy by sustaining intergenerational relationships between moran and elders. Relationships between these two subgroups are strained, as elders convert the product of unmarried men's labor into brideprice to polygynously marry younger women, whereas moran are forbidden to marry for eleven years. The tradition therefore benefits unmarried and married men alike, while ensuring cultural reproduction for the entire group. One group who seemingly does not benefit in any way is young women. During interviews, adolescent girls told of accepting beads under the impression that they were gifts from their mothers, only realizing after the fact that they meant acceptance of full sexual relationships with older, sometimes unknown, moran. The tradition also leads to the sexual initiation of very young girls, sometimes as young as ten to twelve years of age. Because both age at sexual debut and rate of partner change are important parameters in the risk of contracting STIs (Korenromp et al. 2000), the nykeri adolescent sexual tradition represents high-risk sexual behavior.

Ariaal men and women interpreted the large minority of women stating that premarital sex is wrong for a girl as reflecting parental investment in their daughters' education. They stressed that parents would protect the investment they made in their daughters' education by not allowing them to participate in the nykeri tradition, which could lead to pregnancy at an early age and the termination of their daughters' education. This answer was particularly interesting to me, for I had previously investigated the advent and effects of female education in both the lowland Rendille village of Korr and the highland Ariaal community of Karare–Nasakakwe (Roth 1991; Roth et al. 2001). Contrary to Caldwell's (1982) view that parental selection of which children to educate constituted "a lucky dip," I hypothesized that culture-specific factors influence parental decision making. For example, recognizing the Rendille traditions of primogeniture, patrilineal descent, patrilocal postmarital residence, and the economic contribution of children to livestock care, I predicted that children selected for schooling would overwhelmingly be latter-born sons from poor families. These boys would not be in line to inherit the family herd and would not have many animals to care for at home. In contrast to first-born boys who would inherit the family herds, and sons from livestock-rich households, these poor latter-born sons could be spared from the pastoral economy and sent to school. A subsequent analysis of a sample of over 900 children from Korr confirmed this hypothesis through logistic regression methodology. With the use of dichotomous yes–no responses to the question "Has this child ever been to school?" as the dependent variable, independent variables included measures of

Table 5.2. *Results of logistic regressions: boys versus girls selected for schooling*

Date of study	Location	Children (n)	Max. likelihood coeff.	Odds ratio
1987	Korr	931	+0.7822***	2.186
1996	Korr	546	+0.8887***	2.455
1996	Karare	1,065	+0.5532***	1.739

*** $p < 0.001$.

household wealth, birth order, number of sibs ever in school, and child's sex. Results showed that one highly significant variable was offspring sex, with sons selected for schooling more than twice as often as daughters (odds ratio = 2.186).

I conducted subsequent studies of parental decision-making strategies in both Rendille and Ariaal communities. Although different cultural settings demanded different independent variables, offspring sex remained a highly significant variable in all studies, as shown in Table 5.2. The reason why parents favor boys over girls for schooling is apparently embedded in Rendille or Ariaal household economics. Time-allocation studies by Fratkin and Smith (1994) show that girls provide a significant amount of household labor from an early age, making them hard to remove from the family household labor pool for schooling. Later, girls marry and move away from the natal home. Although bridewealth is an effort to compensate the bride's family for her lost labor, a daughter's children, and the potential labor they constitute, are also lost to the natal home, transferring to the husband's patriline with marriage. Under these cultural conditions, a daughter make a poor choice for schooling, because parental investment will be lost upon her marriage.

In spite of this parental economic rationality, some girls *are* selected for schooling. Beginning with Caldwell's (1979) seminal analysis of Nigerian survey data, two decades of research link maternal education with decreased fertility and child–infant mortality (United Nations 1995; Cleland and Kaufmann 1998). Given this history, there are surprisingly few studies establishing culture-specific pathways between fertility and child schooling at the household level in Africa. This are even fewer studies seeking links between female education and STIs. Noting this dearth of information and guided by the results of the 1996 survey, my colleague Dr. Elizabeth Ngugi of the University of Nairobi and I returned to Karare–Nasakakwe in 1998 with the goal of testing a model linking female education negatively to the nykeri tradition and positively with the

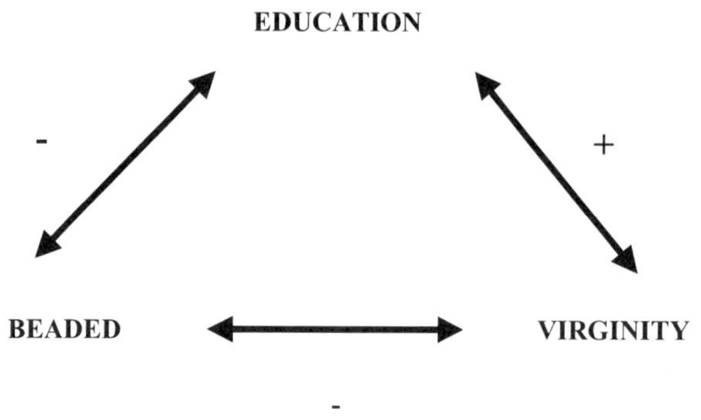

Figure 5.1. Hypothesized relationships between variables in a model linking female education to the nykeri tradition of adolescent sexuality.

concept of virginity at marriage, as shown in Figure 5.1. We interviewed 127 adolescent girls, using a shortened form of the 1996 questionnaire combining attitudinal questions about premarital sex with questions about education and whether the interviewee had ever been beaded. We used a log-linear model that generated maximum likelihood coefficients for variable interaction, that is, attitudes about virginity × ever educated, ever beaded × ever educated, to analyze the data. Figure 5.2 presents the coefficients linking the three independent variables. All three interactions were signed correctly, and all were statistically significant.

These results were encouraging, but to more rigorously test the hypothesis, we looked for differences in age at sexual initiation between beaded and never-beaded women to ascertain if parents were holding their

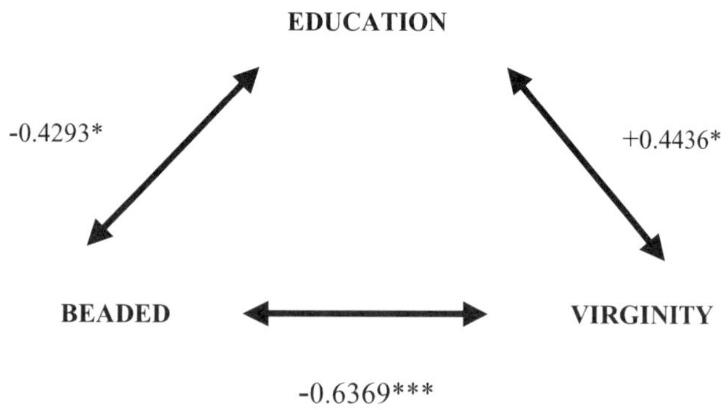

Figure 5.2. Realized relationships between variables in a model linking female education to the nykeri tradition of adolescent sexuality, shown by maximum likelihood coefficients denoting variable interaction.

educated daughters back from the nykeri tradition. To this end I surveyed 181 married and unmarried men and women in Karare–Nasakakwe from May through June, 2001. Survey questions asked men and women about age at sexual debut, number of partners in the past three years, and what subpopulation the partners were from (nkeryi, moran, married men, and married women). Men were asked if they had ever beaded nkeryi and, if so, how many nkeryi they beaded. Women were asked if they were ever beaded and, if so, at what age and by how many warriors.

Results were analyzed by using the SAS survival analysis procedures LIFETEST and PHREG routines, which modeled the time to sexual debut as "failure event." We first compared male and female age distributions for sexual initiation, regardless of beading history. Men (n = 97) featured significantly ($p = 0.009$) later average age (median = 18.0) than women ($n = 84$, median = 16.0). These results initially appear to be contradictory to the Ariaal view that men have strong sexual drives that must be fulfilled. However, this biological perspective is culturally mediated by the Ariaal definition of "manhood," which only begins after circumcision. Male respondents in this survey reported entering their first sexual activity only after they were circumcised. Male education does not alter this pattern, with LIFETEST revealing no significant difference in average age at sexual debut for educated relative to never educated men.

For females the situation is quite different, with analysis revealing a highly significant ($p < 0.0001$) difference between average age at sexual debut for beaded ($n = 20$, median = 13.0) versus nonbeaded ($n = 64$, median = 17.0) women. These different survival curves, shown in Figure 5.3, confirmed our hypothesis that beaded girls began sexual activities at an earlier age than never-beaded females.

Next, we used the SAS procedure PROC PHREG to calculate covariate effects on failure time distribution, by use of the Cox (1972) proportional hazard model. Our covariates were categorical variables for education and beading, respectively dichotomized as never versus ever educated in the variable Education and ever versus never beaded for the variable Beaded. Results of this analysis showed a risk ratio associated with Education of 0.340, meaning that educated females have approximately one-third the hazard of sexual debut as uneducated women. In contrast, the risk ratio for the Beaded covariate yielded a value of 2.693, indicating that beaded girls feature more than two and one-half times the hazard relative to nonbeaded girls.

All these results are based on very small samples, and therefore they must be treated with caution. It is, however, very encouraging to see samples collected at different times exhibiting such consistent results. In this case, a seemingly innocent question about premarital virginity revealed sex-specific cultural constructs of sexual behavior that helped us

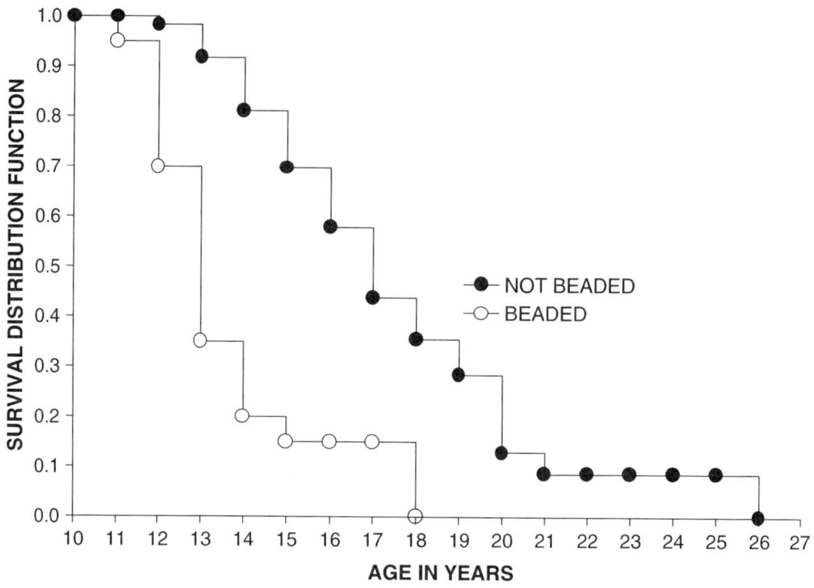

Figure 5.3. Survival distribution curves for age at sexual debut (beaded vs. never-beaded women).

understand the role of sexuality, defined both biologically and culturally, in maintaining the traditional Ariaal pastoral economy as well as the new feature of female education in initiating change in Ariaal sexual culture. In addition, analyses helped delineate pathways through which female education may affect parameters other than fertility and mortality.

On a broader scale, these results show that both anthropological demography and human evolutionary ecology could benefit from considering human sexuality as a meeting ground of culture and biology. Such a joint emphasis has the potential to provide valuable information and insights into topics ranging from the resistance to behavioral change in light of the AIDS pandemic to the unlinking of sex and procreation in noncontracepting and contracepting populations, both historical and contemporary.

Final Ground: Demographic Transitions

This book's main theme is that anthropological demographers and human evolutionary ecologists have many shared, if unrecognized, common research interests. To conclude this section, and this book, I touch on the topic of how these groups could benefit from adopting the strong points of each perspective by using the example of demographic transitions. As pointed out in the book, *The Continuing Demographic Transition* (Jones et al. 1997), there are two major demographic transitions. One is the historic reduction of European fertility levels. The second, sometimes referred to as "The Contraceptive Revolution," was the recent dramatic lowering of fertility rates throughout Asia, South America, and selected countries within sub-Saharan Africa. Anthropological demography and human evolutionary ecology have important theoretical interests in both transitions. The former's interest, and perhaps its very reason for being taken seriously by classically trained demographers, stems from the Princeton European Fertility Project's findings that historic European fertility decline is best explained with reference to regional ideational and behavior patterns, read culture, rather than standard economic variables (Coale and Watkins 1986). Human evolutionary ecology sees both transitions as challenges to their overall paradigm of fitness maximization; in particular, fertility declines in the face of increasing resources break linkages between cultural and reproductive success as well as overall lowered fitness levels (see Borgerhoff Mulder 1998).

In response to these challenges, anthropological demographers stressed the role of culture as ideology and used qualitative data to understand demographic change within a cultural context, exemplified in the work of Schneider and Schneider (1998), who detail the roles of regional political economy and cultural processes in the fertility decline of Sicilian artisans. Predictably, human evolutionary ecology took a quantitative approach, represented by Perusse's (1993) argument that the linkage between cultural and biological success is not truly broken because wealthier men achieve higher copulation rates than their less successful counterparts. Where will each field go in the near future, and what can one learn from the other?

Anthropological demography is most united on what is *not* helpful in investigating past and contemporary fertility decline. They join rank in rejecting ideational diffusionism (Kreager 1998; Carter 2001), a position hearkening back to Malinowski's (1928:37) remark:

> [W]henever one culture "borrows" from another, it always transforms and readapts the objects or customs borrowed. . . . In this process of readaptation the form and function, often the very nature, of the object is deeply modified, it has to be, in short reinvented.

We have already seen one concrete example of this position in the Bledsoe et al. (1998) analysis of Gambian women's use of Western contraceptive technology to maximize a mother's physical endowment, or hapo. A second example of new behavior arising from the context of long-established models is found in Fricke's (1997a) analysis of male contraceptive innovators in Tamang society described in Chapter 3. Part of his fieldwork focused on five men who first consented to undertake vasectomies in the village of Timling. None of these men exhibited any "innovative" behavior before this operation. All had their marriages arranged by senior family members, the most traditional arrangement as described in Chapter 3. Four of the five married cross cousins, a preferred Tamang marriage form, and the same number contributed labor services to their in-laws after marriage. Only one was literate, and only one had spent any time outside his natal village for a month or more prior to marrying. Where, then, did the motivation to limit family size through a new, foreign, and highly intrusive operation originate?

Fricke suggests that this innovative behavior arises from conservative Tamang behavior and is linked to the ethos of exchange and reciprocity that permeates Tamang culture. In this case, the reciprocity is not between exogamous clans but rather between parents and children. Parents feel that they benefit from children's labor, and that children cement the ties between households united in marriage. In exchange, parents believe children should be provided for through inheriting parental property; too many children and the inheritance may be too small to start their own household. Hence there is the need to limit children even in this pronatalist culture, so that each receives a "fair" inheritance. Rather than constituting innovative behavior, Tamang incipient male fertility limitation is interpreted by Fricke as reflecting the established moral good of exchange and reciprocity.

For anthropological demographers, the process of reinventing objects or customs also negates recent attempts to scientifically study the spread of memes, or the new field of memetics (Blackmore 1999). Dawkins (1989:12) coined the term "memes" as the cultural analogue to the biological concept of selfish genes. Like the latter, memes are seen as essentially mindless replicators:

> I think that a new kind of replicator has recently emerged on this very planet. . . . It is still in its infancy, still drifting clumsily about in its primeval soup, but already it is achieving evolutionary change at a rate that leaves the old gene panting far behind. . . . The new soup is the soup of human culture.

Cultural anthropologists for the most part object to memes because of their emphasis on imitation and replication per se. As the previous quote from Malinowski points out, they think emphasis should be on change in borrowing, not merely replication and imitation.

If anthropological demographers reject memes, what do they have to offer? One important contribution is the emphasis on giving voice to the people they study. In his influential article on the concept of culture in demography, Hammel (1990:456) suggested that this elusive property could be considered an "evaluative conversation." Anthropological demography has led the way in presenting and evaluating actual conversations people have about familial demographic concerns. With respect to the ongoing demographic transition, one of the strongest examples of this is the Rutenberg and Watkins (1997) article, "The Buzz Outside the Clinics: Conversations and Contraception in Nyanza Province, Kenya." Here we are presented with the words of Kenyan women as they attempt to understand new contraceptive alternatives on a wide variety of levels, ranging from understanding how the clinic actually works to coping with the concept of Western fertility limitation and its effects on family life.

Human evolutionary ecology, which sees itself as an "anomaly within sociocultural anthropology due to its hypothetico-deductive research strategies" (Winterhalder and Smith 2001:51), has not embraced qualitative data in general and instead successfully focused on raising the standard of excellence for quantitative analyses of sociocultural human behavior. Yet, Worthman (1995:597) made the following important comment on the human evolutionary ecologist Monique Borgerhoff Mulders' (1995) inclusion of quotations in her analysis of changing Kipsigis bride-price:

> A statistical approach can, as in this case, identify outliers, but the significance of the outliers in reinforcing normative behavior may be missed. In this regard Borgerhoff Mulder's use of direct quotes and specific cases bears as important a methodological message for behavioral ecologists as statistical methods do for ethnographers. Quotes and cases provide glimpses of working logic and social life essential to the task of studying emic considerations of value. We need much more of this.

We do indeed need much more of this, that is, qualitative data and peoples' voices in human evolutionary ecology, where it can support, instead of replace, quantitative data and hypothesis testing. At the same time, I think anthropological demography can benefit greatly by at least partially adopting human evolutionary ecology's well-articulated hypothetico-deductive framework. This is well represented in Borgerhoff Mulder's (1998; Luttbeg, Borgerhoff Mulder, and Mangel 2000) outline of three alternative hypotheses to account for recent demographic transitions. The first proposes that fertility declines represent an adaptive adjustment to the quantity–quality fitness tradeoff predicted by life history theory, a train of thought represented by Kaplan and Lancaster's (1999) Competitive Labor-Market Model. The second views lowered fertility rates as stemming from Darwinian, but cultural, mechanisms of inheritance, represented by Boyd and Richerson's (1985) model of the historic demographic transition as mass imitation of behavior linking small family size to socioeconomic success. The third sees reduced fertility as maladaptive outcomes arising from the ill fit between rapidly changing technological and environmental change, exemplified by Barkow's (1989) consideration of contraceptives as breaking the evolutionary linkage between sex and reproduction. Respectively, these correspond to the subfields of human evolutionary ecology discussed in Chapter 2, human behavioral ecology, Dual Inheritance Theory, and evolutionary psychology. Because each field can generate specific, testable hypotheses, each can proceed on the basis of the verification or rejection of previously constructed models. With its roots in cultural anthropology's concern with meaning, description, and personal interpretation, anthropological demography simply cannot compete with this scientific firepower.

Generating hypotheses also leads to methodological advances. Human evolutionary ecology has fruitfully tested theories of demographic transitions by means of dynamic computer simulation, attempting to delineate optimization strategies by which couples attempt to maximize the number of children or the amount of wealth they can leave their descendents. Using either theoretical values (Rogers 1995) or data derived from empirical field studies (see Luttbeg, Borgerhoff Mulder, and Mangel 2000; Mace 2000) as input variables, these exercises have yielded important results. Mace's (2000) simulations based on data from Gabbra pastoralists of northern Kenya revealed that neither improving subsistence base reliability nor reducing the risk of child mortality has nearly as much impact on fertility as does raising parental costs of children and providing them with an inheritance. In a similar manner, Luttbeg, Borgerhoff Mulder, and Mangel (2000), working with data from Kenyan Kipsigi agropastoralists, delineated a culture-specific decision rule weighted toward "wealth maximization" as a combined function of maximizing children and wealth.

Of course, simulation has a strong history in anthropological demography (Wachter 1978; Howell 1979), and today it uses the tools of agent-based modeling (Kohler and Gumerman 2000). Anthropological applications of these principles range from modeling the evolution of cooperation (Pepper and Smuts 2000), through assessing the effects of different marriage rules on demographic structure (Small 2000), to the study of prehistoric culture change (Dean et al. 2000). One theme uniting all this work is the ability, in the words of Gould (1990:320), "to rewind the tape," that is, to repeatedly simulate processes from beginning to end in order to observe both midpoint and cumulative effects of simple decision rules applied over time. Demographic applications are just now emerging, represented by an upcoming book derived from a Max Planck conference in 2000 on Agent Based Computational Demography (Billari and Fürnkranz-Prskawetz 2003). There is great potential for this approach to test evolutionary hypotheses by using historical demographic databases listed by Voland (2000) and Clark and Low (2001). Basing simulations on historic, empirical data can also avoid the construction of agent-based models representing what Maynard-Smith (1995) called "fact-free science."

Finally, we can ask this question: What can mainstream demography offer anthropological demography or human evolutionary ecology? First, with respect to the historic demographic transition, there are now numerous historical databases amenable to historic demographic methodologies of family reconstruction. Voland (1995) and Clark and Low (2001) provide concrete examples of how these can be utilized for testing evolutionary hypotheses. Second, with regard to the ongoing demographic transition, one of the strengths of recent demographic analyses has been to consider the unit of analysis the couple, rather than the individual. Rather than focusing exclusively on women, or, far more infrequently, men, recent research has delineated reproductive couples' decision-making processes with respect to family fertility. For human evolutionary ecology, such an approach parallels Low's (2000) emphasis on coalitions as a valid unit of natural selection and analysis. For anthropological demography, consideration of couples, rather than an exclusive focus on wives, or husbands, or separate lovers, incorporates Greenhalgh's (1995b:24) point that gender entails the study of men as well as women.

Yet by far the most important feature of current demography that can benefit both anthropological demography and human evolutionary ecology is the sense of interest and openness that pervades demography today. Whether this results from a lack of demographic theory or a true intellectual curiosity, the result is a distinct lack of dogma within demographic circles, at least relative to the other two anthropological approaches. Whether assessing evolutionary theories in light of recent fertility reduction (Wachter and Bulatao 2003) or seeking "thicker" data than normally found in survey data (see Orubuloye, Caldwell, and Caldwell 1997:1197), today's demographers appear fully capable of considering either cultural or biological explanations of demographic patterns. Only when anthropological demographers and human evolutionary ecologists exhibit the same openness can there be true hope for a future in which both perspectives can contribute to a synthetic theory of human demography. If this text contributes to this openness by initiating a dialogue based on common research interests, then it has made a worthwhile contribution.

References Cited

Abramson, Paul R. and Steven D. Pinkerton. 1995a. *Sexual Nature Sexual Culture*. Chicago: University of Chicago Press.

1995b. *With Pleasure: Thoughts on the Human Nature of Sexuality*. New York: Oxford University Press.

Abu-Lughod, Lila. 1986. *Veiled Sentiment: Honor and Poetry in a Bedouin Society*. Berkeley: University of California Press.

Alcock, John. 2001. *The Triumph of Sociobiology*. Oxford: Oxford University Press.

Alexander, J. C. 1988. *Action and its Environments: Towards a New Synthesis*. New York: Columbia University Press.

Alexander, Richard. 1974. The evolution of social behavior. *Annual Review of Ecology and Systematics* 5:325–383.

1987. *The Biology of Moral Systems*. New York: Aldine de Gruyter.

1993. Evolution and ethics. In *Evolutionary Ethics*. Matthew H. Nitecki and Doris V. Nitecki, editors, pages 163–198. Albany: State University of New York.

Alexander, Richard and K. Noonan. 1979. Concealment of ovulation, parental care and human social evolution. In *Evolutionary Biology and Human Social Behavior: An Evolutionary Perspective*. Napoleon Chagnon and William Irons, editors, pages 436–453. North Scituate, MA: Duxbury Press.

Aries, Phillipe. 1962. *Centuries of Childhood*. London: Cape.

Arnhart, Larry. 1998. *Darwinian Natural Right: The Biological Ethics of Human Nature*. Albany: State University of New York.

Axelrod, R. 1984. *The Evolution of Cooperation*. New York: Basic Books.

Bailey, Robert C. and Phillip Aunger. 1995. Sexuality, infertility and sexually transmitted diseases among farmers and foragers in Central Africa. In *Sexual Nature, Sexual Culture*. Paul Abramson and Steven Pinkerton, editors, pages 195–222. Chicago: University of Chicago Press.

Balk, Deborah. 2000. To marry and bear children? The demographic consequences of infibulation in Sudan. In *Female "Circumcision" in Africa: Culture, Controversy and Change*. Bettina Shell-Duncan and Ylva Hernlund, editors, pages 55–72. Boulder, CO: Lynne Rienner.

Ball, Helen and Catherine Panter-Brick. 2001. Child survival and the modulation of parental investment: Physiological and hormonal considerations. In *Reproductive Ecology and Human Evolution*. Peter T. Ellison, editor, pages 249–267. New York: Aldine de Gruyter.

Barkow, Jerome. 1989. *Darwin, Sex and Status*. Toronto: University of Toronto Press.

Barkow, Jerome and Nigel Burley. 1980. Human fertility, evolutionary biology and the Demographic Transition. *Ethology and Sociobiology* 1:163–180.

Barkow, J. H., Cosmides, L. and J. Tooby. 1992. *The Adapted Mind: Evolutionary Psychology and the Generation of Culture*. Oxford: Oxford University Press.

Barrett, Louise, Robin Dunbar, and John Lycett. 2002. *Human Evolutionary Psychology*. Princeton, NJ: Princeton University Press.

Barth, Frederick. 1959a. *Political Leadership among the Swat Pathans*. London School of Economics Monograph Series. New York: Humanities Press.

1959b. Segmentary opposition and the theory of games: A study of Pathan organization. *Journal of the Royal Anthropological Institute* 89: 5–21.

Bartlett, Thad, Robert Sussman, and J. Cheverud. 1993. Infant killing in primates: A review of observed cases with specific reference to the sexual selection hypothesis. *American Anthropologist* 95:958–990.

Basu, Alaka Malwade. 1997. Underinvestment in children: A reorganization of the evidence on the determinants of child mortality. In *The Continuing Demographic Transition*. Gavin W. Jones, Robert W. Douglas, John C. Caldwell, and Rennie M. D'Souza, editors, pages 307–332. Oxford: Clarendon Press.

Basu, Alaka Malwade and Peter Aaby. 1998. *The Methods and Uses of Anthropological Demography*. Oxford: Clarendon Press.

Beaman, Ann. 1981. *The Rendille Age-Set System in Ethnographic Context: Adaptation and Integration in a Nomadic Society*. Ph.D. Dissertation, Boston University.

Bates, Daniel and Elliot Fratkin. 1998. *Cultural Anthropology*. Boston: Pearson, Allyn and Bacon.

Beckerman, Stephen and Paul Valentine. 2002a. *Cultures of Multiple Fathers: The Theory and Practice of Partible Paternity in Lowland South America*. Gainesville: University Press of Florida.

2002b. Introduction: The concept of partible paternity among native South Americans. In *Cultures of Multiple Fathers: The Theory and Practice of Partible Paternity in Lowland South America*. Stephen Beckerman and Paul Valentine, editors, pages 1–3. Gainesville: University Press of Florida.

Beckerman, Stephen, Roberto Lizarralde, Manuel Lizarralde, Jie Bai, Carol Bellew, Sissel Schroeder, Din Dajani, Lisa Walkup, Mayhsin Hsuing, Nikole Rawlins, and Michelle Palermo. 2002. The Bari partible paternity project, Phase One. In *Cultures of Multiple Fathers: The Theory and Practice of Partible Paternity in Lowland South America*. Stephen Beckerman and Paul Valentine, editors, pages 27–41. Gainesville: University Press of Florida.

Bell, Duran. 1998. Wealth transfers occasioned by marriage: A comparative reconsideration. In *Kinship, Networks and Exchange*. Thomas Schweizer and Douglas R. White, editors, pages 187–209. Cambridge: Cambridge University Press.

Berlin, B. and Paul Kay. 1969. *Basic Color Terms: Their Universality and Evolution*. Berkeley: University of California Press.

Betzig, Laura. 1997a. People are animals. In *Human Nature: A Critical Reader*. Laura Betzig, editor, pages 1–20. Oxford: Oxford University Press.

1997b. *Human Nature: A Critical Reader*. Oxford: Oxford University Press.

Betzig, Laura, Monique Borgerhoff Mulder, and Paul Turke. 1988. *Human Reproductive Behavior: A Darwinian Perspective*. Cambridge: Cambridge University Press.

Billari, Francesco C., Fürnkranz-Prskawetz, Alexia. 2003. *Agent-Based Computational Demography: Using Simulation to Improve our Understanding of Demographic Behavior*. Heidelberg: Physica-Verlag.

Blackmore, Susan J. 1999. *The Meme Machine*. Oxford: Oxford University Press.

Bledsoe, Caroline. 1990. The politics of children: Fosterage and the social management of fertility among the Mende of Sierra Leone. In *Births and Power: Social Change and the Politics of Reproduction*. W. Penn Handwerker, editor, pages 81–100. Philadelphia: University of Pennsylvania Press.

2002. *Contingent Lives: Fertility, Time, and Aging in West Africa*. Chicago: University of Chicago Press.

Bledsoe, Caroline and Allan G. Hill. 1998. Social norms, natural fertility and the resumption of post-partum "contact" in the Gambia. In *The Methods and Uses of Anthropological Demography*. Alaka M. Basu and Peter Aaby, editors, pages. 268–297. Oxford: Clarendon Press.

Bledsoe, Caroline, Fatoumatta Banja, and Allan G. Hill. 1998. Reproductive mishaps and Western contraception: An African challenge to fertility theory. *Population and Development Review* 24:15–58.

Bledsoe, Caroline, Allan G. Hill, G. d'Alessandro, and P. Langerock. 1994. Constructing natural fertility: The use of Western contraceptive technologies in rural Gambia. *Population and Development Review* 20:81–113.

Bledsoe, Caroline, John Casterline, Jennifer Johnson-Kuhn, and John Haaga. 1999. *Critical Perspectives on Schooling and Fertility in the Developing World*. Washington, DC: National Academy Press.

Blurton-Jones, Nicholas. 1987. Bushman birth spacing: A test for optimal interbirth spacing. *Ethology and Sociobiology* 7:91–105.

1990. Three sensible paradigms for research on evolution and human behavior. *Ethology and Sociobiology* 11:353–359.

Blurton-Jones, Nicholas and R. Sibley. 1978. Testing adaptiveness of culturally determined behavior: Do Bushmen women maximize their reproductive success by spacing births widely and foraging seldom? In *Human Behavior and Adaptation*. Society for the Study of Human Behavior, Symposium 18. Nicholast Blurton-Jones and Vernon Reynolds, editors. Pages 135–158. London: Taylor and Francis.

Bock, John. 2002. Evolutionary theory and the search for a unified theory of fertility. *American Journal of Human Biology* 14(2):145–148.

Boddy, Janice. 1982. Womb as oasis: The symbolic content of pharaonic circumcision in rural northern Sudan. *American Ethnologist* 9:682–698.

1989. *Wombs and Alien Spirits: Women, Men and the Zar Cult in Northern Sudan*. Madison: University of Wisconsin Press.

Boehm, Christopher. 1996. Emergency decisions, cultural-selection mechanics and group selection. *Current Anthropology* 37:763–793.

Bongaarts, John. 1980. Does malnutrition affect fecundity: A summary of the evidence. *Science* 208:565–569.

1982. The fertility inhibiting effects of the intermediate fertility variables. *Studies in Family Planning* 13:179–189.

Boone, James. 1983. Noble family structure and expansionist warfare in the Late Middle Ages: A socioecological approach. In *Rethinking Human Adaptation: Biological and Cultural Models*. Rada Dyson-Hudson and Michael A. Little, editors, pages 79–96. Boulder, Co: Westview.

1986. Parental investment and elite family structure in preindustrial states: A case study of late Medieval-Early Modern Portuguese genealogies. *American Anthropologist* 88:859–878.

1988. Parental investment, social subordination, and population processes among 15th and 16th century Portuguese nobility. In *Human Reproductive Behaviour: A Darwinian Perspective*. Laura Betzig, Monique Borgerhoff Mulder, and Paul Turke, editors, pages 201–219. Cambridge: Cambridge University Press.

Borgerhoff Mulder, Monique. 1987. Adaptation and evolutionary approaches to anthropology. *Man* 22:25–41.

1988a. Kipsigis brideprice payments. In *Human Reproductive Behavior: A Darwinian Perspective*. Laura Betzig, Monique Borgerhoff Mulder, and Paul Turke, editors, pages 65–82. Cambridge: Cambridge University Press.

1988b. Early maturing Kipsigi women have higher reproductive success than later maturing women, and cost more to marry. *Behavioral Ecology and Sociobiology* 24:145–153.

1990. Kipsigi's preference for wealthy men: Evidence for female choice in mammals. *Behavioural Ecology and Sociobiology* 27:255–264.

1992. Reproductive decisions. In *Evolutionary Ecology and Human Behavior*. Eric Alden Smith and Bruce Winterhalder, editors, pages 339–374. New York: Aldine de Gruyter.

1995. Bridewealth and its correlates: Quantifying change over time. *Current Anthropology* 36:573–603.

1996. Response to environmental novelty: Changes in men's marriage strategies in a rural Kenyan community. In *Evolution of Social Behaviour Patterns in Primates and Man*. W. Runciman, John Maynard Smith, and R. I. M. Dunbar, editors, pages 203–233. Oxford: Oxford University Press.

1998. The demographic transition: Are we any closer to an evolutionary explanation? *Trends in Ecology and Evolution* 13(7):266–270.

1999. Brothers and sisters: How sibling interactions affect optimal parental allocation. *Human Nature* 9:119–162.

Borgerhoff Mulder, Monique and Daniel Sellen. 1994. Pastoral decision-making: A behavioural ecological perspective. In *African Pastoralist Systems: An Integrated Approach*. Elliot Fratkin, Kathleen Galvin, and Eric Abella Roth, editors, pages 231–237. Boulder, Co: Lynne Rienner.

Bosserup, Ester. 1970. *Women's Roles in Economic Development*. New York: St. Martin's Press.

Boswell, John. 1988. *The Kindness of Strangers: The Abandonment of Children in Western Europe From Late Antiquity to the Renaissance*. Harmondsworth, England: Penguin Books.

Bourdieu, P. 1976. Marriage strategies as strategies of social reproduction. In *Family and Society: Selections from Annales*. R. Forster and O. Ranum, editors, pages. 117–144. Baltimore: Johns Hopkins University Press.

Bowlby, John. 1988. *A Secure Base: Parent-Child Attachment and Healthy Human Development*. New York: Basic Books.

Boyd, Robert and Peter Richerson. 1985. *Culture and the Evolutionary Process*. Chicago: University of Chicago Press.

1990. Culture and cooperation. In *Beyond Self-Interest*. J. J. Mansbridge, editor. Pages 111–132. Chicago: University of Chicago Press.

1992. Punishment allows the evolution of cooperation (or anything else) in sizeable groups. *Journal of Theoretical Biology* 145:331–342.

Bradley, Candice. 1995. Women's empowerment and fertility decline in western Kenya. In *Situating Fertility*. Susan Greenhalgh, editor, pages 157–178. Cambridge: Cambridge University Press.

Brown, Donald E. 1991. *Human Universals*. Philadelphia: Temple University Press.

Brown, Judith, B. Okako, B. Ayowa, and Richard C. Brown. 1993. Dry and tight: Sexual practices and potential AIDS risk in Zaire. *Social Science and Medicine* 37:989–994.

Brown, L. 1975. *The Evolution of Behaviour*. New York: Norton.

Bulatao, R. and R. D. Lee. 1983. *Determinants of Fertility in Developing Countries*. New York: Academic Press.

Cain, Mead. 1988. The consequences of reproductive failure: Dependence, mobility, and mortality among the elderly of rural South Asia. *Population Studies* 40:375–88.

Caldwell, John. 1977. The economic rationality of high fertility: An investigation illustrated with Nigerian survey data. *Population Studies* 31:5–27.

1979. Education as a factor in mortality decline: An examination of Nigerian data. *Population Studies* 33:395–413.

1982. *Theory of Fertility Change*. New York: Academic Press.

1985. Strengths and limitations of the survey approach for measuring and understanding fertility change: Alternative approaches. In *Reproductive Change in Developing Countries: Insights from the World Fertility Survey*. John Cleland and John Hobcroft, editors, pages 45–63. London: Oxford University Press.

1994. How is greater maternal education translated into lower child mortality? *Health Transition Review* 4:224–229.

1997. The global fertility transition: The need for a unifying theory. *Population and Development Review* 23:803–812.

1999. Reasons for limited sexual behavioural change in the sub-Saharan African AIDS epidemic and possible future intervention strategies. In *Resistances to Behavioural Change to Reduce HIV/AIDS Infection in Predominantly Heterosexual Epidemics in Third World Countries*. John Caldwell, Pat Caldwell, John Anarfi, Kofi Awusabo-Asare, James Ntozi, I. O. Orubuloye, Jeff Marck, Wendy Cosford, Rachel Colombo, and Elaine Hollings, editors, pages 241–256. Canberra: Health Transition Centre, Australia National University.

Caldwell, John and Pat Caldwell. 1989. High fertility in sub-Saharan Africa. *Scientific American* 262:118–131.

Caldwell, John, Allan Hill, and Valerie J. Hull. 1988. *Micro-Approaches to Demographic Research.* London: Kegan Paul International.

Caldwell, John, I. O. Orubuloye, and Pat Caldwell. 1992. Underreaction to AIDS in sub-Saharan Africa. *Social Science and Medicine* 34:1169–1182.

1999. Obstacles to behavioural change to lessen the risk of HIV infection in the African AIDS epidemic: Nigerian research. In *Resistances to Behavioural Change to Reduce HIV/AIDS Infection in Predominantly Heterosexual Epidemics in Third World Countries.* John Caldwell, Pat Caldwell, John Anarfi, Kofi Awusabo-Asare, James Ntozi, I. O. Orubuloye, Jeff Marck, Wendy Cosford, Rachel Colombo, and Elaine Hollings, editors, pages 113–124. Canberra: Health Transition Centre, Australia National University.

Caldwell, John, Pat Caldwell, and Bruce Caldwell. 1987. Anthropology and demography: The reinforcement of mutual speculation. *Current Anthropology* 28:25–33.

Caldwell, John, Pat Caldwell, John Anarfi, Kofi Awusabo-Asare, James Ntozi, I. O. Orubuloye, Jeff Marck, Wendy Cosford, Rachel Colombo, and Elaine Hollings. 1999. *Resistances to Behavioural Change to Reduce HIV/AIDS Infection in Predominantly Heterosexual Epidemics in Third World Countries.* Canberra: Health Transition Center, Australian National University.

Carael, Michele. 1997. Urban-rural differences in HIV/STDs and sexual behaviour. In *Sexual Cultures and Migration in the Era of AIDS.* Gilbert Herdt, editor, pages 107–126. Oxford: Clarendon Press.

Carey, James R. and Debra S. Judge. 2001. Life span extension in humans is self-reinforcing: A general theory of longevity. *Population and Development Review* 27:411–436.

Carey, James R. and Shripad Tuljapukar. 2003. *Life Span: Evolutionary, Ecological and Demographic Perspectives.* New York: Population Council.

Caro, Tim and Borgerhoff Mulder. 1987. The problem of adaptation in the study of human behaviour. *Ethology and Sociology* 8:61–72.

Carroll, John B. 1956. *Language, Thought and Reality: Selected Writings of Benjamin Lee Whorf.* Boston: MIT Technical Press.

Carr–Saunders, A. M. 1922. *The Population Problem: A Study in Human Evolution.* Oxford: Clarendon Press.

Carter, Anthony. 1995. Agency and fertility: For an ethnology of practice. In *Situating Fertility.* Susan Greenhalgh, editor, pages 55–85. Cambridge: Cambridge University Press.

1998. Cultural models and human behavior. In T*he Methods and Uses of Anthropological Demography.* Alaka Basu and P. Aaby, editors, pages 246–267. Oxford: Clarendon Press.

2001. Social processes and fertility change: Anthropological perspectives. In *Diffusion Processes and Fertility Transition: Selected Perspectives.* John B. Casterline, editor, pages 138–178. Washington, DC: National Academy Press.

Cassidy, Claire. 1980. Benign neglect and toddler malnutrition. In *Social and Biological Predictors of Nutritional Status, Growth and Neurological Development.* Lawrence S. Green and Francis Johnson, editors, pages 109–139. New York: Academic Press.

Cavalli-Sforza, Luca-Luigi and M. W. Feldman. 1981. *Cultural Transmission and Evolution.* Princeton, NJ: Princeton University Press.

Chagnon, Napoleon. 1988. Male Yanomamo manipulations of kinship classifications of female kin for reproductive advantage. In *Human Reproductive Behaviour: A Darwinian Perspective*. L. Betzig, M. Borgerhoff Mulder, and P. Turke, editors, pages 23–48. Cambridge: Cambridge University Press.

2000. Manipulating kinship rules: A form of male Yanomamo reproductive competition. In *Adaptation and Human Behavior: An Anthropological Perspective*. Lee Cronk, Napoleon Chagnon, and William Irons, editors, pages 115–132. New York: Aldine de Gruyter.

Chagnon, Napoleon and William Irons. 1979. *Evolutionary Biology and Human Social Behaviour: An Anthropological Perspective*. North Scituate, MA: Duxbury Press.

Chisholm, John. 1999. The evolutionary ecology of attachment organization. *Human Nature* 7:1–38.

Clark, Alice L. and Bobbi S. Low. 2001. Testing evolutionary hypotheses with demographic data. *Population and Development Review* 27:633–660.

Cleland, John and Georgia Kaufmann. 1998. Education, fertility and child survival: Unraveling the links. In *The Methods and Uses of Anthropological Demography*. A. Basu and P. Aaby, editors, pages 128–152. Oxford: Clarendon Press.

Cleland, John and Van Ginnekan, Jon. 1988. Maternal education and child survival in developing countries: The search for pathways of influence. *Social Science and Medicine* 27:1357–1368.

Coale, Ansley and Susan Watkins. 1986. *The Decline in Fertility in Europe*. Princeton, NJ: Princeton University Press.

Corsini, C. 1977. Self-regulating mechanisms of traditional populations before the demographic revolution: European civilizations. *International Proceedings of the International Conference for Scientific Study of Population, Mexico, 1977*, Vol. 3: 5–22. Liege: Ordina.

Comoroff, J. L. 1980. *The Meaning of Marriage Payments*. New York: Academic Press.

Cosmides, L. and J. Tooby. 1992. Cognitive adaptations for social exchange. In *The Adapted Mind*. J. Barkow, L. Cosmides, and J. Tooby, editors, pages 163–225. New York: Academic Press.

Cox, D. R. 1972. Regression models and life tables. *Journal of the Royal Statistical Society* 34:186–220.

Cowan, Jane K., Marie-Benedicte Dembour, and Richard A. Wilson 2001 *Culture and Rights: Anthropological Perspectives*. Cambridge: Cambridge University Press.

Cowlishaw, Guy and Ruth Mace. 1996. Cross-cultural patterns of marriage and inheritance: A phylogenetic approach. *Ethology and Sociobiology* 17:87–97.

Cronk, Lee. 1989. From hunters to herders: Subsistence change as a reproductive strategy among the Mukogodo. *Current Anthropology* 30:228–234.

1989a. From hunters to herders: Subsistence change as a reproductive strategy among the Mukogodo. *Current Anthropology* 30:228–234.

1989b. Low socioeconomic status and female-biased parental investment: the Mukogodo example. *American Anthropologist* 93:345–360.

1991a. Human behavioral ecology. *Annual Review of Anthropology* 20:25–53.

1991b. Intention versus behavior in parental sex preferences among the Mukogodo of Kenya. *Journal of Biosocial Science* 23:229–240.
1993. Parental favoritism towards daughters. *American Scientist* 81:272–273.
1994. Evolutionary theories of morality and the manipulative use of signals. *Zygon* 29:81–101.
1995. Is there a role for culture in human behavioral ecology? *Ethology and Sociobiology* 16:181–205.
1999. *That Complex Whole: Culture and the Evolution of Human Behavior*. Boulder, Co: Westview.
2000. Female-biased parental investment and growth performance among the Mukogodo. In *Adaptation and Human Behavior: An Anthropological Perspective*. Lee Cronk, Napoleon Chagnon, and William Irons, editors, pages 203–222. New York: Aldine du Gruyter.
Cronk, Lee, Napoleon Chagnon, and William Irons. 2000. *Adaptation and Human Behavior: An Anthropological Perspective*. New York: Aldine du Gruyter.
Curtin, R. and Phyllis J. Dolhinow. 1997. Infanticide among languars – a solution to overcrowding? *Science Today* 13:35–41.
Dahl, Grum and Hjort, Anders. 1976. *Having Herds: Pastoral Herd Growth and Household Economy*. Stockholm University Studies in Social Anthropology, Stockholm.
Daly, Martin and Margo Wilson. 1980. Discriminative parental solicitude: A biological perspective. *Journal of Marriage and the Family* 42:277–288.
1984. A sociobiological analysis of human infanticide. In *Infanticide: Comparative and Evolutionary Perspectives*. Glenn Hausfater and Sarah Blaffer Hrdy, editors, pages 487–502. New York: Aldine.
1985. Child abuse and other risks of not living with other parents. *Ethology and Sociobiology* 6:155–176.
1988. Evolutionary psychology and family homicide. *Science* 242:519–24.
1994. Stepparenthood and the evolved psychology of discriminative parental solicitude. In *Infanticide and Parental Care*. S. Parmigiani and F. S. vom Saal, editors, pages 121–134. Chur, Switzerland: Harwood.
1996. Evolutionary psychology and marital conflict: The relevance of stepchildren. In *Sex, Power, Conflict – Evolutionary and Feminist Perspectives*. David Buss and N. Malamuth, editors, pages 9–28. Oxford: Oxford University Press.
D'Andrade, Roy. 1992. Cultural meaning systems. In *Human Motives and Cultural Models*. Roy D'Andrade and Claudia Strauss, editors, pages 88–119. Cambridge: Cambridge University Press.
D'Andrade, Roy and Claudia Strauss. 1992. *Human Motives and Cultural Models*. Cambridge: Cambridge University Press.
Damon, William. 1999. The moral development of children. *Scientific American* 281(August):72–78.
Das Gupta, Monica. 1997. Kinship systems and demographic processes. In *Anthropological Demography: Towards a New Synthesis*. David Kertzer and Tom Fricke, editors, pages 36–53. Chicago: University of Chicago Press.
Dawkins, Richard. 1976. *The Selfish Gene*. Oxford: Oxford University Press.
1979. *The Extended Phenotype*. Oxford: Oxford University Press.

1989. *The Selfish Gene*. Oxford: Oxford University Press.
Dean, Jeffrey S., George J. Gumerman, Joshua M. Epstein, Robert L. Axtell, Alan C. Swedlund, Miles T. Parker, and Steven McCarroll. 2000. Understanding Anasazi culture change through agent-based modeling. In *Dynamics in Human and Primate Societies*. Timothy Kohler and George J. Gumerman, editors, pages 179–206. New York: Oxford University Press.
Degler, C. N. 1991. *In Search of Human Nature: The Decline and Rise of Darwinism in American Social Thought*. New York: Oxford University Press.
Dennett, Daniel. 2003. *Freedom Evolves*. New York: Viking.
Dickemann, Mildred. 1979a. The ecology of mating systems in hypergynous dowry societies. *Social Science Information* 19:163–195.
1979b. Female infanticide, reproductive strategies, and social stratification: A preliminary model. In *Evolutionary Biology and Human Social Behavior: An Anthropological Perspective*. Napoleon Chagnon and William Irons, editors, pages 312–367. North Sciute, MA: Duxbury Press.
1984. Concepts and classification in the study of human infanticide: Sectional introduction and some cautionary notes. In *Infanticide: Comparative and Evolutionary Perspectives*. Glenn Hausfater and Sarah Blaffer Hrdy, editors, pages 427–438. New York: Aldine.
1991. Women, class and dowry. *American Anthropologist* 93:944–946.
Ditz, Toby. 1990. Ownership and obligation: Inheritance and patriarchal households in Connecticut, 1750–1820. *The William and Mary Quarterly* 47:235–265.
Douglas, Mary. 1966. Population control in primitive groups. *British Journal of Sociology* 17:263–273.
Dowsatt, Gary W. 1993. Sustaining safe sex: Sexual practices, HIV and social content. *AIDS* 7(Suppl. 1):S257–S262.
1999. Understanding cultures of sexuality: Lessons learned from HIV/AIDS education and behavior change among gay men in Australia. In *Resistances to Behavioural Change to Reduce HIV/AIDS Infection in Predominantly Heterosexual Epidemics in Third World Countries*. John Caldwell, Pat Caldwell, John Anarfi, Kofi Awusabo-Asare, James Ntozi, I. O. Orubuloye, Jeff Marck, Wendy Cosford, Rachel Colombo, and Elaine Hollings, pages 223–233. Canberra: Health Transition Centre, Australia National University.
Draper, Pat. 1989. African marriage systems: Perspectives from evolutionary biology. *Ethology and Sociobiology* 10:145–169.
Drotar, D. 1991. The family context of non-organic failure to thrive. *American Journal of Orthopsychiatry* 61(1):23–34.
Duby, G. 1977. *The Chivalrous Society*. London: Edward Arnold.
Dukers, N., J. de Wit, J. Goudsmit et al. 2000. Recent increase in sexual risk behaviour and sexually transmitted disease in a cohort of homosexual men: The price of highly active antitretroviral therapy? Paper presented at the 13th International Conference on AIDS, July 9–14, Durban, South Africa (Abstract ThOrC715).
Durham, William H. 1991. *Coevolution: Genes, Culture and Human Diversity*. Stanford CA: Stanford University Press.

Edgerton, Robert B. 1992. *Sick Societies: Challenging the Myth of Primitive Harmony*. New York: Free Press.

El Din, M. 1977. The economic value of children in rural Sudan. In *The Persistence of High Fertility, Vol. 2*. John Caldwell, editor, pages 617–632; Canberra: Australian National University.

Ennew, J. 1995. Outside children: Street children's rights. In *Handbook of Children's Rights: Comparitive Policy and Practice*. B. Franklin, editor, pages 201–214. New York: Routledge.

Falkenstein, M. 1995. Concepts of ethnicity and inter-ethnic migration among the Ariaal of Kenya. *Zeitschrift fur Ethnologie* 120:1–26.

Ferraro, Gary, Wenda Trevanthan, and Janet Levy. 1994. *Anthropology: An Applied Perspective*. Minneapolis: West.

Fildes, Valerie. 1990. Maternal feelings reassessed: Child abandonment and neglect in London and Westminster, 1550–1800. In *Women as Mothers in Pre-Industrial England*. Valerie Fildes, editor, pages 141–165. London: Routledge.

Fisher, Ronald. 1958. *The Genetic Theory of Natural Selection*. New York: Dover.

Fix, Alan. 1990. Comment on "Explaining biased sex ratios in human populations" by Daniela Sieff. *Current Anthropologist* 31:36–37.

Flannery, Kent and Robert Reynolds. 1989. *The Flocks of the Wamani: A Study of Llama Herders on the Punas of Ayacucho, Peru*. New York: Academic Press.

Flowers, Paul, Graham Hart, and Claire Marriott. 1999. Constructing sexual health: Gay men and "risk" in the context of a public sex environment. *Journal of Health Psychology* 4:483–495.

Food and Agricultural Organization. 1967. *FAO Production Yearbook*. Rome: Food and Agriculture Organization.

Foster, Caroline. 2000. The limits to low fertility: A biosocial approach. *Population and Development Review* 26:209–234.

Frank, Andre Gunner. 1967. *Capitalism and Underdevelopment in Latin America*. New York: Monthly Review of Books.

Frank, Robert H. 1988. *Passions Within Reason: The Strategic Role of the Emotions*. New York: Norton.

Fratkin, Elliot. 1991. *Surviving Drought and Development: Ariaal Pastoralists of Northern Kenya*. Boulder, CO: Lynne Rienner.

1998. *Ariaal Pastoralists of Northern Kenya: Surviving Drought and Development in Africa's Arid Lands*. Boston: Allyn and Bacon.

Fratkin, Elliot and Eric Abella Roth. 1996. Who survives drought: Measuring winners and losers among the Ariaal Rendille pastoralists of Kenya. In *Case Studies in Human Ecology*. Daniel Bates and Susan Lees, editors, pages 159–174. New York: Plenum Press.

Fratkin, Elliot and Kevin Smith. 1994. Labor, livestock and land: The organization of pastoral production. In *African Pastoralist Systems: An Integrated Approach*. Elliot Fratkin, Kathleen Galvin, and Eric Roth, editors, pages 91–112. Boulder, Co: Lynne Reinner.

Fratkin, Elliot, Eric Roth, and Martha Nathan. 1999. When nomads settle: commoditization, nutrition and child education among Rendille pastoralists. *Current Anthropology* 40(5):729–735.

Freeman, Derek. 1983. *Margaret Mead and Samoa: The Making and Unmaking of an Anthropological Myth*. Cambridge, MA: Harvard University Press.

Fricke, Tom. 1990. Elementary structures in the Nepal Himalayas: Reciprocity and the politics of hierarchy in Ghale–Tamang Marriage. *Ethnology* 29:135–158.

1994. *Himalayan Households: Tamang Demography and Domestic Processes*. New York: Columbia University Press.

1997a. Culture theory and demographic process: Toward a thicker demography. In *Anthropological Demography: Toward a New Synthesis*. David. Kertzer and Tom Fricke, editors, pages 248–278. Chicago: University of Chicago Press.

1997b. Marriage change as moral change: Culture, virtue and demographic transition. In *The Continuing Demographic Transition*. G. Jones, R. M. Douglas, J. M. Caldwell, and R. M. D'Souza, editors, pages 183–212. Oxford: Clarendon Press.

Frisch, Rose. 1975. Critical weights, a critical body composition menarche and the maintenance of menstrual cycles. In *Biosocial Interelations in Population Adaptation*. Elizabeth Watts, Francis E. Johnston, and Gabriel W. Lasker, editors, pages 319–351. The Hague: Mouton.

Frisch, Rose and Robert L. Barieri. 2002. *Female Fertility and the Body Fat Connection*. Chicago: University of Chicago Press.

Fuchs, Rachel G. 1984. *Abandoned Children: Foundlings and Child Welfare in Nineteenth-Century France*. Albany: State University of New York.

Fuchs, Rachel G. and Leslie Page Moch. 1995. Invisible cultures: Poor women's networks and reproductive strategies in nineteenth century Paris. In *Situating Fertility: Anthropology and Demographic Inquiry*. S. Greenhalgh, editor, pages 86–107. Cambridge: Cambridge University Press.

Fukui, Katsuyoshi and David Turton. 1979. *Warfare Among East African Herders*. Osaka: Japan National Museum of Ethnology.

Galaty, John. 1979. Pollution and pastoral antipraxis: The issue of Maasai inequality. *American Ethnologist* 6:803–816.

Gaulin, Stephen and James Boster. 1990. Dowry as female competition. *American Anthropologist* 93:946–48.

Gaulin, Stephen and Carole Robbins. 1991. Trivers–Willard Effect in contemporary North American societies. *American Journal of Physical Anthropology* 85:61–69.

Gavitt, Phillip. 1990. *Charity and Children in Renaissance Florence: The Ospedale degli Innocenti*. Ann Arbor: University of Michigan Press.

1994. "Perche non avea chi la ghovernass." Cultural values, family resources and abandonment in the Florence of Lorenzo de' Medici, 1467–85. In *Poor Women and Children in the European Past*. John Henderson and Richard Wall, editors, pages 65–94. Routledge: London.

Geertz, Clifford. 1973. *The Interpretation of Culture*. New York: Basic Books.

Giddens, A. 1979. *Central Problems in Social Theory*. Berkeley: University of California Press.

Goodman, Alan H. and Thomas L. Leatherman. 1998. Transversing the chasm between biology and culture: An introduction. In *Building a New Bio-Cultural*

Synthesis: Political Economic Perspectives on Human Biology. Alan H. Goodman and Thomas L. Leatherman, editors, pages 3–42. Ann Arbor: University of Michigan Press.

Goody, John R. 1973. Bridewealth and dowry in Africa and Eurasia. In *Bridewealth and Dowry*. John Goody and S. J. Tambiah, editors, pages 1–58. Cambridge: Cambridge University Press.

1976. *Production and Reproduction: A Comparative Study of the Domestic Domain*. Cambridge: Cambridge University Press.

Goody, John, J. Thrisk, and E. Thompson. 1976. *Family and Inheritance*. Cambridge: Cambridge University Press.

Goody, Esther. 1984. Parental strategies: Calculation or sentiment? In *Interest and Emotions: Essays on the Study of Family and Kinship*. H. Medick and D. W. Sabean, editors, pages 266–267. Cambridge: Cambridge University Press.

Gould, Stephen J. 1982. Sociobiology and the theory of natural selection. In *Sociobiology: Beyond Nature/Nurture?* G. Barlow and J. Silverberg, editors, pages 257–263. Boulder, Co: Westview.

1990. *Wonderful Life: The Burgess Shale and the Nature of History*. New York: Norton.

Gould, Stephen J. and Richard Lewontin. 1979. The spandrels of San Marcos and the Panglossian paradigm: A critique of the adaptionist programme. *Proceedings of the Royal Society of London Series B* 2–5:581–598.

Grafen, A. 1984. Natural selection, kin selection and group selection. In *Behavioral Ecology: An Evolutionary Approach,* 2nd edition. J. R. Krebs and N. B. Davies, editors. Pages 62–84. Berkeley: University of California Press.

Grandin Barbara. 1988. Wealth and pastoral dairy production: A case study from Maasailand. *Human Ecology* 16:1–21.

Gray, J. Patrick. 2000. Twenty years of evolutionary biology and human social behavior: Where are we now? In *Adaptation and Human Behavior: An Anthropological Perspective*. Lee Cronk, Napoleon Chagnon, and William Irons, editors, pages 475–496. New York: Aldine de Gruyter.

Green, Margaret and Ann Biddlecom. 2000. Absent and problematic men: Demographic accounts of male reproductive roles. *Population and Development Review* 26:81–115.

Greenhalgh, Susan. 1990. Toward a political economy of fertility. *Population and Development Review* 16:85–106.

1995a. *Situating Fertility: Anthropology and Demographic Inquiry*. Cambridge: Cambridge University Press.

1995b. Anthropology theorizes reproduction: Integrating practice, political economic, and feminist perspectives. In *Situating Fertility: Anthropology and Demographic Inquiry*. Susan Greenhalgh, editor, pages 3–28. Cambridge: Cambridge University Press.

Greenhalgh, Susan and Jiali Li. 1995. Engendering reproductive policy and practice in peasant China: For a feminist demography of reproduction. *Signs* 20:601–641.

Gruenbaum, Ellen. 2000. Is female "circumcision" a maladaptive cultural pattern. In *Female "Circumcision" in Africa: Culture, Controversy and Change?*

Bettina Shell-Duncan and Ylva Hernlund, editors, pages 41–54. Boulder, CO: Lynne Rienner.

Grum, Anders. 1977. The Rendille calendar. Mimeograph on file, Integrated Project on Arid Lands, Nairobi: UNESCO.

Haaga, John G. 2001. Comment: The pace of fertility decline and the utility of evolutionary approaches. *Population and Development Review, Supplement* 27:53–59

Hajnal, H. J. 1965. European marriage patterns in perspective. In *Population in History*. David Glass and D. Coleman, editors, pages 101–143. Chicago: Aldine.

Hamilton, W. D. 1964. The genetical evolution of social behavior. *Journal of Theoretical Biology* 7:1–52.

1998. *Narrow Roads of Gene Land*. Oxford: Freeman.

2002. *Narrow Roads of Gene Land: Evolution of Sex*. Oxford: Oxford University Press.

Hammel, Eugene. 1990. A theory of culture for demography. *Population and Development Review* 3:433–454.

1995. Economics 1: Culture 0. Fertility change and differences in the Northwest Balkans, 1700–1900. In *Situating Fertility: Anthropological and Demographic Inquiry*. Susan Greenhalgh, editor, pages 225–258. Cambridge: Cambridge University Press.

Hammel, Eugene and Diana Friou. 1997. Anthropology and demography: Marriage, liaison or encounter. In *Anthropological Demography: Towards a New Synthesis*. David Kertzer and Tom Fricke, editors, pages 175–200. Chicago: University of Chicago Press.

Harding, Garret. 1967. The tragedy of the Commons. *Science* 162:1243–1244.

Handwerker, W. Penn. 2002. The construct validity of cultures: Cultural diversity, culture theory, and a method for ethnography. *American Anthropologist* 104:106–122.

Harms, William. 2000. The evolution of cooperation in hostile environments. In *Evolutionary Origins of Morality: Cross-Disciplinary Perspectives*. Leonard D. Katz, editor, pages 308–313. Bowling Green, OH: Imprint Academic.

Harpending, Henry C., Pat Draper, and Renee Pennington. 1991. Cultural evolution, parental care and mortality. In *Disease in Populations in Transition*. Alan Swedlund and George Armelagos, editors, pages 251–265. South Hadley, MA: Bergin and Garvey.

Harris, Marvin. 1995. *Cultural Anthropology, 4th Edition*. New York: Harper Collins College.

Harris, Marvin and Eric Ross. 1987. *Death, Sex and Fertility: Population Regulation in Preindustrial and Developing Societies*. New York: Columbia University Press.

Hartung, John. 1976. On natural selection and the inheritance of wealth. *Current Anthropology* 17:607–622.

1981. Paternity and inheritance of wealth. *Nature* 291:652–654.

1982. Polygyny and inheritance of wealth. *Current Anthropology* 23:1–12.

Hausfater, Glenn and Sarah Blaffer Hrdy. 1984. *Infanticide: Comparative and Evolutionary Perspectives*. New York: Aldine.

Hawkes, Kristen, James F. O'Connell, Nicholas Blurton-Jones, Helen Alvarez, and Eric L. Charnov. 2000. The grandmother hypothesis and human evolution. In *Adaptation and Human Behavior: An Anthropological Perspective*. Lee Cronk, Napoleon Chagnon, and William Irons, editors, pages 115–132. New York: Aldine de Gruyter.

Heinrich, Joseph, Robert Boyd, Samuel Bowles, Colin Camerer, Ernst Fehr, Herbert Gintis, and Richard McElreath. 2001. In search of *Homo Economicus*: Behavioral experimentation in 15 small-scale societies. *American Economic Review*, 91:73–78.

Heise, L. and Elias, C. 1995. Transforming AIDS prevention to meet women's needs: A focus on developing countries. *Social Science and Medicine* 40:931–943.

Herdt, Gilbert. 1984. *Ritualized Homosexuality in Melanesia*. Berkeley: University of California Press.

1997a. Sexual cultures and population movement: Implications for AIDS/STDs. In *Sexual Cultures and Migration in the Era of AIDS*. Gilbert Herdt, editor, pages 3–22. Oxford: Clarendon Press.

1997b. *Sexual Cultures and Migration in the Era of AIDS: Anthropological and Demographic Perspectives*. Oxford: Clarendon Press.

1999. *Sambia Sexual Cultures: Essays from the Field*. Chicago: University of Chicago Press.

Hill, Allan. 1997. Truth lies in the eye of the beholder. In *Anthropological Demography: Towards a New Synthesis*. D. Kertzer and T. Fricke, editors, pages 223–247. Chicago: University of Chicago Press.

Hill, Kim and A. Magdalena Hurtado. 1996. *Ache Life History: The Ecology and Demography of a Foraging People*. New York: Aldine de Gruyter.

Hill, Kim and Hillard S. Kaplan. 1999. Life history traits in humans: Theory and empirical studies. *Annual Review of Anthropology* 28:397–430.

Hinton, Alexander. 1999. *Biocultural Approaches to the Emotions*. Cambridge: Cambridge University Press.

Holy, Ladislav and Milan Stuchlik. 1983. *Actions, Norms and Representations: Foundations of Anthropological Inquiry*. Cambridge: Cambridge University Press.

Howell, Cecilia. 1976. Peasant inheritance customs in the Midlands, 1280–1700. In *Family and Inheritance*. J. Goody, J. Thrisk, and E. Thompson, editors, pages 112–155. Cambridge: Cambridge University Press.

Howell, Nancy. 1979. *Demography of the Dobe !Kung*. New York: Academic Press.

2000. *Demography of the Dobe !Kung*. Hawthorne, NY: Aldine de Gruyter.

Hrdy, Sarah Blaffer. 1977. *The Languars of Abu-Female and Male Strategies of Reproduction*. Cambridge, MA: Cambridge University Press.

1979. Infanticide among animals: A review, classification and examination of the implications for the reproductive strategies of females. *Ethology and Sociobiology* 1:1–13.

1990. Sex bias in nature and history. *Yearbook of Physical Anthropology* 33:25–37.

1997. Fitness tradeoffs in the history and evolution of delegated mothering with special reference to wet-nursing, abandonment and infanticide. In

Human Nature: A Critical Reader. Laura Betzig, editor, pages 402–422. Oxford: Oxford University press (originally published as *Ethology and Sociobiology* 14:409–442).

1999. *Mother Nature: Maternal Instincts and How They Shape the Human Species.* New York: Ballentine.

Hrdy, Sarah and Debra S. Judge. 1993. Darwin and the puzzle of primogeniture: An essay on biases in parental investment. *Human Nature* 4:1–46.

Hunecke, Volker. 1994. The abandonment of legitimate children in nineteenth-century Milan and the European context. In *Poor Women and Children in the European Past.* John Henderson and Richard Wall, editors, pages 117–138. London: Routledge.

Huxley, Thomas H. 1894. Evolution and ethics and other essays. In *Collected Essays.* Thomas H. Huxley, editor, pages v–ix. London: MacMillan.

Im-Em, Wassana. 1999. Changing partner relations in the era of AIDS in Upper-North Thailand. In *Resistances to Behavioural Change to Reduce HIV/AIDS Infection in Predominantly Heterosexual Epidemics in Third World Countries.* John Caldwell, Pat Caldwell, John Anarfi, Kofi Awusabo-Asare, James Ntozi, I. O. Orubuloye, Jeff Marck, Wendy Cosford, Rachel Colombo, and Elaine Hollings, editors, pages 157–170. Canberra: Health Transition Centre, Australia National University.

Irons, William. 1979. Cultural and biological success. In *Evolutionary Biology and Human Social Behavior: An Anthropological Perspective.* Napoleon Chagnon and William Irons, editors, pages 257–272. North Sciute, MA: Duxbury Press.

1991. How did morality evolve? *Zygon* 26:49–89.

1996. Morality as an evolved adaptation. In *Investigating the Biological Foundations of Human Morality.* J. Hurd, editor, pages 1–34. Lewiston, ID: Edwin Mellen.

Isaac, B. and W. Feinberg. 1982. Marital form and infant survival among the Mende of rural upper Bambara Chiefdom, Sierra Leone. *Human Biology* 54:627–634.

Jejeebhoy, S. J. 1995. *Women's Education, Autonomy and Reproductive Behavior: Experiences from Developing Countries.* Oxford: Clarendon Press.

Johnson, Kay. 1993. The politics of the revival of infant abandonment in China, with special reference to Hunan. *Population and Development Review* 22:77–98.

Johnson, Kay, Huang, Banghan and Wang Liyao. 1998. Infant abandonment and adoption in China. *Population and Development Review* 24:469–510.

Johnson-Hanks, Jennifer. 2002. On the modernity of traditional contraception: Time and the social context of fertility. *Population and Development Review* 28:229–249.

Jones, Doug. 2000. Physical attractiveness, race and somatic prejudice in Bahia, Brazil. In *Adaptation and Human Behavior: An Anthropological Perspective.* Lee Cronk, Napoleon Chagnon, and William Irons, editors, pages 133–154. New York: Aldine de Gruyter.

Jones, Gavin W., Robert M. Douglas, John C. Caldwell, and Rennie D'Souza. 1997. *The Continuing Demographic Transition.* Oxford: Clarendon Press.

Judge, Deborah and Sara Blaffer Hrdy. 1992. Allocation of accumulated resources among close kin: Inheritance in Sacramento, California, 1890–1984. *Ethology and Sociobiology* 13:495–522.

Kacelnik, Alejandro and John R. Krebs. 1997. Yanomamo dreams and starling payloads: The logic of optimality. In *Human Nature: A Critical Reader*. Laura Betzig, editor, pages 21–35. Oxford: Oxford University Press.

Kaplan, Hillary. 1994. Evolutionary and wealth flows theories of fertility: Empirical tests and new models. *Population and Development Review* 20:753–791.

1996. A theory of fertility and parental investment in traditional and modern human societies. *Yearbook of Physical Anthropology* 39:91–135.

1997. The evolution of the human life course. In *Between Zeus and the Salmon: The Biodemography of Longevity*. Kenneth W. Wachter and Caleb E. Finch, editors, pages 175–211. Washington, DC: National Academy Press.

Kaplan, Hillard S. and Jane B. Lancaster. 2000. The evolutionary economics and psychology of the demographic transition to low fertility. In *Adaptation and Human Behavior: An Anthropological Perspective*. Lee Cronk, Napoleon Chagnon, and William Irons, editors, pages 283–322. New York: Aldine de Gruyter.

2003. An evolutionary and ecological analysis of human fertility, mating patterns and parental investment. In *Offspring: Human Fertility Behavior in Biodemographic Perspective*. Kenneth W. Wachter and Rudolfo A. Bulatao, editors, pages 170–221. Washington, DC: National Academy Press.

Katz, Leonard D. 2000. *Evolutionary Origins of Morality: Cross-Disciplinary Perspectives*. Bowling Green, OH: Imprint Academic.

Keen, M. H. 1976. Chivalry, nobility and the man-at-arms. In *War, Literature and Politics in the Late Middle Ages*. C. T. Allmand, editor, pages 33–57. New York: Barnes & Noble.

Keesing, Roger. 1974. Theories of culture. *Annual Review of Anthropology* 3:73–97.

Keller, Matthew C., Randolph M. Nesse, and Sandra Hofferth. 2001. The Trivers–Willard Hypothesis of parental investment: No effect in the contemporary United States. *Evolution and Human Behavior* 22:343–360.

Kellog, T., W. McFarland and M. Katz. 1999. Recent increases in HIV seroconversion among repeat anonymous testers in San Francisco [Correspondence]. *AIDS* 13:2303–2304.

Kertzer, David. 1984. Anthropology and family history. *Journal of Family History* 9:201–203.

1992. Child abandonment in European history. *Journal of Family History* 17:13–19.

1993. *Sacrificed for Honor: Infant Abandonment and the Politics of Reproductive Control*. Boston: Beacon Press.

1995. Political-economic and cultural explanations of demographic behavior. In *Situating Fertility: Anthropological and Demographic Enquiry*. S. Greenhalgh, editor, pages. 29–52. Cambridge: Cambridge University Press.

1998. The proper role of culture in demographic explanation. In *The Continuing Demographic Transition*. G. Jones, J. Caldwell, R. Douglas, and R. D'Souza, editors, pages 137–157. London: Oxford University Press.

2001. The lives of foundlings in nineteenth century Italy. In *Abandoned Children*. Catherine Panter-Brick and Malcolm T. Smith, editors, pages 41–56. Cambridge: Cambridge University Press.

Kertzer, David and Tom Fricke. 1997. *Anthropological Demography: Toward a New Synthesis*. D. Kertzer and T. Fricke, editors, pages 248–278. Chicago: University of Chicago Press.

Kertzer, David and M. White. 1994. Cheating the angel-makers: surviving infant abandonment in nineteenth century Italy. *Continuity and Change* 9:451–480.

Kimura, M. 1979. The neutral theory of molecular evolution. *Scientific American* 241:98–126.

Kleinbaum, David G. 1996. *Survival Analysis: A Self-Learning Text*. New York: Springer Verlag.

Kluckhorn, Clyde. 1939. The place of theory in anthropological studies. *The Philosophy of Science* 6:328–344.

Knodel, John. 1988. *Demographic Behavior in the Past*. Cambridge: Cambridge University Press.

Knodel, John and Etienne van de Walle. 1979. Lessons from the past: Policy implications of historical fertility studies. In *The Decline of Fertility in Europe*. Ansley Coale and Susan C. Watkins, editors, pages 420–449. Princeton, NJ: Princeton University Press.

Knodel, John, Mark VanLandingham, Chanpen Saengtienchai, and Anthony Pramualratana. 1996. Thai views of sexuality and sexual behavior. *Health Transition Review* 6:179–201.

Kohler, Timothy and George J. Gumerman. 2000. *Dynamics in Human and Primate Societies*. New York: Oxford University Press.

Korenromp E. L., Vliet C. van, Bakker R., Vlas S. J, de, Habbema J. D. F. 2000. HIV spread and partnership reduction for different patterns of sexual behaviour – a study with the microsimulation model STDSIM. *Mathematical Population Studies* 8(2):135–173.

Kreager, Phillip. 1982. Demography *in situ*. *Population and Development Review*, 8:237–266.

1986. Demographic regimes as cultural systems. In *The State of Population Theory*. D. Coleman and R. Schofield, editors, pages 131–155. Oxford: Basil Blackwell.

1998. The limits to diffusionism. In *The Methods and Uses of Anthropological Demography*. Alaka Basu and Peter Aaby, editors, pages 298–322. Oxford: Clarendon Press.

Krebs, J. R. 1978. Optimal foraging: Decision rules for predators. In *Behavioural Ecology: An Evolutionary Approach*. J. R. Krebs and N. B. Davies, editors, pages 23–63. Oxford: Blackwell Scientific.

Krebs, J. R. and N. B. Davies. 1978. *Behavioural Ecology: An Evolutionary Approach*. Oxford: Blackwell Scientific.

Kuper, Adam. 1988. *The Invention of Primitive Society: Transformations of an Illusion*. London: Routledge.

Laland, Kevin N. and Gillian R. Brown. 2002. *Sense and Nonsense: Evolutionary Perspectives on Human Behaviour*. Oxford: Oxford University Press.

Lam, David. 2003. Evolutionary biology and rational choice in models of fertility. In *Offspring: Human Fertility Behavior in Biodemographic Perspective*. Kenneth W. Wachter and Rodolfo A. Bulatao, editors, pages 322–338. Washington, DC: National Research Council.

Lancaster, Jane B. and Hilary S. Kaplan. 2000. Parenting other men's children: Costs, benefits and consequences. In *Adaptation and Human Behavior: An Anthropological Perspective*. Lee Cronk, Napoleon Chagnon, and William Irons, editors, pages 179–202. New York: Aldine de Gruyter.

Lave, J. 1988. *Arithmetic Practices and Cognitive Theory: An Ethnographic Inquiry*. Cambridge: Cambridge University Press.

Lebrun, Francois. 1971. *Les hommes et la morte en Anjou aux 17e et 18e Siecles*. Paris: Mouton.

Lee, Richard. 1979. *The !Kung San: Men, Women and Work in a Foraging Society*. Cambridge: Cambridge University Press.

Leete, Richard. 1997. *Dynamics of Values in Fertility Change*. Oxford: Oxford University Press.

Leibenstein, H. 1981. Economic decision theory and fertility behaviour. *Population and Development Review* 6:441–462.

Lesthaeghe, Ron. 1980. On the social control of human reproduction. *Population and Development Review* 4:527–548.

1989. Production and reproduction in sub-Saharan Africa: An overview of organizing principles. In *Reproduction and Social Organization in sub-Saharan Africa*. Ron Lesthaeghe, editor, pages 15–39. Berkeley: University of California Press.

Levine, Robert A. and Susan Scrimshaw. 1983. Effects of culture on fertility: Anthropological contributions. In *Determinants of Fertility in Developing Countries, Vol. 2*. Rodolfo A. Bulatao and Ronald D. Lee, editors, pages 666–695. New York: Academic Press.

Levine, R. A., S. E. Levine, A. Richman, F. M. Tapia Uribe, C. Sunderland Correa, and P. M. Miller. 1991. Women's schooling and child care in the demographic transition: A Mexican case study. *Population and Development Review* 17:459–496.

Lewis, Ioan M. 1976. *Social Anthropology*. London: Penguin.

Lewontin, Richard, Stephen Rose, and L. J. Kamin. 1984. *Not in Our Genes*. New York: Pantheon.

Lindenbaum, Shirley. 1991. Anthropology rediscovers sex. *Social Science and Medicine* 33:865–907.

Lock, Margaret M. 1995. *Encounters With Aging: Mythologies of Menopause in Japan and North America*. Berkeley: University of California Press.

Lockwood, Matthew. 1995. Structure and behavior in the social demography of Africa. *Population and Development Review* 21:1–32.

Lovejoy, C. Owen. 1981. The origin of man. *Science* 211:341–350.

Low, Bobbi S. 1996. Behavioral ecology of conservation in traditional societies. *Human Nature* 7(4):353–379.

2000. Sex, wealth and fertility: Old rules, new environments. In *Adaptation and Human Behavior: An Anthropological Perspective*. Lee Cronk, Napoleon Chagnon, and William Irons, editors, pages 323–344. New York: Aldine de Gruyter.

2000. *Why Sex Matters: A Darwinian Look at Human Behavior.* Princeton, NJ: Princeton University Press.

Low, Bobbi S., Alice L. Clarke, and Kenneth Lockridge. 1992. Towards an ecological demography. *Population and Development Review* 18:1–32.

Luttbeg, Barney, Monique Borgerhoff Mulder, and Marc Mangel. 2000. To marry or not: A dynamic model for demographic transition. In *Adaptation and Human Behavior: An Anthropological Perspective.* Lee Cronk, Napoleon Chagnon, and William Irons, editors, pages. 345–370. New York: Aldine de Gruyter.

Mace, Ruth. 1996a. When to have another baby: A dynamic model of reproductive decision-making and evidence from the Gabbra pastoralists. *Ethology and Sociobiology* 17:263–273.

1996b. Biased parental investment and reproductive success in Gabbra pastoralists. *Behavioural Ecology and Sociobiology* 38:75–81.

2000. An adaptive model of human reproductive rate where wealth is inherited: Why people have small families. In *Adaptation and Human Behavior: An Anthropological Perspective.* Lee Cronk, Napoleon Chagnon, and William Irons, editors, pages 261–282. New York: Aldine De Gruyter.

Mackie, Gerrie. 1996. Ending footbinding and infibulation: A conventional account. *American Sociological Review* 18:499–518.

MacClellan, Hugh. 1945. *Two Solitudes.* Toronto: Duell, Sloan and Pearce.

Malotki, Ekkehart. 1983. *Hopi Time: A Lingustic Analysis of the Temporal Concepts in the Hopi Language.* Berlin:Mouton.

Malinowski, Branislow. 1927. *Sex and Repression in Savage Society.* Cleveland, OH: Meridan.

1928. The life of culture. In *Culture: The Diffusion Controversy.* G. E. Smith, B. Malinkowski, H. Spindon, and A. Goldenweiser, editors, pages 23–44. New York: Norton.

1929. *The Sexual Life of Savages in North-Western Melanesia.* New York: Harcourt, Brace & World.

Malowist, M. 1964. Les aspects sociaux de la premeire phas de l' expansion coloniale. *Africana Bulletin* 1:11–40.

Martindale, Steve, Kevin Craib, Kevin Chang, Mary Lou Miller, Darrel Cook, and Robert Hogg. 2001. Increasing rate of new HIV infections among young gay and bisexual men in Vancouver, 1995–99 vs. 2000. Paper presented at the Canadian Conference on HIV/AIDS Research, May 31–June 3, Toronto, Ontario.

Mason, Karen Oppenheim. 1993. The impact of women's position on demographic change during the course of development. In *Women's Position and Demographic Change.* N. Federici, K. Mason, and S. Sogneer, editors, pages 19–42. Oxford: Clarendon Press.

1997. Gender and demographic change. In *The Continuing Demographic Transition.* G. Jones, R. Douglas, J. Caldwell, and R. D'Souza, editors, pages 158–182. Oxford: Clarendon Press.

May, D. and D. May. 1968. Son survivorship motivation and family size in India: A computer simulation. *Population Studies* 22:199–210.

Maynard-Smith, John. 1974. *Models in Ecology.* Cambridge: Cambridge University Press.

1982. *Evolution and the Theory of Games*. Cambridge: Cambridge University Press.
1995. Life at the edge of chaos. *New York Review of Books* March (2):28–30.
McCabe, J. Terrance. 1990. Turkana pastoralism: A case against the tragedy of the commons. *Human Ecology* 18:81–103.
McDade, Thomas and Carol M. Worthman. 1998. The weanling's dilemma reconsidered: A biocultural analysis of breastfeeding ecology. *Journal of Developmental and Behavioral Pediatrics* 19(4):286–299.
McElroy A. and P. K. Townsend. 1989. *Medical Anthropology in an Ecological Perspective*. Boulder, CO: Westview.
McNicoll, Geoffrey. 1994. Institutional analysis of fertility. In *Population, Development and the Environment*. Kerstin Lindahl-Kiessling and Hans Landberg, editors, pages 201–222. Oxford: Oxford University Press.
Mead, Margaret. 1927. *Coming of Age in Samoa*. New York: William Morrow.
1935. *Sex and Temperment in Three Primitive Societies*. New York: Dutton.
Miller, Barbara. 2001. Female selective abortion in Asia: Patterns, policies and debates. *American Anthropologist* 103:1083–1095.
Miller, Jane, German Rodriguez, and Anne Pebley. 1994. Lactation, seasonality and mothers' post-partum weight change in Bangladesh: An analysis of maternal depletion. *American Journal of Human Biology* 6:511–524.
Mills, S. and J. Beatty. 1984. The propensity interpretation of fitness. In *Conceptual Issues in Biology*. E. Sober, editor. Pages 34–57. Cambridge, MA: MIT Press.
Moch, L. Leslie. 1987. Historians and family strategies. *Historical Methods* 20:114–123.
Moore, Kirsten and Sondra Zeidenstein. 1996. *Learning about Sexuality: A Practical Beginning*. New York: Population Council and International Woman's Health Coalition.
Moran, Emilio. 1979. *Human Adaptation: An Introduction to Ecological Anthropology*. North Sciute, MA: Duxbury.
Morris, Martina and Mirjam Kretzschmar. 1997. Concurrent partnerships and the spread of HIV. *AIDS* 11:641–648.
Mosley, William H. and Lincoln C. Chen. 1984. An analytical framework for the study of child survival in developing countries. In *Child Survival: Strategies for Research, Population and Development Review Supplement* 10:25–48.
Murdock, George. 1967. *Ethnographic Atlas*. Pittsburgh, PA: University of Pittsburgh Press.
1986. Ethnographic atlas. *World Cultures* 2:4.
Murdock, George and Douglas White. 1969. Standard cross-cultural sample. *Ethnology* 8:329–369.
Nathan, Martha, Elliot Fratkin, and Eric Roth. 1996. Sedentism and child health among Rendille pastoralists of Northern Kenya. *Social Sciences and Medicine* 43:503–515.
Nations, Marilyn K. and Linda-Ann Rebhun. 1988. "Angels with wet wings can't fly": Maternal sentiment in Brazil and the image of neglect. *Culture, Medicine and Psychiatry* 12:141–200.

Nesse, Randolph and George C. Williams. 1994. *Why We Get Sick: The New Science of Darwinian Medicine*. New York: Time Books.

Newell, W. 1986. Inheritance on the maturing frontier: Butler County, Ohio 1803–1865. In *Long Term Factors in American Economic Growth*. R. Engerman and R. Gallman, editors, pages 261–303. Chicago: University of Chicago Press.

Nowak, Martin A. and Karl Sigmund. 1998. Evolution of indirect reciprocity by image scoring. *Nature*, 393:573–579.

Orians, G. H. 1969. On the evolution of mating systems in birds and mammals. *American Naturalist* 103:589–603.

Ortner, Sherry. 1973. On key symbols. *American Anthropologist* 75:1338–1346.

1984. Theory in anthropology since the sixties. *Comparative Studies in Society and History* 26:126–166.

Orubuloye, I. O., John Caldwell, and Pat Caldwell. 1997. Perceived sexual needs and male sexual behaviour in southwest Nigeria. *Social Science and Medicine* 44:1195–1207.

Panter-Brick, Catherine. 2001. Nobody's children? A reconsideration. In *Abandoned Children*. Catherine Panter-Brick and Malcolm T. Smith, editors, pages 1–23. Cambridge: Cambridge University Press.

Panter-Brick, Catherine and Malcolm T. Smith. 2001. *Abandoned Children*. Cambridge: Cambridge University Press.

Pelletier, David L. 1994. The potentiating effects of malnutrition on child mortality: Epidemiological evidence and policy implications. *Nutritional Reviews* 52:409–415.

Pepper, John W. and Barbara W. Smuts. 2000. The evolution of cooperation in an ecological context: An agent-based model. In *Dynamics in Human and Primate Societies*. Timothy Kohler and George J. Gumerman, editors, pages 19–45. New York: Oxford University Press.

Perusse, D. 1993. Cultural and reproductive success in industrial societies: Testing relationships at the proximate and ultimate levels. *Behavioural and Brain Sciences* 16:267–322.

Pinker, Stephen. 1997. *How the Mind Works*. New York: Norton.

2002. *The Blank Slate: The Modern Denial of Human Nature*. New York: Viking Press.

Pinkerton, Steven and Paul Abramson. 1992. Is risky sex rational? *The Journal of Sex Research* 29:561–568.

Pollack, Stephen and Susan Coates Watkins. 1994. Cultural and economic approaches to fertility: Proper marriage or *mesalliance*? *Population and Development Review* 19(3):467–496.

Rao, Aparna. 1998. Prestations and progeny: The consolidation of well-being among the Bakkarwal of Jammu and Kashmir (Western Himalayas). In *Kinship, Networks and Exchange*. Thomas Schweizer and Douglas R. White, editors, pages 210–233. Cambridge: Cambridge University Press.

Reed, Holly, Rona Briere, and John Casterline. 1999. *The Role of Diffusion Processes in Fertility Change in Developing Countries*. Washington, DC: National Academy Press.

Richerson, Peter J. and Robert Boyd. 1992. Cultural inheritance and evolutionary ecology. In *Evolutionary Ecology and Human Behavior*. Eric Alden Smith and Bruce Winterhalder, editors, pages 61–94. New York: Aldine de Gruyter.

Riley, Nancy. 1997a. Similarities and differences: Anthropological and demographic perspectives on gender. In *Anthropological Demography: Toward a New Synthesis*. D. Kertzer and T. Fricke, editors, pages 115–138. Chicago: Chicago University Press.

1997b. American adoptions of Chinese girls: The socio-political matrices of individual decisions. *Women's Studies International* 20:87–101.

Robinson, W. 1992. Kenya enters the fertility transition. *Population Studies* 46:445–457.

Rogers, Alan. 1995. For love or money: The evolution of reproductive and material motivations. In *Human Reproductive Decisions: Biological and Social Perspectives*. R. Dunbar, editor, pages 76–95. London: MacMillan.

Romaniuk, Anatole. 1968. The demography of the Democratic Republic of the Congo. In *The Demography of Tropical Africa*. William Brass and Ansley Coale, editors, pages 241–341. Princeton, NJ: Princeton University Press.

Romney, Kimball, Susan C. Weller, and William Batchelder. 1986. Culture as consensus. *American Anthropologist* 88:313–338.

Rose, Hilary and Stephen Rose. 2000. *Alas Poor Darwin: Arguments Against Evolutionary Psychology*. New York: Harmony Books.

Roth, Eric A. 1990. Modelling Rendille household herds. *Human Ecology* 18:441–457.

1991. Education, tradition and household labor among Rendille pastoralists of northern Kenya. *Human Organization* 50:136–141.

1993. A reexamination of Rendille population regulation. *American Anthropologist* 95:597–611.

1994a. Demographic systems: Two East African examples. In *African Pastoralist Systems: An Integrated Approach*. Elliot Fratkin, Kathleen Galvin, and Eric Roth, editors, pages 133–146. Boulder, CO: Lynne Rienner.

1996. Traditional pastoral strategies in a modern world: An example from Northern Kenya. *Human Organization* 55:219–224.

1999. Proximate and distal variables in Rendille demography. *Human Ecology* 27:517–536.

2000. On pastoralist egalitarianism: Consequences of primogeniture among the Rendille. *Current Anthropology* 41:269–271.

2001.

Roth, Eric Abella and Balan Kurup. 1988. Demography and polygyny in a Southern Sudanese agro-pastoralist society. *Culture* 8:67–73.

Roth, Eric Abella, Elliot Fratkin, Anne Eastman, and Leah Nathan. 1999. Knowledge of AIDS among Ariaal Pastoralists of northern Kenya. *Nomadic Peoples (NS)* 3(2):161–175.

Roth, Eric Abella, Elliot Fratkin, Elizabeth N. Ngugi, and Barry Glickman. 2001. Female education, adolescent sexuality and the risk of sexually transmitted infection in Ariaal Rendille culture. *Culture, Health and Sexuality* 3:35–48.

Rottschaefer, William A. 1998. *The Biology and Psychology of Moral Agency*. Cambridge: Cambridge University Press.

Rutenberg, Naomi and Susan Cotts Watkins. 1997. The buzz outside the clinics: Conversations and contraception in Nyanza Province, Kenya. *Studies in Family Planning* 28:290–307.

Sa, Isabel Do Guimaraes. 1994. Child abandonment in Portugal. Legislative and institutional care. *Continuity and Change* 9:69–89.

2001. Circulation of children in eighteenth-century Portugal. In *Abandoned Children*. Catherine Panter-Brick and Malcolm T. Smith, editors, pages 27–40. Cambridge: Cambridge University Press.

Sahlins, Marshall. 1976. *The Use and Abuse of Biology: An Anthropological Critique of Sociobiology*. Ann Arbor: University of Michigan Press.

Salzman, Phillip Carl. 1999. Is Inequality Universal? *Current Anthropology* 40(1):31–62.

Sato, Shun. 1980. Pastoral movements and the subsistence unit of the Rendille of northern Kenya. *Senrie Ethnological Series* 6:1–78.

Saucier, J.-F. 1972. Correlates of the long postpartum taboo: A cross-cultural study. *Current Anthropology* 13:238–249.

Scheper-Hughes, Nancy. 1992. *Death Without Weeping: The Violence of Everyday Life in Brazil*. Berkeley: University of California Press.

1997. Demography without numbers. In *Anthropological Demography: Towards a New Synthesis*. David Kertzer and Tom Fricke, editors, pages 201–222. Chicago: University of Chicago Press.

Scheper-Hughes, Nancy and D. Hoffman. 1998. Brazilian apartheid: Street kids and the struggle for urban space. In *Small Wars: The Cultural Politics of Childhood*. Nancy Scheper-Hughes and Carolyn Sargent, editors, pages 1–33. Berkeley: University of California Press.

Scheper-Hughes, Nancy and Margaret M. Lock. 1987. The mindful body: A prolegomenon to future work in medical anthropology. *Medical Anthropology Quarterly*: 6–41.

Schlee, Gunther. 1989. *Identities on the Move: Clanship and Pastoralism in Northern Kenya*. Manchester, England: Manchester United Press.

Schlegel, Alice. 1993. Dowry? Who competes for what? *American Anthropologist* 95:155–157.

Schlegel, Alice and R. Eloul. 1987. A new coding of marriage transactions. *Behavioral Science Research* 22:111.

Schneider, Jane and Peter Schneider. 1998. Political economy and cultural processes in the fertility decline of Sicilian artisans. In *The Methods and Uses of Anthropological Demography*. Alaka M. Basu and Peter Aaby, editors, pages 177–197. Oxford: Clarendon Press.

Schoenmaeckers, Ronny, Iqbal Shah, Ron Lesthaeghe, and Oleko Tambashe. 1981. The child-spacing tradition and the post-partum taboo in tropical Africa: Anthropological evidence. In *Child-Spacing in Tropical Africa: Traditions and Change*. Hilary Page and Ron Lesthaeghe, editors, pages. 25–72. London: Academic Press.

Scrimshaw, Nancy. 1978. Infant mortality and behaviour in the regulation of family size. *Population and Development Review* 4:383–403.

1983. Infanticide as deliberate fertility control. In *Determinants of Fertility in Developing Countries*. R. Bulatao and Ronald D. Lee, editors, pages 245–266. New York: Academic Press.

1984. Infanticide in human populations: Societal and individual concerns. In *Infanticide: Comparative and Evolutionary Perspectives*. Glenn Hausfater and Sarah Blaffer Hrdy, editors, pages 439–462. New York: Aldine.

Scrimshaw, Neville, Charles Taylor, and John Gordon. 1989. *Interaction of Nutrition and Infection*. Geneva: World Health Organization Monograph Series 57.

Sear, Rebecca, F. Steele, I. A., McGregor, and Ruth Mace. 2001. The effects of kin on child mortality in rural Gambia. *Demography* 39(1):43–63.

Sellen, Daniel W., Monique Borgerhoff Mulder, and Daniela F. Sieff. 2000. Fertility, offspring quality and wealth in Datoga Pastoralists: Testing evolutionary models of intersexual selection. In *Adaptation and Human Behavior: An Anthropological Perspective*. Lee Cronk, Napoleon Chagnon, and William Irons, editors, pages 91–114. New York: Aldine De Gruyter.

Shell-Duncan, Bettina and Ylva Hernlund. 2000a. Female "circumcision" in Africa: Dimensions of the practices and debates. In *Female "Circumcision" in Africa: Culture, Controversy and Change*. Bettina Shell-Duncan and Ylva Hernlund, editors, pages 1–40. Boulder, CO: Lynne Rienner.

2000b. *Female "Circumcision" in Africa: Culture, Controversy and Change*. Bettina Shell-Duncan and Ylva Hernlund, editors, Boulder, CO: Lynne Rienner.

Shore, Bradd. 1996. *Culture in Mind: Cognition, Culture and the Problem of Meaning*. New York: Oxford University Press.

Shorter, Edward. 1977. *The Making of the Modern Family*. New York: Basic Books.

Sieff, Daniel. 1990. Explaining biased sex ratios in human populations: A critique of recent studies. *Current Anthropology* 31:25–48.

Sigmund, Karl, Ernst Fahr, and Martin A. Nowak. 2002. The economics of fair play. *Scientific American* 286:83–87.

Silk, Joan. 1990. Human adaptation in evolutionary perspective. *Human Nature* 1:25–52.

Skinner, G. William. 1997. Family systems and demographic processes. In *Anthropological Demography: Towards a New Synthesis*. David Kertzer and Tom Fricke, editors, pages 53–95. Chicago: University of Chicago Press.

Small, Cathy A. 2000. The political impact of marriage in a virtual Polynesian society. In *Dynamics in Human and Primate Societies*. Timothy Kohler and George J. Gumerman, editors, pages 225–250. New York: Oxford University Press.

Smil, Vaclav. 2002. Eating meat: Evolution patterns, and consequences. *Population and Development Review* 28(4):599–639.

Smith, Eric Alden. 2000. Three styles in the evolutionary study of human behavior. In *Adaptation and Human Behavior*. Lee Cronk, Napoleon Chagnon, and William Irons, editors, pages 27–48. New York: Aldine De Gruyter.

Smith, Eric Alden and Bruce Winterhalder. 1992a. *Evolutionary Ecology and Human Behavior*. Chicago: Aldine De Gruyter.

1992b. Natural selection and decision-making: some fundamental principles. In *Evolutionary Ecology and Human Behavior*. Eric Alden Smith and Bruce Winterhalder, editors, pages 3–24. New York: Aldine De Gruyter.

Smith, Malcolm T. 2001. Modelling the economic and human costs of foundling care in the Azores. In *Abandoned Children*. Catherine Panter-Brick and Malcolm T. Smith, editors, pages 57–69. Cambridge: Cambridge University Press.

Smith, Martin, Bradley Kish, and Charles Crawford. 1987. Inheritance of wealth as human kin investment. *Ethology and Sociobiology* 8:171–182.

Smith, T. C. 1977. *Nakahura: Family, Farming and Population in a Japanese Village*. Stanford: Stanford University Press.

Snow, C. P. 1993. *The Two Cultures*. Cambridge: Cambridge University Press.

Sobania, Neal W. 1980. The historical tradition of the peoples of the Eastern Lake Turkana Basin, c. 1840–1925. Ph.D. Dissertation, University of London.

Sober, Elliot and David S. Wilson. 1998. *Onto Others: The Evolution and Psychology of Unselfish Behaviour*. Cambridge, MA: Harvard University Press.

2000. Summary of *Unto Others: The Evolution and Psychology of Unselfish Behaviour*. In Evolutionary Origins of Morality: Cross-Disciplinary Perspectives. Leonard D. Katz, editor, pages 185–206. Bowling Green, OH: Imprint Academic.

Sommer, Volker. 2001. The holy wars about infanticide. Which side are you on? And why? In *Infanticide by Males and its Implications*. Carel P. van Schaik and Charles H. Janson, editors, pages 9–26. Cambridge: Cambridge University Press.

Spencer, Paul. 1973. *Nomads in Alliance*. London: Oxford University Press.

1988. *The Maasai of Matapato: A Study of Rituals of Rebellion*. Bloomington: University of Indiana Press.

Spiro, Melford E. 1987. Collective representations and mental representations in religious symbol systems. In *Culture and Human Nature: Theoretical Papers of Melford E. Spiro*. B. Kilbourne and L. L. Langness, editors, pages 161–184. Chicago: Universtity of Chicago Press.

Statistical Analysis System. 2000. *SAS/STAT User's Guide, Version 8*. Cary NC: SAS Publishing.

Stearns, S. C. 1992. *The Evolution of Life Histories*. Oxford: Oxford University Press.

Stephen, Peter. 1992. Wie egoistich sind memshchlich Gene? – Versuch einer Deutung vol Differenzen in der Lebersserwartung von Kinder mit und ohne Stiefmutter. *Wissenschafliche Zeitshcrift der Humboldt-Universitat zu Berlin, Reihe Medizin* 41:75–76.

Strassmann, Beverly I. 2000. Polygyny, family structure and child mortality: A Prospective study among the Dogon of Mali. In *Adaptation and Human Behavior*. Lee Cronk, Napoleon Chagnon, and William Irons, editors, pages 49–67. New York: Aldine De Gruyter.

Strassmann, Beverly I. and Robin Dunbar. 1999. Human evolution and disease: Putting the stone age into perspective. In *Evolution in Health and Disease*. S. C. Stearns, editor, pages 91–101. Oxford: Oxford University Press.

Strauss, Claudia. 1992. Models and motives. In *Human Motives and Cultural Models*. Roy D'Andrade and Claudia Strauss, editors, pages 1–20. Cambridge: Cambridge University Press.

Strauss, Claudia and Naomi Quinn. 1997. *Cognitive Theory of Cultural Meaning*. Cambridge: Cambridge University Press.

Sussman, George. 1982. *Selling Mothers' Milk: The Wet-Nursing Business in France, 1715–1914*. Urbana: University of Illinois Press.

Sussman, Robert, James Cheverud, and Thad Barlett. 1995. Infant killing as an evolutionary strategy: Reality or myth? *Evolutionary Anthropology* 3:149–151.

Symons, Donald. 1989. A critique of Darwinian anthropology. *Ethology and Sociobiology* 10:131–144.

Tindenbergen, N. 1963. On aims and methods of ethology. *Zeitschrift fur Tierpsychologie* 20:410–433.

Tooby, John and Leda Cosmides. 1989. Evolutionary psychology and the generation of culture. Part I: Theoretical considerations. *Ethology and Sociobiology* 10:29–49.

1990. The past explains the present: Emotional adaptations and the structure of ancestral environments. *Ethology and Sociobiology* 11:375–424.

Trivers, Robert. 1971. The evolution of reciprocal altruism. *Quarterly Review of Biology* 46:35–57.

1972. Parental investment and sexual selection. In *Sexual Selection and the Descent of Man*. B. Campbell, editor, pages 139–179. Chicago: Aldine.

1974. Parent-offspring conflict. *American Zoologist* 14:249–264.

1985. *Social Evolution*. Menlo Park, CA: Benjamin/Cummings.

2002. The elements of a scientific theory of self-deception. In *Natural Selection and Social Theory: Selected Papers of Robert Trivers*. Oxford: Oxford University Press.

Trivers, Robert and Huey P. Newton. 1982. The crash of Flight 90: Doomed by self-deception? *Science Digest*: 66, 67, 111.

Trivers, Robert and Dan E. Willard. 1972. Parental investment and sexual selection. In *Sexual Selection and the Descent of Man, 1871–1971*. Benjamin Campbell, editor, pages 136–179. Chicago: Aldine.

1973. Natural selection and the ability of parents to vary the sex ratio of offspring. *Science* 179:90–92.

Turke, Paul W. 1989. Evolution and the demand for children. *Population and Development Review* 15:61–90.

Turke, Paul W. and Laura Betzig. 1985. Those who can do:Wealth, status and reproductive success on ifaluk. *Ethology and Sociobiology* 6:79–87.

Tylor, Edward. 1871. *Primitive Culture*. London: J. Murray.

United Nations. 1995. *Women's Education and Fertility Behaviour*. New York: United Nations Department of Social and Economic Affairs.

Valenzuela, M. 1990. Attachment in chronically underweight young children. *Child Development* 61:1984–1996.

Valverde, Lola. 1994. Illegitimacy and the abandonment of children in the Basque country, 1550–1800. In *Poor Women and Children in the European Past*. John Henderson and Richard Wall, editors, pages 51–64. Routledge: New York.

Van De Ven, P. G. Prestage, and J. French. 1998. Increase in unprotected anal intercourse with casual partners among Sydney gay men in 1996–98. *Australian and New Zealand Public Health* 22:814–818.

Van der Walle, Etienne and F. van der Walle. 1990. The private and public child. In *What We Know About Health Transition: The Cultural, Social and Behavioral*

Determinants of Health. John C. Caldwell, editor, pages 150–164. Canberra: Australian National University.

VanLandingham, Mark and Nancy Grandjean. 1997. Some cultural underpinnings of male sexual behavior. In *Sexual Cultures and Migration in the Era of AIDS*. Gilbert Herdt, editor, pages 127–142. Oxford: Oxford University Press.

Van Schaik, Carel P. and Charles H. Janson. 2001. *Infanticide by Males and its Implications*. Cambridge: Cambridge University Press.

Van Velson, J. 1967. The extended-case method and situational analysis. In *The Craft of Social Anthropology*. A. L. Epstein, editor, pages 129–149. London: Tavistock Publications.

Varga, Christine. 1999. South African young people's sexual dynamics: Implications for behavioural responses to HIV/AIDS. In *Resistances to Behavioural Change to Reduce HIV/AIDS Infection in Predominantly Heterosexual Epidemics in Third World Countries*. John C. Caldwell, Pat Caldwell, John Anarfi, Kofi Awusabo-Asare, James Ntozi, I. O. Orubuloye, Jeff Marck, Wendy Cosford, Rachel Colombo, and Elaine Hollings, editors, pages 13–34. Canberra: Australian National University Press.

Vayda, A. P. 1995a. Failures of explanation in Darwinian ecological anthropology: Part I. *Philosophy of the Social Sciences* 25:219–249.

1995b. Failures of explanation in Darwinian ecological anthropology. Part II. *Philosophy of the Social Sciences* 25:360–375.

Viazzo, Piers Paolo. 1994. Family structures and the early phase in the individual life cycle. In *Poor Women and Children in the European Past*. John Henderson and Robert Wall, editors, pages 31–50. New York: Routledge.

Viazzo, Pier Paolo and Katherine A. Lynch. 2002. Anthropology, family history and the concept of strategy. *International Review of Social History* 47:423–452.

Viazzo, Piers Paolo, Maria Bortolotto, and Andrea Zanotto. 2001. Five centuries of foundling history in Florence: Changing patterns of abandonment, care and mortality. In *Abandoned Children*. Catherine Panter-Brick and Malcolm T. Smith, editors, pages 70–91. Cambridge: Cambridge University Press.

Vickers, William T. 2002. Sexual theory, behavior and paternity among the Siona and Secoya Indians of Eastern Ecudor. In *Cultures of Multiple Fathers: The Theory and Practice of Partible Paternity in Lowland South America*. Stephen Beckerman and Paul Valentine, editors, pages 221–246. Gainesville: University Press of Florida.

Vining, D. S. 1986. Social versus reproductive success – the central theoretical problem of human sociobiology. *Behavioral and Brain Sciences* 9:167–200.

Voland, Eckart. 1984. Human sex-ratio manipulation: Historical data from a German parish. *Journal of Human Evolution* 13:99–107.

1989. Differential parental investment: Some ideas on the contact area of European social history and evolutionary biology. In *Behavioural Ecology of Humans and Other Mammals*. Vern Standen and Robert Foley, editors, pages 391–403. Oxford: Blackwell.

1990. Differential reproductive success in the Krummhorn population. *Behavioral Ecology and Sociobiology* 10:223–240.

1995. Reproductive decisions viewed from an evolutionarily informed historical demography. In *Human Reproductive Decisions: Biological and Social Perspectives*. R. I. M. Dunbar, editor, pages 137–159. London: St. Martin's Institute.

2000. Contributions of family reconstruction studies to evolutionary reproductive ecology. *Evolutionary Anthropology* 9:134–146.

Voland, Eckart and R. I. M. Dunbar. 1995. Resource competition and reproduction – the relationships between economic and parental strategies in the Krummhorn population (1720–1874). *Human Nature* 6:33–49.

Voland, Eckart, R. I. M. Dunbar, C. Engel, and P. Stephen. 1997. Population increase and sex-biased parental investment in humans: Evidence from 18th and 19th Germany. *Current Anthropology* 38:129–135.

Voland, Eckart, E. Siegelkow, and C. Engel. 1991. Cost/benefit oriented parental analysis by high status families: The Krummhorn case. *Ethology and Sociobiology* 12:105–118.

Voland, Eckart and Peter Stephan. 2001. "The hate that love generated" – sexually selected neglect of one's own offspring in humans. In *Infanticide by Males and its Implications*. Carel P. van Schaik and Charles H. Janson, editors, pages 447–469. Cambridge: Cambridge University Press.

Wachter, Kenneth. 1978. *Statistical Studies of Historical Social Structure*. New York: Academic Press.

Wachter, Kenneth and Rodolfo A. Bulatao. 2003. *Offspring: Human Fertility Behavior in Biodemographic Perspective*. Washington, DC: National Academy Press.

Wallerstein, Immanuel. 1976. *The Modern World System: Capitalism, Agriculture and the Origin of the European World Market in the Sixteenth Century*. New York: Academic Press.

Waltner, Ann. 1990. *Getting an Heir: Adoption and the Construction of Kinship in Late Imperal China*. Honolulu: University of Hawaii Press.

Watkins, Susan Cotts. 2000. Local and foreign models of reproduction in Nyanza Province, Kenya. *Population and Development Review* 26(4):725–759.

White, Douglas R. 1988. Rethinking polygny: Co-wives, codes and cultural systems. *Cultural Anthropology* 29:529–558.

Wiley, Andrea S. and Leslie C. Carlin. 1999. Demographic contexts and the adaptive role of mother-infant attachment. *Human Nature* 10:135–161.

Williams, George. 1966. *Adaptation and Natural Selection: A Critique of Some Current Evolutionary Thought*. Princeton, NJ: Princeton University Press.

Wilson, David S. 2002. *Darwin's Cathedral: Evolution, Religion, and the Nature of Society*. Chicago: University of Chicago Press.

Wilson, David and Elliot Sober. 1994. Reintroducing group selection to the human behavioural sciences. *Behavioral and Brain Sciences* 17:585–654.

1996. Continuing commentary on reintroducing group selection to the human behavioural sciences. *Behavioural and Brain Sciences* 19:777–787.

Wilson, E. O. 1975. *Sociobiology: The New Synthesis*. Cambridge, MA: Harvard University Press.

1978. *On Human Nature*. Cambridge, MA: Harvard University Press.

1998. *Consilience: The Unity of Knowledge*. New York: Knopf.

Wilson, R., A. Diallo, and K. Wagenaar. 1985. Mixed herding and the demographic parameters of domestic animals in the arid and semi-arid zones of Tropical Africa. In *Population, Health and Nutrition in the Sahel: Issues in the Welfare of Selected West African Communites*. Alan Hill, editor, pages 116–140. London: Kegan Paul.

Winterhalder, Bruce and Eric Alden Smith. 2000. Analysing adaptive strategies: Human behavioural ecology at twenty-five. *Evolutionary Anthropology* 9:51–72.

Wolf, Arthur P. and Huang, Chieh-Shan. 1980. *Marriage and Adoption in China, 1845–1945*. Stanford, CA: Stanford University Press.

Wolf, Eric. 1982. *Europe and the People Without History*. Berkeley: University of California Press.

World Bank. 1999. *Confronting AIDS: Public Priorities in a Global Epidemic*. Oxford: Oxford University Press.

Worthman, Carol M. 1995. Comment on Borgerhoff Mulder's "Bridewealth and its correlates." *Current Anthropology* 36:596–597.

1999. Emotions: You can feel the difference. In *Biocultural Approaches to the Emotions*. Alexander Laban Hinton, editor, pages 41–74. Cambridge: Cambridge University Press.

2003. Energetics, sociality and human reproduction: Life history theory in real life. In *Offspring: Human Fertility Behavior in Biodemographic Perspective*. Kenneth Wachter and Rudolfo Bulatao, editors, pages 289–321. Washington, DC: National Academies Press.

Wrigley, Charles. 1978. Fertility strategies for the individual and the group. In *Historical Studies of Changing Fertility*. C. Tilley, editor, pages 135–154. Princeton, NJ: Princeton University Press.

Wynne-Edwards, V. C. 1962. *Animal Dispersion in Relation to Social Behavior*. New York: Hafner.

Index